# AESTHETIC CREATION

# Aesthetic Creation

NICK ZANGWILL

OXFORD
UNIVERSITY PRESS

# OXFORD

UNIVERSITY PRESS

Great Clarendon Street, Oxford OX2 6DP

Oxford University Press is a department of the University of Oxford.
It furthers the University's objective of excellence in research, scholarship,
and education by publishing worldwide in

Oxford New York

Auckland Cape Town Dar es Salaam Hong Kong Karachi
Kuala Lumpur Madrid Melbourne Mexico City Nairobi
New Delhi Shanghai Taipei Toronto

With offices in

Argentina Austria Brazil Chile Czech Republic France Greece
Guatemala Hungary Italy Japan Poland Portugal Singapore
South Korea Switzerland Thailand Turkey Ukraine Vietnam

Oxford is a registered trade mark of Oxford University Press
in the UK and in certain other countries

Published in the United States
by Oxford University Press Inc., New York

© Nick Zangwill 2007

The moral rights of the author have been asserted
Database right Oxford University Press (maker)

First published 2007

British Library Cataloguing in Publication Data
Data available

Library of Congress Cataloging in Publication Data
Data available

Typeset by Laserwords Private Limited, Chennai, India
Printed in Great Britain
on acid-free paper by
Biddles Ltd., King's Lynn, Norfolk

ISBN 978–0–19–926187–1

3 5 7 9 10 8 6 4 2

For Takahiro

岳洋に捧ぐ

# Contents

# *Preface*

In this book I defend a particular version of the aesthetic theory of art. Many people who have no sympathy with any such view have nevertheless helped me considerably to develop, refine and to defend the view. My greatest debt is to Jerrold Levinson, for written comments and discussion—but not agreement!—on most of the papers from which the chapters derive, and for encouragement over many years. For comments on the whole manuscript I am grateful to John Bender, Malcolm Budd and Peter Kivy. I received very useful written comments on the papers from which the chapters originated from: Stephen Davies, Simon Evnine, Brian Garrett, Berys Gaut, Serge Guilbaut, Alan Goldman, Gary Kemp, Matthew Kieran, Philip Percival and Robert Stecker.

The chapters were all originally published as papers, but they have all been more or less rewritten for this volume. Some new material has been added. Two of the papers were originally given as talks at the national meetings of the American Society of Aesthetics, in Reno, NV, and Washington, DC.

I intend each chapter to stand as far as possible on its own, which leads to some repetition of basic principles about aesthetic properties, dependence and contextualism. Partly this is due to the origin of the chapters as journal articles. And partly it is because I do not flatter myself that people will read this book from cover to cover. There are some places where I rely on arguments and considerations offered in other chapters. Discussion of certain topics is distributed throughout this book, such as the discussion of appropriation, creative thinking and the sociology of art. Those with specific interests in a topic that is dispersed in the book might find the indexes useful.

I would like what I write here to be of interest to non-philosophers. But I recognize that some parts are likely to seem somewhat technical or abstruse, particularly the more metaphysical discussions. I hope that those who are not interested in such matters will skip them and continue with something that speaks to them more directly. I make no apology for metaphysical discussion, however. There is no escaping metaphysics.

This book was more or less complete in 2001. I originally envisaged the material sharing the same covers as what became my book *The*

*Metaphysics of Beauty* (Ithaca: Cornell University Press, 2001) But the pursuit of various other projects kept it from an earlier completion. Some work was done during a year in which I held visiting fellowships at Harvard University, MIT and The University of California at Berkeley. A sabbatical from Glasgow University, with a matching sabbatical from the Arts and Humanities Research Board, made that year possible.

I do not claim much originality for the view defended here. In my view the greatest book on aesthetics written in the twentieth century is probably Monroe Beardsley's *Aesthetics* (Indianapolis: Hackett, 1958), and I am happy to follow in his footsteps in many respects. This book falls comfortably in what was the mainstream trend of aesthetics in Western philosophy since Plato. This tradition is now widely thought to be passé. Some readers will think that any aesthetic approach to art is 'conservative'; but I do not care much about that. One generation's conservative is the next generation's radical, and vice versa. The aesthetic tradition was under attack for much of the twentieth century. However, that tradition, like many good things that we can easily take for granted, needs articulation, nurturing and vigorous defence, not the least so that its glories can be bequeathed to future generations and not squandered.

N.Z., London

# Introduction

## 1 BASIC QUESTIONS

Sometimes it is best not to begin at the beginning. The question "What is art?" might seem to be the obvious starting point for the philosophy of art. Surely, one might think, an inquiry into the nature of art should take the question "What is art?" to be central and therefore ask that question first. After all, if we want to know what art is, what else should we ask?

However, my view is that this is the wrong place to begin. I shall address that question, in a way; and, in a way, I shall propose an answer to it. But I think that there are questions that should precede it. If asked alone, the question, "What is art?", invites us to speculate on what works of art have in common and on how they differ from other things. It invites us to conceive of the project of understanding art as being about finding a description that snugly fits all and only those objects and events that are art. But producing such a description would not address what really puzzles us about art. It would not settle the perplexities that drove us to philosophical reflection on art in the first place. There are other important and pressing questions. Why are we concerned with art? What drives us to make it and behold it? Why does it motivate us? Why do we think it important? Why do we value it? In my view we need to ask these questions *before* we ask the "What is art?" question. Our perplexity was never really about a bizarre class of *objects*, but rather about *us* and our bizarre attitudes to those objects. It is only out of a concern to answer these prior questions that we need to find an answer to the "What is art?" question. In thinking about art, reflection on value and our evaluations should precede more metaphysical questions.[1] And

[1] In my view, this is true in quite a few areas of philosophy where purely metaphysical debates reach stalemate. Reflection on values and our evaluations helps to break the deadlock. The debates over personal identity and free will are examples.

if our inquiry into art turned into a purely metaphysical one, we would have lost the thread of what originally puzzled us.

My guiding methodology in the theory of art is that of seeking a *rational explanation*. I want to explain our art-activities. And I want to make our art-activities intelligible. That is, I want to show how they are rational and worthwhile, or at least how they seem rational and worthwhile to us. I argue for this methodology in Chapter 1. In later chapters, I apply this methodology in order to support the view of art that I favour, and as a way of arguing against rival views.

## 2 THE AESTHETIC CREATION THEORY

I shall develop and defend a particular version of the *aesthetic theory of art*. Aesthetic theories of art form a family. Roughly, according to an aesthetic theory of art, *having an aesthetic purpose* makes a thing art. Monroe Beardsley proposed a particular theory of art which rested on his instrumentalist view of aesthetic appreciation.[2]

The particular aesthetic theory of art that I develop in this book I call the Aesthetic Creation Theory. In a nutshell, this is the view that it is the function of art to have certain aesthetic properties in virtue of having certain nonaesthetic properties; and this function arises from our insight into these dependence relations and the intentional realization of them. Nature *possesses* aesthetic properties, but nature does not have the *function* of possessing them. That function has its origin in aesthetic intentions.

This theory depends on the notion of an aesthetic property, and on the principle that aesthetic properties depend on nonaesthetic properties. Obviously, we should *not* say that aesthetic properties are those possessed by works of art or that they are those properties that it is the function of art to possess. We need an independent definition of aesthetic properties. My view is that aesthetic properties should be delineated with reference to beauty and ugliness. Beauty and ugliness are the central aesthetic properties, and other properties are aesthetic if they stand in a particular, intimate relation to beauty and ugliness. Daintiness, dumpiness, elegance, balance and delicacy are so related,

---

[2] Monroe Beardsley, "An Aesthetic Definition of Art", in (ed.) Hugh Curtler, *What is Art?*, New York: Haven, 1983, but also conveniently reprinted in Peter Lamarque and Stein Olsen (eds.) *Aesthetics and the Philosophy of Art*, Oxford: Blackwell, 2004

unlike nonaesthetic properties such as physical or representational properties. Daintiness, dumpiness, elegance, balance and delicacy are all *ways* of being beautiful or ugly. I pursued this account of aesthetic properties in my book *The Metaphysics of Beauty*.[3]

These are the main assumptions of the specific aesthetic theory that I develop and defend in this book. But for the moment let us stay with the general family of Aesthetic Theories of Art according to which a work of art is something that has an aesthetic purpose.

## 3 OBJECTIONS TO AESTHETIC THEORIES

There are two main sources of hostility to aesthetic theories of art of any sort. One source of hostility springs from a general hostility to the notion of the aesthetic. The notion of the aesthetic has not been popular in the twentieth century. Indeed, considerable dismissiveness has been directed at it. Many believe that the notion is somehow fraudulent and should be jettisoned. I disagree. I am in favour of the notion of the aesthetic. Those who say they reject the notion either fail to do so in practice or else produce patently false or unilluminating theories without the notion.

However, many philosophers and art theorists think that even if the notion of the aesthetic is not itself to be rejected, it is nevertheless a mistake to deploy the notion in trying to understand art. Again, I disagree. The notion of the aesthetic is in fact indispensable in understanding art. It is a fundamental mistake *not* to appeal to the aesthetic in giving an account of art. Deploying the notion of the aesthetic is essential if we are to understand art because it is essential if we are to *explain* our attitudes to art, and it is essential if we are to *justify* our attitudes to art.

The standard objection to aesthetic theories of art, of countless papers, textbooks and monographs, is that there are many works of art with no aesthetic purpose. That is, there are thought to be *counterexamples* to aesthetic theories of art. The usual source of counterexamples is twentieth century avant garde visual art.[4] Very many aestheticians in

---

[3] *The Metaphysics of Beauty*, Ithaca: Cornell University Press, 2001.

[4] I use 'avant garde' in a broad sense so that it includes the artistic movements of the 1920s and 1930s that thought of themselves under that label. Thus, avant garde art includes the ready-mades of the early twentieth century. But I also use it to include pop art and conceptual art of the 1960s and onwards.

the last few decades have thought that it is *obvious* that the avant garde
provides clear counterexamples to aesthetic theories of art, and so they
think that such theories are easily shown to be false. It is common to
hold that these examples *refute* the theory (a remarkably strong claim).
This objection, using avant garde counterexamples, is *so* common that
I want now to indicate, in brief, what my attitude to it is.[5]

## 4 'DEFINING' ART

There is often said to be a project called *defining art,* which is consecrated
in aesthetics anthologies and textbooks. This project usually involves the
search for 'necessary and sufficient conditions' for being art. Avant garde
art enters the stage as a candidate counterexample to certain theories.
The somewhat Hegelian picture that many urge us to accept is that
theories of art attempt to describe art, but meanwhile art itself moves
on and refutes the theories. The theories of art are pitched at something
moving and changing, and they tend to describe art as it was but is
no more.

This project of 'definition' is usually thought of as presenting the
meaning of the word, or concept, "art". But it is in fact odd that
this project is pursued by seeking 'necessary and sufficient conditions'
for being a work of art. Giving necessary and sufficient conditions for
something being X (a modal equivalence) is not the same as giving
the meaning of "X" (a semantic equivalence). Water is necessary and
sufficient for being $H_2O$, but there is no equivalence of meaning between
"water" and "$H_2O$". In fact, the project of 'defining art' is clearly not
coherent; the phrase "defining art" is not well-formed. One can define
the word "art" but not art itself. Are those who seek a 'definition' really
in search of what is sometimes called a 'real definition', which is not a
matter of meanings? I suspect that those who pursue definitions in the
philosophy of art have not made up their minds.

Suppose that the project that is being pursued is the analysis of
the concept of art, and this concept is assumed to include painting,

---

[5] We will see in Chapter 3 that this objection usually rests on a hasty interpretation
of the kinds of counterexamples that the critics have in mind. I argue that in fact there is
not too much to worry about from twentieth century avant garde visual art. Almost all
the usual examples are fairly easily tamed by an aesthetic theory without much difficulty.
But what is more important, and needs to be highlighted now, is the methodologically
naive approach that this kind of dialectic embodies.

sculpture, architecture, literature and music. Then at least the following four issues arise, which caution us on either the feasibility of conceptual analysis or its fruits even if successfully pursued. (1) The project assumes that there *is* a concept of art that it is in good order and that awaits analysis. Taking thesis and counterexample to be the central method of conceptual analysis in the philosophy of art only makes sense if there is something stable and robust to analyse. But it is not obvious that we had such a notion of art before we started studying philosophy. Some but not all English dictionaries list such a meaning for it. (In German, *kunst* might correspond to the word "art" as used in Philosophy, but many other languages lack such a word.) (2) There may be quite a few concepts of art that we might analyse. But if there are competing notions, it raises the question of which concept we *ought* to deploy. In Renaissance Europe and in Japan, for example, there are radically different categorizations that apply to very different things. Perhaps we should think like them. (3) The fact that we have a certain concept, even if it is universally shared, does not mean that the concept succeeds in including a range of objects that share a common nature. It may or may not do so. We are primarily interested in the world, and what art picks out.[6] Not all concepts are equally satisfactory. We need concepts that do justice to the world. (4) Even if there were a concept of art that is in good order and that did pick out a range of things that share a common nature, it is not clear that explanatory issues can be addressed given only a grasp of the concept of art. There would be a lot left to do to understand art and art-activities, even after the conceptual analysis had been successfully achieved. For at least these four reasons, conceptual analysis is not a satisfactory approach to philosophical reflection on art: either it makes questionable assumptions or else it is too limited.

But if we are not overly interested in the concept of art, or we are wary of engaging in 'analysing' that concept, then the concern with counterexamples is no longer paramount. The project of conceptual analysis in the philosophy of art usually consists in the search for necessary and sufficient conditions for something to be art. Hence the search for counterexamples—something that is art but fails to fit the definition, or something that fits the definition but is not art. But with a different methodology, counterexamples need not take centre stage. This is why deploying the avant garde as a source of

---

[6] Compare Hilary Kornblith, *Knowledge and Its Place in Nature,* Oxford: Oxford University Press, 2002, especially chapter 1.

putative counterexamples to aesthetic theories of art makes questionable assumptions about fundamental issues of methodology in the philosophy of art.


## 5 EXPLANATION

We need to ask the meta-question: how should we assess theories of art? What criteria of adequacy should we deploy? The entire method of definition and counterexample is questionable. The project of conceptual analysis and the search for extensional adequacy is vulnerable to a meta-criticism. Even if a theory were good by those lights, it might be uninteresting and unilluminating. In place of an extensional criterion of adequacy, I propose an explanatory criterion of adequacy. We want explanation: we need to explain the consumption and production of art, and perhaps also the sustenance of works of art. These are very broadly the three things we do with art. And they are puzzling. Why do we bother with art? The philosophy of art should address these questions. If it does not, it risks being flawed or superficial.

The explanation we seek is *rational* explanation, or it involves rational explanation. We need an explanation of why art appears to us to be worth making, preserving and using. What do people see in it? This does not imply that all works of art have value. George Dickie unfairly claims that an evaluative definition implies that there is no bad art.[7] This objection is beside the point. What is important is that many works of art seem to be of value. Bad art is presumably not typically thought bad by its makers. In the *Republic*, Plato interestingly gave an explanation of why some of what we call art *seems* to be of value, but it is not. This is the right kind of theory.

Some say that the theory of art can be a metaphysical theory that is neutral on evaluative matters.[8] Two separate theories are thus envisaged: a value-neutral theory of art and a theory of the evaluation of art. The idea is that the theory of art might fit under some broader theory of evaluation, but it need not itself supply that broader evaluation. But this is not feasible. There could only be such a value-neutral theory of art if art were a natural kind, like gold. But works of art are human

---

[7] George Dickie, *Art and Value*, Oxford: Blackwell, 2001, chapter 6.
[8] Stephen Davies, "Essential Distinctions for Art Theorists", in (eds.) Stephen Davies and Anata ch. Sukla, *Art and Essence*, London: Praeger, 2003.

artefacts with purposes that derive from intentions. And artefacts are not understood until we find them intelligible—that is, until we see how it would be rational to make and use them. To understand an artefact is to understand why someone might want to make it and use it. Either a theory of art should itself provide this explanation or else it provides the basis for such an explanation. It can not be a completely unrelated story. The theory of art must be subsumed under a general rational explanatory story. Views about the nature of art should be a by-product of a good rational explanatory story.

Others say that if we want to explain human art-activities, we should bring to bear empirical psychology or empirical sociology. But I think that there are dangers lurking down this path. We need a theory that explains various attitudes that we have and activities that we engage in, by making them intelligible or by showing how they seem worthwhile to those who have them or engage in them. We need a theory that prioritizes the first person point of view—a theory that invokes the reasons that a person has not just causes. So the kind of explanation we need to make a priority is *rational causal* explanation. Other explanations of our actions should, in most cases, respect our own self-understanding of our actions, not replace it. There are of course some areas where our self-understanding is delusory, but this is not generally the case.[9] This is not to rule out the possibility of empirical psychological studies of art or of an empirical sociology of art. But such empirical enquiries must respect our own self-conception, either by vindicating it, or by going beyond it and building on it. Psychological studies of art or the sociology of art without a sound philosophy of art—one that emphasizes the first-person point of view—are likely to be inconclusive at best and irrelevant at worst.

Although I shall proceed directly to theorizing about art and our art-activities, I shall sometimes draw on the concept of art—particularly the idea that it is part of the concept of art that works of art are artefacts. And I will sometimes appeal to 'intuition', particularly when considering the persistence of works of art over time. But much will not turn on conceptual considerations, and much will not turn on

[9] In general, I think that the mental causes of our actions are usually transparent to agents. Here I am probably on Hegel's side against Marx and Freud. We have considerable self-understanding of the source of our actions; for the most part, we know why we act as we do. See further Nick Zangwill, "Perpetrator Motivation: Some Reflections on the Browning/Goldhagen Debate", in (ed.) Eve Garrard and Geoffrey Scarre, *Moral Philosophy and the Holocaust*, Aldershot: Ashgate Press, 2003.

the appeal to intuition. The point of the account I give is to allow for the value of art and the rationality of art-activities and to seek an account of metaphysical issues about art—such as issues about identity or survival—that fits within a plausible rational explanatory story of activities that involve art.

We need to understand the world, including ourselves, and we need concepts that allow us to do that. Our concept of 'art' is not sacrosanct. The question is not: what is our concept of art? But: which concept or concepts *should* we have? If a proposed theory involves reforming ordinary common concepts to a greater or lesser extent, then so be it; that is something we may need to do for an explanatory gain. We want an explanatory theory of our mental life as far as it involves works of art. And we should fashion concepts that allow us to attain that.

## 6 THE VALUE OF THE AVANT GARDE

Let us now return to avant garde art. Such art is controversial. Indeed it is often supposed to be controversial. In particular, its value is controversial. Many people think that avant garde art does not have much value. For example, the popular anti-art-establishment art critic Brian Sewell thinks that these works are by and large not worth producing, conserving or consuming.[10] So, given the rational-explanatory aim of a theory of art, it is surely not a good idea to make such works the centrepiece of one's philosophy of art. This leads to the opposite approach from that of many contemporary writers—the conservative position according to which the priority is to explain central uncontentious examples of valuable art. How about focusing on Uccello and Cranach rather than Duchamp and Warhol?

So when aestheticians object to aesthetic theories of art on extensional grounds, asking "What about such and such works of art that do not have aesthetic ambitions?", the reply is that we are not playing the extensional game but the explanatory game. We can concede that an aesthetic theory does not fit this or that case. Why is that so disastrous? The aesthetic theory gives the essence of a great many works of art. It tells us what they are, and it yields an explanation of the value of these works and of the value of our art-activities. That is interesting. Whether

---

[10] Brian Sewell, *An Alphabet of Villains*, London: Bloomsbury, 1995.

there are some other phenomena that are not explained in this way does not detract from the successful explanation of the many cases with which the theory deals.

We need a theory of art that explains the *apparent* value of most works of art. Someone might, following Plato, maintain the radical thesis that the value of most central cases is merely apparent and not real. But that appearance still needs to be explained. By contrast, where the value of art is widely disputed—as the value of avant garde art is disputed—there is no general appearance of value to be explained. These works differ from mainstream works in that there is no general acceptance of their apparent value. Of course tastes differ; people value mainstream works differently. But we must think that, quite generally, it is not irrational to make and experience most art. By contrast, many people do think that it is irrational to make and view much avant garde art. Hence it is a mistake to make such examples central in the theory of art.

## 7 ART AND INDISCERNIBLE DUPLICATES

There is another reason that avant garde art has been taken to be of special importance in the philosophy of art, particularly by Arthur Danto. This is not so much because it is a putative counterexample to certain theories but because the works themselves allegedly make a philosophical point about the nature of art. Of course, *some* avant garde art may be intrinsically interesting. Perhaps philosophers can reflect on the meaning and value of those works. Some of those works may even raise philosophical issues. However, many philosophers have followed Arthur Danto in thinking that there are quite general morals to be drawn from these works.[11]

Danto thinks that the philosophical content of this art lies in the lesson that examples of indiscernible duplicates teach. These are examples of imaginary or real pairs of things that are intrinsically indiscernible, yet one of them is art while the other is not. Such examples have been influential in getting philosophers to embrace artworld or institutional

---

[11] Arthur Danto, "The Artword", *Journal of Philosophy*, 1964; *The Transfiguration of the Commonplace*, Cambridge, MA: Harvard University Press, 1981; *The Philosophical Disenfranchisement of Art*, New York: Columbia University Press, 1986; *Beyond the Brillo Box*, Berkeley: University of California Press, 1992; *The Abuse of Beauty*, Chicago: Open Court, 2003.

theories, or other theories of that general sort. But what exactly do examples of indiscernible duplicates show? What they show is that being art is a *relational* property. But that leaves open a vast range of theories. In particular it leaves open Monroe Beardsley's aesthetic theory of art. Danto and his followers infer that their preferred kind of relational theory is encouraged. But this is a clear non-sequitur.[12]

Some examples of indiscernible duplicates might not only show that being a work of art is relational but also that the relevant relation is that of having an essential origin of some kind. Thus a piece of 'swamp art', which is just like some artwork except that it came into existence after lightning struck a swamp, is not art, despite its similarity to things that are art. This is because it has the wrong origins. That works of art have essential origins falls out of the fact that they are *artefacts*. Swamp tables are not tables for this reason. Artefacts have essential origins in thought. The possibility of cases of indiscernible duplicates involving works of art follows from the artefactuality of artworks.

There are also indiscernible duplicate examples of two things that are different artworks. Ernst Gombrich explored this in 1959 in his book *Art and Illusion*.[13] Here Gombrich makes explicit the anti-formalist stance that was implicit in the title of his 1950 multi-million selling book *The Story of Art*.[14] Perhaps a relational theory of art is not very controversial, and it does not seem too controversial to say that works of art have essential origins in artistic actions. But to say that they also have essential relations to other works of art is much more controversial. It is true that many works of art do have such essential relational properties; but it is plausible that some, and perhaps many, do not. Their identity does not depend on relations to other works. It is also plausible that there *must* be some cases where art identity is not relational in this way if there is anything for the story of art to be the story of. Granted, there are some works of art that depend on other works of art. But there can only be those works of art because there are other works of art that do not depend on any others.

Thus I doubt that examples of indiscernible duplicates have much to teach us. They should not play the pivotal role in general theorizing about the nature of art that Danto envisages. On the basis of these sort of examples, Danto has been influential in persuading many philosophers

---

12 Whoever thought that being art was an intrinsic property anyway?
13 Ernst Gombrich, *Art and Illusion*, London: Phaidon, 1959, p. 313.
14 Ernst Gombrich, *The Story of Art*, London: Phaidon, 1950.

of art, particularly in the United States, to approach the philosophy of art in a particular way—a way that emphasizes the social and artistic context of art and that turns away from the aesthetic ambitions of the individual artist in making a work. But in fact the examples are no support at all for this theoretical shift.

## 8 AESTHETIC THEORIES AND RATIONAL EXPLANATION

A theory of art needs to explain our art-attitudes and art-activities. It should explain the value that people see in making, sustaining and perceiving works of art. Aesthetic theories of art have a great advantage over theories that privilege ideological, cognitive or emotional purposes of art. Aesthetic theories appeal to *pleasure*; and the desire and pursuit of pleasure is familiar and understandable. The kind of pleasure that aesthetic theories appeal to is likely to be a special kind of pleasure: a pleasure with greater value than more pedestrian kinds of pleasure. Nevertheless, it is pleasure. And the pursuit of pleasure is an intelligible and rational pastime.[15] If aesthetic theories invoke pleasure, they can provide, or can easily be conjoined with, a particularly compelling explanation for the appearance of value of artworks and of our art-activities. Hence aesthetic theories of art give us a rational explanation of the great majority of art and art-activities throughout the world in the last few millennia. This is surely more important than whether a theory can capture a handful of experimental works made in New York in the 1960s.

Aesthetic accounts of art are particularly well placed to account for the rationality of art-activities. The particular aesthetic theory that I develop—the Aesthetic Creation Theory—does that by seeing art as having the purpose of emboding values of a certain sort. These values are aesthetic values—typically beauty and other valuable aesthetic properties. Appreciating and creating beauty and other valuable aesthetic properties yields pleasure. Here I depart from the great Monroe

[15] One speculation about the suspicion of aesthetic theories of art would be that it arises from a Puritanism that frowns on pleasure. Perhaps it is thought that art would be more worthwhile if it provides knowledge, moral uplift or political progress rather than superficial or decadent feelings of pleasure! An example is Nelson Goodman's high-minded dismissal of the 'tingle-immersion theory' in his *Languages of Art*, Oxford: Oxford University Press, p. 112.

Beardsley, who had an instrumentalist theory of aesthetic value. My view is that we see value in making, sustaining and perceiving works of art only because they *have* valuable features. The pleasure we feel in contemplating works of art is pleasure *in* those valuable features; the features are not a mere means of producing pleasure. And we take pleasure *in* producing valuable features. That is, we feel pleasure in making works of art because we think that we are producing things of value; and this is also why we think that it is worth making works of art. If a work turns out to be a failure, then making it has been a wasted effort, unless that failure is part of some larger, ongoing enterprise which can boast later success. (Perhaps this failure was part of a necessary experiment on the path to making something better.)

I do not concur with Beardsley's instrumentalism on aesthetic value. But he was deeply right to embrace an aesthetic theory of art where such a theory privileges beauty and other aesthetic properties among (but not necessarily above) the many values of works of art. All aesthetic theories of art invoke pleasure, although they do so in different ways. I assume that being motivated by pleasure is understandable and rational. If art embodies aesthetic properties, and creating and appreciating aesthetic properties yields pleasure of a special rich sort then art-activities are not just understandable and rational, but also valuable. We can see why creating and appreciating such art might be part of a flourishing life.

# Summary of Chapters

The first chapter of this book addresses the criteria of adequacy of a theory of art. Chapters 2–5 are constructive—they advance a positive view of the nature of art, explore the consequences of this view and defend it against objections. The last two chapters, 6 and 7, are destructive—they argue against other views of the nature of art, and they do so by contrast with the positive view put forward earlier and in the light of the groundrules laid down in the first chapter.

In Chapter 1 ("Groundrules in the Philosophy of Art"), I argue that theories of art should not be measured primarily by whether they apply to things that we intuitively think are art and not to things that we intuitively think are not art. A rational explanatory ambition is more important. We must explain the fact that we desire and value making and experiencing art. What we want is a theoretically reconstructed concept of art that helps us understand certain phenomena—our dealings with the things that we call 'art'. This chapter will provide a reference point for the positive (Chapters 2–5) and negative (Chapters 6–7) parts of the book.

In Chapter 2 ("Art as Aesthetic Creation"), I articulate and defend the view that a work of art is the intentional product of aesthetic creative thought. The view, roughly, is that someone has an insight into an aesthetic/nonaesthetic dependency, and then intentionally endows something with the aesthetic properties in virtue of the nonaesthetic properties. I give an account of aesthetic insight and aesthetic action. The account of aesthetic action is an instance of a familiar means–end model of rational deliberation. But the account of aesthetic, creative insight is non-rational and it coincides with traditional accounts of genius. I defend the notion of creative genius against claims made by sociologists of art.

In Chapter 3 ("Are There Counterexamples to Aesthetic Theories of Art?"), I address the objection that Aesthetic Theories of Art, such as the Aesthetic Creation Theory, fall short in what they say about the twentieth century avant garde. I argue that Arthur Danto misinterpreted, and overreacted to, the phenomena of ready-mades. I supply various ways in which various avant garde phenomena can be tamed by aesthetic theories. I then address the assumptions underlying the objection that aesthetic theories of art are subject to counterexamples. I consider what we should think about narrative arts that lack an aesthetic function. This leads to methodological reflections on the concepts of 'art' that we should take to demarcate the target for explanation in the philosophy of 'art'.

In Chapter 4 ("Art Essence, Identity and Survival") I consider the view that the survival of a work of art is determined by its aesthetic properties, and I compare that view with the view that the survival of a work of art is determined by its compositional origins. I argue that both theories have virtues and both have vices, and that the virtues of one theory are the vices of the other. This points us towards the kind of view we need.

In Chapter 5 ("Aesthetic Functionalism"), I put forward a view of the metaphysics of art that delivers conditions for the identity or survival of a work of art across time. This metaphysics is a consequence of the Aesthetic Creation Theory put forward in Chapter 2. I call this metaphysical consequence, 'Aesthetic Functionalism'. I propose an account of the cross-time identity of functional things in general, which also applies to works of art. I contest the view that the material composition of a work of art is essential to it. I then propose a way of understanding the fact that particular works of art may have many nonaesthetic functions that are essential to them along with their essential aesthetic functions. After that I discuss appropriation—artistic and non-artistic.

In Chapter 6 ("Art and Audience"), I argue against all theories of the nature of art that make essential reference to an audience. I argue that there should be *no* reference to an audience in a theory of art. The initial problem for audience theories arises from the fact that there seem'to be counterexamples. But there are more fundamental objections. I argue that, when we consider the content of the audience's experiences, audience theories are crucially incomplete; and that when they are completed, they are either false or else the reference to the audience drops out. I refine the argument to cope with complex dispositional theories. I argue that we do not always create for the eyes and ears of others, nor do we always create so that we can experience our own work. This leads me to insist on some measure of artistic autonomy from social pressures, and to give some account of the rational aspect of creative activity. In the Appendix to Chapter 6, I discuss Dickie's institutional approach.

Lastly, in Chapter 7 ("Against the Sociology of Art") I return to the theme of rational explanation. I argue against non-rational sociological explanations in favour of aesthetic rational explanations. Sociologists of art illegitimately slide from giving sociological explanations of *some* aspects of art-production to thinking that they can offer a complete explanation of art-production in which the aesthetic has no place. But aesthetic and sociological factors might both be significant. Moreover it is plausible that nonaesthetic explanations are only possible because there are aesthetic factors at work. I end by filling out what aesthetic explanations of art-production and consumption would look like. I appeal to the pleasure that people derive from art-making and consuming. Since it is rational and understandable that people pursue pleasure, aesthetic explanations are rational explanations.

# 1

# Groundrules in the Philosophy of Art

What do we want from a theory of art? What would make one theory of art better than another? What criteria of adequacy should we use for assessing theories of art? What are the groundrules in the philosophy of art? Much speculation and debate about the nature of art, by philosophers and others, proceeds without explicit reflection on these questions. But this means that debate and speculation to some extent proceeds in the dark. It is not satisfactory merely to assume some goal for a theory of art without examining that goal. We might be lucky and happen to have the right goal. But we might not. Furthermore, if different theories aspire to different goals, it may mean that apparently different theories do not compete with each other. Or else they try to engage with each other but fail to do so, given their different goals. In order to put the philosophy of art on a firm footing we need to establish its proper goals. Then theory construction and debate will be more fruitful. Theories can be constructed on a firm basis, and different theories will be measured against an independent source of assessment. In this first chapter, I shall consider what goals we should set ourselves when we consider the nature of art.

## 1 EXTENSION

Many contemporary aestheticians take extensional adequacy to be the sole or primary criterion of adequacy of a theory of art. (Philosophers use the word "extension" to mean the things a word picks out.) That is, they seek a theory of art that classifies as art all or most of the things that we intuitively call "art", and that excludes all or most of the things that we intuitively do not call "art". Aesthetics is supposed to make progress by thesis and counterexample. Debate proceeds as follows: some aestheticians propose theories with the aspiration that they apply to most or all of the cases we intuitively call "art" and they hope the theories exclude most or all of the cases that we intuitively do not call "art". Other aestheticians then try to refute such theories by offering counterexamples that the theory fails to fit. If the counterexamples are genuine and significant, then the original theory must be abandoned or modified. This is how the game is played given the extensional criteria of adequacy.

This extensional methodology is particularly common among contemporary aestheticians.[1] Extensional inadequacy is seen as the prime theoretical flaw. It is because aestheticians place such a high premium on avoiding extensional inadequacy that they are anxious to say the right thing about avant garde art. A certain sort of aesthetician is terribly concerned with keeping up with the latest developments in experimental avant garde art. Such aestheticians tend to hold a theory of art that appeals to the 'artworld'—for example, an institutional or historical theory of art. There is a respectable motive behind this. They want to avoid a priorism. They worry that a theory might be produced on purely speculative or a priori grounds that does not fit the messy empirical facts about what art is actually like. And in particular, these aestheticians do not want to be caught being behind the artistic times. Surely—it seems reasonable to suppose—theories of art must fit the facts, including the facts of recent art history.

Thus, many aestheticians have made extension their God. One can understand why they have done so. If someone produces a theory of art according to which red Rams-horn water-snails are the only works of art, then something has gone sadly wrong. But my objection is that there is a lot more to a theory of art than its extensional adequacy. I shall try to say what this 'more' is. In the light of my alternative criterion of adequacy, I shall try to show why the extensional methodology is limited and inadequate as a sole or primary criterion of adequacy. But this will not mean that extensional adequacy counts for nothing. From the alternative point of view that I shall recommend, we shall see what can be said for extensional adequacy.

---

[1] Some prominent examples of contemporary aestheticians who are motivated by extensional adequacy are the following. Arthur Danto, "The Artworld", *Journal of Philosophy*, 1964, and *The Transfiguration of the Commonplace*, Cambridge, MA: Harvard University Press, 1981; George Dickie, *Art and the Aesthetic*, Ithaca: Cornell University Press, 1974, and *The Art Circle*, New York: Haven, 1984; Jerrold Levinson, *Music, Art, and Metaphysics*, Ithaca: Cornell University Press, 1990.

## 2 INTUITION AND REFUTATION

While extensional adequacy is the tacit and sometimes explicit ground-rule of much contemporary philosophy of art, it is worth noting the historical or sociological point that philosophy rarely operates exclusively with the extensional methodology. When one philosopher holds a thesis analogous to "All swans are white" and a second philosopher points out a black swan, that is rarely the end of the argument, because the first philosopher typically replies: "What black swan?—I can't see a black swan". We can hang on to a theory if we can reject purported counterexamples to it. It almost never happens that philosophical theories are subject to straightforward refutation by counterexample. The connection between theory and data is far more elastic than this extensional methodology suggests.

However, the relation between theory and data is not infinitely elastic. We do have *intuitions* about examples, and such intuitions are important: they are the basis for extensional methodology. But it is also important that intuitions differ. I often find that my intuitions differ from those of artworld or institutional theorists (such as Danto and Dickie). For example, such theorists tend to say things like "Some photographs are works of art, but ordinary unappropriated holiday snapshots are not". I don't agree. I think that many of the latter may be classified as works of art. The correctness or incorrectness of my intuitions does not matter particularly. But it is absolutely certain that it is not absolutely certain that ordinary unappropriated holiday snapshots are *not* works of art. There is no intuitional rock bottom. There are only shifting sands. The intuitions of artworld and institutional theorists, I would claim, have been corrupted by their theories. My intuitions, presumably, have been differently corrupted. But all the more reason not to make intuitions about examples to the final court of appeal.

The extensional methodology, and its concomitant appeal to intuitions, embodies a naive and limited methodology. My suspicion is that many aestheticians assume the extensional methodology because of the heritage of mid-twentieth century 'conceptual analysis' in philosophy. But that heritage in philosophy in general has for the most part been superseded—and for good reason. The irony is that while some aestheticians have been keen to show obsequious sensitivity to 'radical' developments in the artworld, the philosophical methodology that led them to this approach is crude and stale and, at the very least, unexamined.

## 3 THEORY AND EXPLANATION

If we are not to be guided by extension then—it will be asked—what else should we be guided by? We might even be tempted to think that we cannot argue for our assessment of theories of art. Perhaps this judgement is ultimately a matter of choice—a kind of theoretical existential leap! Such pessimism is not warranted. We can attain a neutrally agreed fulcrum in the following way.

We are pursuing a good theory (or account) of a general phenomenon. I say 'theory' (or 'account') rather than 'definition' since the latter sounds as if it has to do with the words or concepts. If philosophers pursue the philosophy of X (mind, mathematics, science, art), it is because they are interested in the phenomenon itself, not in our words or concepts. We want to know what X *is,* not what the word or concept 'X' means. We are interested in something that is sometimes called a 'real definition'. That is not to say that we can only have such an account of a phenomenon when we have a natural kind, of the sort that Saul Kripke and Hilary Putnam describe.[2] For example, many people think that biological kinds have real essences that are partly or wholly historical.

A *theory* of X is at very least a set of beliefs about X things: it is a further description of X things apart from merely saying that these things are called 'X'. But all sorts of descriptions are possible. So what sort of descriptions do we want? What we want, I think, is a description that *explains much that we independently believe about X things.* This is the kind of explanation of the phenomenon that we want.

The outline of a criterion of adequacy of a theory of X now begins to emerge: a good theory about the nature of X things would be a set of claims about X things that yields a good explanation of properties that we independently believe X things to possess. It could not be the case that the *only* beliefs we had about X things is that they are *called* "X". Suppose that we also believe that they are P, Q and R. These beliefs might be part of our everyday 'folk' wisdom about X things, or they

[2] Saul Kripke, *Naming and Necessity,* Cambridge, MA: Harvard University Press, 1980. Hilary Putnam, "The Meaning of Meaning", *Philosophical Papers, vol. 2,* Cambridge: Cambridge University Press, 1975.

might be empirical discoveries. A good theory of X things, then, would be a theory which attributes properties, say, F, G and H, to Xs, such that the fact that Xs are F, G and H explains the fact that they are P, Q and R.

Now, this very general schematic statement covers extensional adequacy as one factor but not as the only factor. For *one* of our beliefs about Xs is that certain things are X and that certain things are not. That is, we have beliefs about the extent of the phenomenon. Or if we want to semantically ascend, we can say that we believe that the word "X" applies to certain things and not to others; we have beliefs about the extension of "X". But it is important that there are many *other* things that we believe about Xs. And these beliefs might be equally important, or more important, from the explanatory point of view. Fitting the extension of the word "X" is one part of the explanatory methodology, but not all of it.

## 4 ART AND INTERPRETATION

When we strive to understand and explain *art,* we are concerned to understand and explain a common *human* phenomenon. Understanding and explaining art is not like understanding and explaining black holes or seaweed; for art is a product of human agency and it is the object of human perception. I shall argue that in the philosophy of art, we need to connect the explanatory methodology with issues that arise in the theory of the *interpretation* of mental states and artefacts such as texts.

When we explain the behaviour of bearers of propositional attitudes (mental states with contents)—that is, when we want to explain by attributing states such as beliefs, hopes, expectations, thoughts or wishes—we explain *by* interpreting. Were we dealing with black holes or seaweed then we would not have to deal with interpretation: a purely scientific account would suffice. Of course, works of art themselves can sometimes be interpreted, but only in as far as they are the product of creative activity or are appreciated. In considering art, what we need to explain by interpretation is not works of art themselves, but *behaviour involving works of art*. The kinds of behaviour in question are primarily *creative* and *appreciative* activities. The question is: how can we make such art-involving activities intelligible? We cannot understand works of art themselves independently of this enterprise. Imagine someone setting about describing all the works of art that there are in purely scientific terms. It is pretty clear that there will be nothing physical that is common to all works of art in intrinsic respects: some are made of canvas and paint; others of sounds; others of people in action; and others of words. We need to shift from focusing on works of art themselves to focusing on our propositional attitudes concerning works of art.[3]

If we are dealing with interpretation, we need to look to its fundamental principle. The principle is sometimes said to be the principle of 'charity', and it is sometimes said to be the weaker principle of 'humanity'; but we need not worry about the difference here. As Donald Davidson has emphasized, we could not know how to begin interpreting an organism as possessing propositional attitudes unless we assume that it shares many propositional attitudes with us.[4] Whether—contra Davidson—there could be propositional attitudes transcending our interpretational epistemic access is a question I leave open. If we want to understand some phenomenon, X, which is a product of human action or which is the object of human perception, then we must assume—at least as a regulative principle—that the people in question believe of X things much that we believe of them. We must assume that they share many of our beliefs about X things. This is surely correct as a regulative principle, even if we reject the transcendental consequences that Davidson draws—that massive error is incoherent.

Suppose we suspect that some alien being has been making or contemplating works of art in the way that we do. Then we must suppose that it believes of its products, or of what it is contemplating, much of what we also believe of our products. There is a holism point here: one cannot *just* believe that certain things are works of art without having further beliefs about those things. In belief attribution we must take into account other things believed about the object in question. There will be many of these beliefs, and they will be connected with many other beliefs. As Davidson emphasized, a propositional attitude is inevitably part of a wider system of propositional attitudes, and propositional attitude attribution must take account of this.

---

[3] Presumably it is not the case that the contents of propositional attitudes concerning works of art are determined in part by our causal interactions with works of art; for as physical things, there is nothing significant in common between them. The case will not be like our thoughts about natural kinds, on the Kripke/Putnam account.

[4] See his *Essays on Actions and Events*, Oxford: Clarendon, 1980; and *Inquiries into Truth and Interpretation*, Oxford: Clarendon, 1982.

## 5 ART AND DESIRE

Although I have just drawn attention to the *beliefs* that we must assume are possessed by a person who makes or experiences art, it would be a mistake to think that all we have to take into account in interpretation are beliefs. We must also take into account other sorts of propositional attitudes, such as desires, hopes and fears. In interpretation, we are interested in people's cognitive states and also their non-cognitive states. We need to explain behaviour, and we can only do that if we know about both the cognitive and the non-cognitive sides of the mind. For these two combine together to produce behaviour. To know only what someone believes is not sufficient.[5] We must interpret beliefs, desires and actions all at once.

What this means for the philosophy of art is that it is not enough to seek to understand the *beliefs* of those we are interpreting as making or contemplating works of art. We must also seek to understand their *desires* concerning works of art. And here I approach the main theme of this chapter.

People think that producing and consuming art is *worthwhile*. We have beliefs about the *value* of art and about its role in our lives. Among the things we believe about art is at very least that art-making and appreciation is a rational pursuit and not a waste of time. Sometimes we believe that it is worthwhile. And sometimes we believe that it is of very great worth. These beliefs about the value of art are closely tied up with our desires concerning art. It is an important fact that art *motivates* people to do various things—to produce and consume works of art. I do not want to commit myself to any view about the priority of desiring and valuing art. It may be possible to desire something without valuing it, and it may be possible to value something without desiring it. Moreover, it may be that we desire art because we value it, or it may be that we value it because we desire it. But at any rate, in the case of art, we both desire and value it, or at least quite a lot of it. And this desiring and valuing plays an essential role in art-related behaviour.

Hence a theory of art and art-behaviour must make sense of our desires and evaluations concerning art. If we have not made sense of these desires and evaluations, we will have made little progress in interpreting the

[5] See my "The Indifference Argument", *Philosophical Studies*, 2007.

behaviour of those who make and consume art. And, since the only form of understanding here is explanation by interpretation, it would mean that we would have made little progress in understanding art itself. We must understand how art can motivate anyone to do anything. And we must understand how art can seem valuable to its makers and consumers. We must understand why we bother with art. A good theory of art gives us such an understanding. And a theory that provides little or no understanding of this is a failure.

## 6 MOTIVATION AND THEORIES OF ART

This, then, is what there must be in a theory of art, beside extensional adequacy: we need a theory of art according to which it is understandable that people pursue the activities of making and contemplating art. And we need a theory of art according to which it is understandable that people value making and contemplating it. This is where many theories of art fall down. They fail to be theories that could contribute to the explanation of our interest in art. The list of failures probably includes: artworld theories, institutional theories, historical theories, ideology theories, semantic theories, emotion-expression theories, semiotic theories and many more. These theories fail to illuminate the question of how art-making or consuming could seem desirable or valuable.[6] Yet without that, a theory has not even begun as an explanatory theory. In this first chapter of this book, I do not want to get too involved in arguing for or against particular theories of art—there will be plenty of time for that later on. For the moment, I want to keep the discussion on a 'meta-level', as far as possible. But I shall indicate very briefly why I say that the above theories fail to be satisfactory on explanatory grounds, and I want to illustrate how the debates will go when we look at matters from the perspective of the methodology of rational explanation.

Consider, for example, the kind of view according to which works of art communicate some truth to us or enable us to experience some emotion. A common sort of debate then unfolds. Two worrying possibilities seem to be allowed. First, we could gain the same truth or emotion by making or perceiving a quite different work of art (say a work of literature rather than a painting), and so we ought to be

---

[6] See Roger Scruton, *The Aesthetic Understanding,* London: Carcanet, 1983, chapter 1.

indifferent between making or perceiving the one or the other of the two works of art. Second, we could gain the same truth or emotion by doing something that is nothing to do with art at all, and so we ought to be indifferent between making or perceiving a work of art and that other thing. In fact it is often likely that doing something else would produce the truth or emotion more effectively, and if so we ought to prefer that. Let us call these *substitution* arguments. We need to avoid theories of art which allow substitution arguments to succeed. For if they succeed, making or perceiving artworks would be irrational.

Of course, we are sometimes indifferent between making or perceiving two very different works of art, and we are sometimes indifferent between making or perceiving a work of art and doing something else. But *what* we find valuable in a particular work of art is not the same as what we find valuable in another work of art or in something else, even if we find both of equal value. What is problematic is the idea that what is of value in a work of art lies in some truth or emotion that we gain from it, even though something quite different would as easily yield the very same truth or emotion. For what is of value in the creation or experience of a particular work of art is not detachable from the creation or experience of the characteristics of that particular work of art (except in the unusual case where another work of art happens to be very similar). If what is valuable were detachable, art-activities would be rendered irrational. Suppose one wants a good milkshake and one knows that café A serves much better milkshakes than café B; then other things being equal it is irrational to go to café B for a milkshake. Similarly, if one's prime concern is with the truth or emotion one can get from a work of art, then it would be irrational to experience art as a means to that truth or emotion rather than pursuing some more effective non-artistic means; and we should be indifferent between experiencing two very different works of art if they are both equally a means to that truth or emotion.

The reply at this point might be that we are dealing with a rather special sort of truth or emotion—one which, somehow, only a work of art, and only a particular work of art, can state or express. However, then the problem will be to explain this without playing with the words "truth" or "emotion". Such theories might or might not be objectionable depending on the meaning that these words are given. However, given that art is said to convey truths or express emotions in the usual senses of these terms, these theories seem, on the face of it, to make it irrational to go in for making or contemplating art.

There are, of course, possible replies; but they tend not to be very convincing. Such theories have unpaid explanatory debts. Similar sorts of problems afflict other theories of art. Schematically, we are told that the essential thing about works of art is that they do F. But if some other work of art, or something which is not a work of art at all, would do F just as well, or better, then the rationality of our interest in art will have evaporated. What is important is that these are the *sort* of arguments that we need to discuss. This is more important than whether such arguments go through in the case of particular theories.

## 7 AESTHETIC THEORIES AND RATIONAL EXPLANATION

To anticipate matters that we will encounter in more detail in later chapters, my view is that the more traditional *aesthetic* approach to the philosophy of art does comparatively well in respect of motivational and evaluational considerations. Aesthetic accounts make room for the possibility of explaining the fact that we value and desire making and consuming art. Aesthetic theories come in many forms, but they all say that *pleasure* is derived from making or contemplating works of art. To be sure, it is pleasure of a special sort, but it is pleasure all the same.[7] If so, it is not difficult to see why we are motivated to go in for this kind of activity: it is understandable that people pursue pleasure. And if pleasure is derived from making or contemplating particular works of art, then it is also not difficult to see why the same pleasure cannot be obtained by contemplating a different work of art, perhaps in another medium, or something which is not a work of art at all. For the pleasure is an 'intentional' pleasure—a pleasure that is directed onto the work of art, a pleasure *in* characteristics of the work. So the pleasure taken in a particular piece of music could not be the same pleasure as that taken in a painting or in a game of cards.

If we say that pleasure is involved, we can explain the fact that we are motivated. And if we say that the pleasure is intentionally directed to the work of art, we can explain why substitution arguments do not go through. This is not yet enough to explain the peculiar *value* we ascribe

---

[7] The aesthetic theorist might deploy the notion of function and say that works of art do not necessarily *succeed* in possessing the aesthetic properties that it is their function to possess; works can fail to fulfil their purpose, at least to some degree.

to art. To explain that, we have to explain the peculiar value we ascribe to aesthetic pleasure. And to do that we have to say more about aesthetic pleasure than just saying that it is a pleasure. We see aesthetic pleasure as having a certain importance. What *kind* of pleasure is it? This is a deep and difficult question. I shall not pursue this issue further here. It is a fundamental issue in the theory of beauty and aesthetic pleasure.

Aesthetic theories not only do not rule out the possibility of explaining questions of value, they are particularly well placed to explain it. There may be objections to aesthetic theories, but such theories *do* seem to be able to provide the basis for an explanation of our interest in art.

This has been an incursion into, and a foretaste of, some of the issues that will occupy us in later chapters. But for the purpose of this chapter, it does not matter much if I am wrong about the virtues of aesthetic theories and about the weaknesses of truth- and emotion-inducing theories. What is crucial is that if such theories are assessed as succeeding or failing, it is on rational explanatory grounds.


## 8 CLASSIFICATORY VS. EVALUATIVE CONCEPTIONS OF ART

One important corollary of this argument is that the attempt to find a neutral, non-evaluative notion of art is doomed. Many philosophers have wanted to separate the question of what art is, from the question of its value. George Dickie, for example, has distinguished *classificatory* from *evaluative* senses of "art".[8] But to insist on a distinction along these lines is a mistake. For to classify something as art is—among other things—to make it intelligible that someone might value making or appreciating it. If so, an account of art must explain the fact that we value it; and in order to explain that, we must explain the fact that we value the activities of making and appreciating art.

Dickie defended his distinction by arguing that we need a theory that allows for bad art.[9] But only the crudest theory linking art and value would deny the possibility of bad art, and Dickie makes things too easy for himself by taking weak theories as his target. Of course, there is plenty of bad art. Nevertheless we need a theory that explains our positive evaluation of many creative and contemplative activities, and

---

[8] For example, George Dickie, *Aesthetics* pp. 98–99.
[9] George Dickie, *Art and Value*, Oxford: Blackwell, 2001, chapter 6.

this is compatible with allowing the possibility of some, or even quite a lot of, bad art. Indeed, such a theory may even require the existence of bad art, since we are pursuing an explanation of our positive evaluation of some but not all creative and contemplative activities.

Others have defended a classificatory 'definition' of art without deploying this bad argument from bad art. They argue that the project of explaining art activities or showing that they are valuable, or are reasonably thought to be valuable, is perfectly fine but need not be part of the project of 'defining' art or saying what art is.[10] This is quite a common view, but it is wrong for the reason that it overlooks the artefactuality of art. An artefact is something created to play a role, and as such it must be intelligible, merely in virtue of being an artefact, that someone could be motivated to use and value it, given that they have desires concerning the role in question. Consider hammers. We cannot separate classificatory and evaluative conceptions of hammers. For one thing, the nature of hammers dictates what good hammers are—a good hammer is good *as* a hammer. Furthermore, given a good theory of what hammers are, it is immediately clear why people might be interested in hammers. Presumably being a hammer implies that its maker intended to give it a nail-knocking role. This is a role that others apart from its maker can recognise and use. Thus, given that people have an interest in knocking in nails, it is understandable and rational that they make and use hammers. The idea that we should have one theory of what hammers are and a completely different theory of why hammers are thought valuable to make or use is clearly wrong. So we should not split hammer-theory into two separate parts—a metaphysical part and an evaluative part. Similarly with art. Works of art, like hammers, are artefacts; and that immediately implies that we cannot separate metaphysics from evaluation. What kind of artefact works of art are determines the kind of value that they can have as artefacts of that kind. Furthermore, given that one shares the goals of the art-makers—whatever they are—or one can at least imagine sharing them, art-activities are understandable and rational. Those goals in part determine the kind of artefacts that works of art are. They determine the kinds of value that they have as works of art of specific kinds. And they make making and using works of art intelligible. Hence the nature

---

[10] See for example Stephen Davies, *Definitions of Art*, Ithaca: Cornell University Press, 1991, pp. 42–47, and his "Essential Distinctions for Art Theorists", in (eds.) Stephen Davies and Ananta ch. Sukla, *Art and Essence*, London: Praeger, 2003, pp. 3–16.

of works of art, and the intelligibility of making and using art, are inextricably intertwined.

Being an artefact does not imply being a physical object that has been altered. We can understand artefactuality in a broader sense. An event such as a dance, or an abstract object such as a theory, are artefacts in a wide sense, since they are intentionally created, or brought into being, for a purpose. Can there be works of art that are not artefacts even in this wide sense? Suppose that someone exhibits unaltered driftwood in a gallery. They might merely be exhibiting interesting driftwood, but suppose that the driftwood is also a work of art. Is this a work that is not an artefact?[11] Here we should say that the work of art is indeed an artefact but it is *constituted* in part by the piece of driftwood, which is not an artefact. The work of art is always something brought into existence with a purpose.

A purely classificatory theory of *any* artefact would be mistaken, and so it is also mistaken in the case of art. But the error would be compounded in the case of art if it turns out that many or all works are *evaluative artefacts*, in the sense that sustaining certain values is the function of art, as knocking in nails is the function of hammers. That would make the art–value link even closer. It would not be so close that it would imply that there cannot be bad art. What it implies is that understanding what art is is not separable from understanding the minds of those who traffic with art; and understanding their minds means understanding how and why they value art. Furthermore if works of art are evaluative artefacts, it means that we value art because of the values it embodies.


## 9 KINDS OF KINDS

There is a preliminary question that we often have to ask in philosophy: what kind of kind are we dealing with? For example, an important preliminary question in the philosophy of mind is whether mental kinds are natural kinds. Many programmes in the philosophy of mind simply assume that they are. But some dispute this. Even if mental kinds are natural kinds, it needs to be argued, not assumed. If something is a natural kind, it has underlying properties that are essential to it and that

---

[11] See Stephen Davies' discussion in his *Definitions of Art*, chapter 5.

explain its causal properties; this is often accompanied by the epistemic claim that this essence may be unknown by those thinking in terms of the kind in question.

Gold is a natural kind. So a theory of the nature of gold and a theory of its value would be distinct projects. Artefactual things, by contrast, have value *as* things of their kinds, as well as having other values; and to conceive of a thing as an artefact of a kind is to grasp norms that apply to it in virtue of it being a thing of that kind. That is, if we know what kind of artefact something is, then we know what it is for it to be working well or malfunctioning. Artefactual natures and norms both derive from the intentions and desires of the maker of the artefact. And we need only imagine someone having those desires to understand using the artefact. Activities involving are intelligible to those who desire to open tins, or at least who can imagining desiring to open tins. (Something good might be inside!)

A colonic irrigator is a device for performing 'colonic irrigation', a spiritually purifying, ritual washing of one's bowels. Some people, it appears, desire to wash their bowels in this ritual, spiritual way. And something might be a device for doing just that. We might think that this desire is odd. No matter. There can still be better or worse colonic irrigators and they can work better or worse. And given that people have such desires, odd though they may be, the use and making of colonic irrigators is intelligible and rational.[12]

The theory of any artefact kind must tie in with a rational explanation of our traffic with artefacts of that kind. A theory of chairs must make it intelligible that we should make them and sit on them. Since chairs are artefacts that are for sitting on, it is easy to see why we might desire and value chair-involving activities. A pure 'descriptive' theory of chairs, which was severed from such explanations, would be misguided and inadequate. Similarly with a purely descriptive theory of art.[13]

## 10 COMPLEX ARTEFACTS

In an interesting recent discussion—one of the few to reflect on the goals of a theory of art—Stephen Davies opposes the kind of

---

[12] I assume a conception of rationality that is sometimes called 'internalist' or 'instrumentalist'.

[13] Contrast Richard Wollheim's puzzling 'deliberate omission' at the end of the main text of *Art and Its Objects*, Cambridge: Cambridge University Press, 1980.

evaluational account that I favour, and he sides with Dickie on this question. He pursues this by comparing the kind 'art' to the kind 'parking ticket'. Both, he thinks are what he calls 'human' kinds, not natural kinds, like gold, which may have a hidden microstructural essence. Parking tickets, Davies says, only have a 'nominal' essence, not a 'real' essence. Davies' view is that art is a human kind but not a simple one. Nevertheless he thinks that art is not a natural kind.[14] I am not sure that this categorization of kinds is helpful. First, it assumes that natural kind essences are always intrinsic. Although many natural kinds have intrinsic microstructural essences, some, it seems, also have *relational* essences, such as essential histories. There are historical kinds, such as biological kinds, which have historical essences. Ruth Millikan, for example, argues that a historical conception of function delivers explanatory generalities that a non-historical conception lacks.[15] And artefacts are similar. Second, although some kinds may have unknown essences, other kinds may have essences that must be known by those thinking in the terms in question. And artefact kinds such as "chair" or "parking ticket" are plausible examples. Such kinds still have real essences; it is just that those essences are transparent to thinkers. (In the jargon, they have *both* 'real' and 'nominal' essences.)

Although he thinks that works of art are not natural kinds, Davies thinks that the notion of 'art' is unlike the notion of a 'chair' (or 'tin-opener' or 'parking ticket') in that the function of chairs is simple and obvious to those who use the category, whereas the purposes of works of art, by contrast, are much more varied and obscure than those of chairs—and we know this. This point should be granted. Nevertheless both are artefact kinds, even if it is not clear exactly what specific kind of artefact works of art are. To think of something as a work of art is at least to conceive of the thing as an artefact. So artefactuality is essential to art and this principle has conceptual status, as it does for 'chair' (and 'tin-opener' and 'parking ticket'). This does not imply that works of art have no essential properties (and only 'nominal essences'), but it may be that their essential properties are not as transparent to those thinking in

---

[14] Davies, "Essential Distinctions for Art Theorists", *Art and Essence*, p. 5.

[15] See Ruth Millikan, "Biofunctions: Two Paradigms", in (eds.) Andre Ariew, Robert Cummins and Mark Perlman, *Functions*, Oxford: Oxford University Press, 2002; and see also her *White Queen Psychology*, Cambridge, MA: MIT Press, 1993, especially chapters 1 and 2.

the terms in question in the way that it is for those who think in terms of 'chair'.

Religious artefacts are more profitably compared with works of art. Religious artefacts have complex symbolic and ritual purposes that may be opaque to those who think in terms of them. In particular, there might be a division of labour and deference to authority in the knowledge of what kind of religious artefact something is. We may not really know what some religious artefact is for, but we may think that the rabbis, mullahs, priests or whoever, know what it is for. Thus while we might know that something is a religious artefact of some kind or other, we might not know exactly what it is for and thus we might not have a grasp of when the artefact is malfunctioning or functioning well as an artefact of its sort. Still, to know that it has some symbolic or ritual religious function is to know quite a lot. It is to know something about the broad kind of value that it can have. And given religious desires and values, our making and using artefacts of that sort is intelligible and rational. For example, many people wear a pendant round their neck that has an eye design. I recognize that artefact as something that is intended to ward off the 'evil eye'. So in a sense I know what it is *for*. Wearers believe that their pendant does this. The trouble, I confess, is that I do not really know what the 'evil eye' is, which means that I don't really know what it is that they are trying to neutralize with their pendants. In such a case I only partially grasp what this artefact is. And I only have a partial grasp of the rationality of wearing and making such pendants.

Works of art are in many ways like religious artefacts. They often have complex purposes and those purposes may be obscure to those who think in terms of them. Even so, this does not help those (such as Davies) to defend a purely 'descriptive' account of what art is. For even if we only have a partial grasp of an artefact kind, we have a partial grasp of what the norms are for the artefact, and we also have a partial grasp of the rationality of activities involving the artefact. What we do not have in the religious artefact case is a purely descriptive account. A religious artefact is one that is supposed to serve the religious purposes of those with religious desires and projects, such as warding off the evil eye. One might not share those desires and projects, just as one might not desire to have one's bowels ritually, spiritually washed. Still, a theory of such artefacts needs to dovetail with the actual desires, intentions and projects of human beings. And if it does not do so, the theory is inadequate. Fitting with the rational explanation of human activities is a criterion of adequacy of theories of any artefact type.[16] So this is also true of theories of art.


## 11 THREE REMARKS

(A) An interesting figure, when we think about the value of the arts, is Plato. For in the *Republic*, he rejects the value we tend to think much art possesses. But at the same time, he does attempt to provide an explanation of its *apparent* value. Plato thought that some art purports to give us something—knowledge—which it does not in fact give us, or perhaps it gives us knowledge, but of an inferior sort. Plato's theory attempted to explain why such art-making and art-consuming is desired and thought valuable even though in fact, according to him, it is not worthy of desire and it does not have the value we think it has. Plato thought that this art purports to give us knowledge, which is something we desire and value. Plato held an 'error theory' about our commitment to the value of such art. To his eternal credit, he tried to explain why it is we *think* that this art is valuable, even though he thought that we are mistaken about that. However, I take it that most theorists of art would want to explain why people desire and think that artistic activities are valuable, as well as holding that these activities really are of value.

(B) In the light of the criterion of adequacy according to which we must understand how making or experiencing a work of art might be thought to be desirable, we should be circumspect about the role that avant garde art plays in the philosophy of art. We do not have to be outrageously old-fashioned to doubt whether it is *obvious* that making and contemplating very radical avant garde works is worthwhile. The artworld has lapped it up, as have some philosophers of art, but the general public has been more circumspect.[17] I do not want to endorse any view on the value of such works. This is not the issue. The point is simply that it is misguided to make such examples one's *paradigm* in the philosophy of art, as many art theorists do. For in these cases,

---

[16] Compare Daniel Dennett, "The Interpretation of Texts, People and Other Artefacts", *Philosophy and Phenomenological Research* L, 1990, 177–194.
[17] One popular critic who criticises avant garde art harshly (but amusingly) is Brian Sewell, *An Alphabet of Villains*, London: Bloomsbury, 1995.

the value of art and its contemplation is at least controversial.[18] It may seem a little dull, but aestheticians who want to understand art would do better to concentrate on the more usual cases where the value of art is not in doubt.

(C) At this stage, I leave open the possibility that what people get out of making or contemplating works of art might vary from person to person or from one art form to another. The values of the arts are indeed many and varied, and so is what people get out of them. I only require that there is *something* that people get out of them. However, my view is that even though there are many differences between people and between different art forms, there is in fact also *some* sort of value that is shared by many art forms, which everyone can appreciate, even though there are *other* values that differ between people and between art forms. This value is aesthetic value.


## 12 PRIORITY

Where does this leave things with extensional adequacy? A theory of art explains nothing if it gets the extension right but fails to explain why anyone bothers with art. For most contemporary aestheticians, such a theory would be notched up as a success, but it should instead be marked down as a failure. What about a theory that explains the point of art but which is extensionally inadequate? There is no easy answer here. It depends how extensionally inadequate it is. It cannot be *majorly* extensionally inadequate. It must explain the point of many or most of those things that we normally categorize as works of art. But if the theory has minor extensional quirks in an otherwise good explanatory theory, these could be overlooked.

It would be a mistake to contrast the extensional and explanatory methodologies too dramatically. For what the extensional methodology tacitly does is to elevate one sort of belief about art into the only interpretational constraint. But, as I emphasized, not only do we have other beliefs about art, but also desires, which we need to respect in a theory of our transactions with art. Of course, our beliefs about which

---

[18] Perhaps there is something to be said for the appeal to 'paradigm cases' in the philosophy of art!

*Aesthetic Creation*

things are works of art are important. Otherwise how do we know what we are talking about? But these could not be our only beliefs about works of art. And in particular, we need to be interested in those beliefs about art that tie in with our desires concerning art, so as to yield action. The inadequacy of the extensional methodology stems from the fact that the mere belief that certain things are instances of a certain kind is a belief with limited consequences. It is not by itself a particularly motivationally significant belief to have. It is not the kind of belief that could move one to act unless one had other more exciting beliefs about things of that kind.

For this reason, the extensional criterion of adequacy is indeed second-rate. It is shallow and unilluminating.


## 13 CODA

What I have tried to do is to suggest a perspective from which we can think about various different and competing criteria of success for theories of art. I have proposed that rational explanation provides us with such a perspective. From this perspective, I have argued in favour of the motivational criterion and against the extensional criterion. I argued that the motivational constraint is a more fundamental constraint in the theory of art than extensional adequacy. For a theory of art must explain the behaviour of those who traffic with art. If it does not do that, there is no sense in which the theory has succeeded in telling us something about the nature of art. So purely extensional theorists cannot plead that they are simply interested in a different project. They cannot escape like that! To explain the behaviour of those who traffic with art, a theory must explain both our beliefs and our desires concerning art. We have to tailor our philosophy of art to the beliefs and desires that we actually have concerning art. Such an explanatory perspective grants a role to extensional adequacy, but it is a limited role. Motivational adequacy subsumes extensional adequacy. The motivational constraint is more fundamental. A theory of art according to which art could never have been thought to have a point is inadequate because it could not help to explain the behaviour of those who make and consume works of art. And given that art is a human product, it means that we have not understood it at all.

In this chapter, I have not entered much into the first-order debate concerning the correct theory of art. What I have done is to argue for a certain way of assessing theories of art. I have tried to lay down some groundrules in the philosophy of art.

# 2

# Art as Aesthetic Creation

In this chapter, I shall expound the theory of art that I call the 'Aesthetic Creation Theory'. It is a version of the aesthetic theory of art. I shall give an explicit statement of the theory and deal with minor queries. In sections 2 and 3 of this chapter, I focus on the main elements of the theory. In section 4, I add a number of supplementary remarks and caveats, which serve to clarify minor points and remove minor objections. And in section 5, I defend the theory against the charge that it ignores the social context in which works of art are produced. A full defence of the theory will then be provided in later chapters. I delay arguing against objections arising from avant garde art until the next chapter (Chapter 3), since it raises methodological issues. In the two chapters after that (Chapters 4 and 5) I tackle metaphysical issues that are generated by the Aesthetic Creation Theory. I shall not, in this chapter, attempt to argue against rival views of art. That is something I do in Chapters 6 and 7. My purposes in this chapter are constructive and defensive.

## 1 BASIC ELEMENTS

### 1.1 The Aesthetic Creation Theory

A bare statement of the Aesthetic Creation Theory is this:

Something is a work of art because and only because someone had an insight that certain aesthetic properties would depend on certain nonaesthetic properties; and because of this, the thing was intentionally endowed with some of those aesthetic properties in virtue of the nonaesthetic properties, as envisaged in the insight.

This statement makes various assumptions about aesthetic properties that I want to acknowledge immediately. After that I shall examine the intentional production of art and aesthetic insight.

## 1.2 Aesthetic Properties

I rely on the notion of an aesthetic property, and on there being a significant distinction between aesthetic and nonaesthetic properties. Which properties are 'aesthetic' properties? Aesthetic properties may be purely *verdictive* or *evaluative* properties, such as beauty and ugliness, or aesthetic merit and demerit, if indeed these are different from beauty and ugliness. Aesthetic properties also include *substantive* aesthetic properties, such as elegance, daintiness, balance or frenzy. Nonaesthetic properties include physical properties, such as shape and size, and secondary qualities, such as colours or sounds. In my view, nonaesthetic properties also include semantic or representational properties. I shall not expand upon this division here. I assume that it is in good order.

## 1.3 Aesthetic Dependence

I am also going to assume that aesthetic properties *depend* on nonaesthetic properties. The idea is that if something has an aesthetic property then it has it *in virtue of* its nonaesthetic properties or *because* of them. This dependence relation implies that a 'supervenience' relation holds between aesthetic and nonaesthetic properties. Supervenience is best characterized in terms of the existence of necessities running from nonaesthetic to aesthetic properties: if something instantiates an aesthetic property, it instantiates some nonaesthetic property that is *sufficient* for the instantiation of the aesthetic property. This implies that two things that are similar in all relevant nonaesthetic respects must be similar in all aesthetic respects, and that something which is unchanged in all relevant nonaesthetic respects must also be unchanged in all aesthetic respects. There are various complex and controversial issues over the exact characterization of supervenience that we need not discuss here.[1]

---

[1] One way of characterizing supervenience is as follows. A *particular* property A supervenes on a *particular* property N if and only if necessarily if something is N then it is M. If we want to make the supervenience claim one about *families* of properties, we can say that the *family* of properties *F* supervenes on the *family* of properties *G* if and only if something has an *F* property M then it has some *G* property N and necessarily if something is N then it is M. (See Jaegwon Kim, "Concepts of Supervenience", *Philosophy and Phenomenological Research*, 1984, reprinted in his *Supervenience and Mind*, Cambridge: Cambridge University Press, 1993.) The idea of aesthetic-nonaesthetic dependence can be found in Frank Sibley's important paper "Aesthetic/Nonaesthetic", *Philosophical Review*, 1965 (which was completed in 1959).

There are also complex issues about the relation between dependence and supervenience.

In my view, aesthetic/nonaesthetic dependence is a fundamental principle in ordinary aesthetic thought.[2] In making an aesthetic judgement, for example that something is beautiful, we cannot judge simply that it is beautiful, we must judge that it is beautiful by virtue of how it is in other respects. Not to do so would be irresponsible, or else bizarre and crazy. If something is beautiful it is so because of its other characteristics, and if we judge that something is beautiful we must judge that it is so because of its other characteristics. Thus aesthetic/nonaesthetic dependence is fundamental to aesthetic thought. It is an a priori or conceptual constraint governing aesthetic thought.[3] If aesthetic/nonaesthetic dependence is fundamental for all aesthetic thought, it means that it is fundamental to our aesthetic judgements, to our aesthetic intentions and also to our aesthetic insights.

Furthermore, there are dependence and supervenience relations *among* aesthetic properties, as well as a dependence and supervenience relation between aesthetic and nonaesthetic properties. Verdictive aesthetic properties depend on substantive aesthetic properties. Something may be beautiful in virtue of being graceful.

These are my assumptions. I defended these assumptions at length in my book *The Metaphysics of Beauty*. Some dispute these assumptions, and this is not the place to defend them. But many others say that even if these assumptions are granted, a tenable theory of art cannot be constructed around them. I shall do what they say cannot be done.

---

The idea of dependence without laws can be found in these papers some time before the same combination became popular in the philosophy of mind.

[2] For a defence of a parallel thesis in moral philosophy, see my "Moral Supervenience", *Midwest Studies in Philosophy*, vol. 20, 1996; "Moore, Essence, Dependence, Supervenience, Epistemology", *American Philosophical Quarterly*, 2005, and "Moral Epistemology and the Because Constraint", in (ed.) Jamie Dreier, *Contemporary Debates in Moral Theory*, Blackwell: Oxford, 2005.

[3] Alan Goldman argues against aesthetic supervenience in his *Aesthetic Value*, Boulder, CO: Westview, 1995, pp. 39–44. But his argument there takes as a premise a particular dispositional view of aesthetic value. He writes: ". . . even fully developed and informed tastes can differ between ideal critics. Supervenience therefore fails." (ibid., p. 42). But the dialectic cuts the other way. Given the common-sense nature of aesthetic supervenience, there must be something wrong with Goldman's theory of aesthetic value. It should also be noted that not all 'response-dependence' theories of aesthetic value are like Goldman's. For example, some response-dependence theories do not allow that ideal critics can disagree. And some response-dependence theories specify that things have dispositions to affect people in virtue of their intrinsic properties, in which case aesthetic supervenience can be respected.

## 2 THE INTENTIONAL PRODUCTION OF ART: BASIC ELEMENTS

### 2.1 Aesthetic Intentions

Let us start with the *production* of art. According to the Aesthetic Creation Theory of art, we try to achieve substantive aesthetic effects when we make a work of art, and in doing that we try to make something of aesthetic value. Art is the creation or construction of aesthetic value. Just as a joke is something created with the intention that it will be funny, and funny in a certain way, so, a work of art is something created with the intention that it will have aesthetic value in virtue of a specific aesthetic character.[4] It would not be very inaccurate to state the Aesthetic Creation Theory by saying that a work of art is something made to be *beautiful*, so long as 'beauty' is construed to amount to no more than having 'aesthetic value'. Talk of beauty and aesthetic value may sound old-fashioned to some ears, and I shall deal with this concern in the next chapter.

Exactly *how*, on the Aesthetic Creation Theory, do we go about producing aesthetic properties? According to the Aesthetic Creation Theory, works of art bear an essential relation to an intention that certain aesthetic properties will be *realized* by an object or event with certain nonaesthetic properties—for example, marks on canvas, sounds or words. In a sense, to create the one *is* to create the other. That is: we intend to realize certain aesthetic properties; we intend to realize certain nonaesthetic properties; and we intend to realize the aesthetic properties *by* realizing the nonaesthetic properties. (I assume that works of art have *positive* aesthetic functions, though we can imagine someone deliberately trying to make something ugly for some further purpose.)

There is a *metaphysical* dependence here. It is not that the realization of the aesthetic properties is intended to be a *causal consequence* of the re-alization of the nonaesthetic properties. The relation is tighter than that. The aesthetic properties hold *in virtue of* the nonaesthetic properties.

It is not as though a person first decides which aesthetic property is to be realized—elegance, say—and then wonders how that property

---

[4] The essential role of intention in defining what it is to be a joke can be seen if we consider that someone who unintentionally says something funny does not thereby make a joke; there is a difference between 'laughing at' and 'laughing with'.

can be produced. That would leave matters somewhat open since it is plausible that aesthetic properties are variably realized by nonaesthetic properties: many very different sorts of things can be elegant. The person does not just want to produce *elegance* but *elegance that depends on or is realized in certain nonaesthetic properties.*

We cannot *intend* to create aesthetic properties in virtue of nonaesthetic properties unless we *believe* that the aesthetic properties depend on the nonaesthetic properties. So it is not enough that aesthetic properties *do* depend on nonaesthetic properties, the producer of art must also *believe* that they do.

The claim, then, is that in artistic activity, there is an intention that by creating an object or event with certain nonaesthetic properties, certain dependent aesthetic properties will be produced. The existence of such an intention or set of intentions, I maintain, is essential for something to be a work of art.

## 2.2  The Success Condition

Two other supplementary essential conditions need to be added if we are to understand how we act on aesthetic intentions so as to produce a work of art.

We must add some kind of *success* condition as a second condition for art status: it is not enough that someone merely *intends* to realize a certain range of aesthetic properties by realizing a certain configuration of nonaesthetic properties. The strongest success condition would be that the intended aesthetic properties do in fact depend on the nonaesthetic properties that are produced. So something is art only if a person intended to make a thing possess certain aesthetic properties by giving it certain nonaesthetic properties *and* it does in fact have those aesthetic properties because it has the nonaesthetic properties.

But this seems too strong. Things can go wrong in the production of art in two ways. Someone might get particular dependence relations wrong. A nonaesthetic set-up might in fact realize the aesthetic properties of ugliness and clumsiness, rather than of beauty and elegance as was nobly intended. Or someone might have excellent aesthetic intentions that were not properly executed because the nonaesthetic properties were not successfully produced. There are unsuccessful works of art just as there are unfunny jokes. But can works of art or jokes be *completely* unsuccessful? It is true that some jokes are not as funny as they are intended to be, but perhaps they must be funny to some non-zero degree.

As Donald Davidson says in passing, they must have brought something off even if it was not worth bringing off.[5] 'Unfunny' jokes are somewhat funny, otherwise they have not succeeded in being a joke. Similarly, works of art are not all as good as they were intended to be. But no work of art is a *complete* failure. Elements of success can be found in the most abysmal works. Bad works of art are aesthetically successful in *some* respects. Success and failure is not black and white. Not every aesthetic ambition need be successfully achieved; but they cannot all fail. We can leave this requirement deliberately vague: *some significant proportion* of aesthetic intentions must be successfully executed.[6] Dysfunctional works of art will be examined further in Chapter 5.

## 2.3 Non-deviant Causal Chains

There is one more element of the intentional production of art. The relation between the aesthetic properties produced and the artist's intentions must be a causal relation of the right kind. Imagine that someone has an aesthetic intention that by realizing certain nonaesthetic properties, certain aesthetic properties will be thereby realized. The object then comes into existence by a miraculous coincidence, and the object does in fact have the aesthetic properties in virtue of the nonaesthetic properties. Our first two conditions include this in the class of artworks. But it should be excluded because the aesthetic properties of the object are not the causal upshot of the person's intentions and subsequent endeavours. The object with its aesthetic properties is not a consequence of what the artist did. We therefore need to add to the definition that the requirement that the object together with its aesthetic properties is a causal consequence of what someone did so as to realize aesthetic intentions.

But even this is not enough. It fails to exclude the following case. I am sitting in a chair, and the inspired thought strikes me: "Ah Ha! If I paint a blue splodge in the middle of the canvas, it will look dynamic and frenzied". I then leap out of my chair to perform the deed, only to knock over the pot of blue paint from the arm of the chair onto the canvas, thereby creating a blue splodge exactly like the one I had in

---

[5] Donald Davidson, "What Metaphors Mean", *Inquiries into Truth and Interpretation*, Oxford: Blackwell, 1984, p. 245.

[6] We can imagine someone querying even this weakened success requirement. Perhaps only aesthetic intentions matter and completely failed works of art can be admitted as unusual cases. However, we can ignore this since little turns on it.

mind and was about to create with painstaking care.[7] That would be what is called a 'deviant causal chain'. Although there is a causal relation between the intention and the splodge, it is not the right kind of causal relation to make the result art. For something to be a work of art, it is necessary that the aesthetic effect is produced by means of a non-deviant causal chain between intention and result. There is a general problem about saying what it is for causal chains to be deviant. But since this is a quite *general* problem, and not something that afflicts only the philosophy of art, we need not tackle it here.

At any rate, according to the Aesthetic Creation Theory, there are three components of the intentional production of art. (A) There are aesthetic intentions, the content of which is that by realizing certain nonaesthetic properties, certain aesthetic properties will thereby be realized. (B) Many of the intended aesthetic properties are realized in the nonaesthetic properties, as intended. And (C) these aesthetic properties must be the non-deviant causal upshot of the aesthetic intentions.

## 3 AESTHETIC INSIGHT: BASIC ELEMENTS

### 3.1 Insufficiency

A parallel story—connecting intention, success and non-deviant causal chains—also applies to other activities, such as making bookshelves and boats. All I have really said so far is that art is the product of a certain sort of rational activity. The only differential feature has been that it is aesthetic properties that we strive to realize in artistic rational activity. But more must be said. The intentional realization of aesthetic properties is not enough for art. For example, one might cultivate potted plants for their beauty. Or one might appreciate the beauty of some natural thing—a shell for example—and decide to make an artificial replica of it using a rubber mould. But neither the potted plant nor the replica shell are works of art (if that is all there is to it). Furthermore, someone might produce works of art without being an artist. For example, a studio assistant might work in the studio of an artist, carrying out the artist's instructions, but with enough understanding to see what is being aiming at. Or someone might work

---

[7] Or paint-staking care?

in a factory, mass-producing something that someone else has designed but with enough understanding to see what the designer was aiming at. What is it that artists do that distinguishes them from aesthetically aware studio assistants or factory workers? What is produced by such studio assistants or factory workers is indeed art, but they are not the artists of the works of art they produce. More needs to be said.

## 3.2 Aesthetic Insight

What we need to add is that a work of art must have its origin in a piece of *aesthetic insight*. Aesthetic insight involves, but is not exhausted by, the acquisition of the knowledge that a specific aesthetic property depends on a specific configuration of nonaesthetic properties. It is an insight into a nonaesthetic-to-aesthetic dependency. And the insight into the dependency is put into practice by means of an intention that has the content of the insight. However, the acquisition of this knowledge of the dependency is not sufficient for aesthetic insight. For in normal aesthetic appreciation, one is aware of how a thing's aesthetic properties depend on its nonaesthetic properties. One is struck by the fact that something with certain nonaesthetic properties has certain aesthetic properties. What I have called "insight" also involves the acquisition of knowledge of aesthetic/nonaesthetic dependence relations. So what's the difference?

The difference is that an insight is not derived from perceiving an existing thing with the nonaesthetic properties. The artist either has a vision of a *non-actual* thing with the aesthetic/nonaesthetic property combination or of an actual thing that lacks these properties. The content of the insight is that certain aesthetic properties *would be* realized by certain nonaesthetic properties. Those aesthetic properties would be realized by those nonaesthetic properties because the aesthetic properties depend on the nonaesthetic properties. This implies that a counterfactual conditional holds: *if* the nonaesthetic property were instantiated *then* the aesthetic properties would be instantiated. And the artist thinks that if certain nonaesthetic property instantiations were produced *then* certain aesthetic property instantiations would be produced. The artist strives to actualize an object like the possible one envisioned in the insight. Both insight and appreciation share the cognition of aesthetic-nonaesthetic dependence relations. But the cause of the insight is not actual instantiation of the combination.

Someone with no capacity for appreciation could have no creative insight. (As Kant would say, genius involves taste.)[8] But the reverse is not true. One could be appreciative but uncreative. Aesthetic creativity or talent might be defined as the capacity to envisage non-actual things that would have a high degree of aesthetic value. (*Artistic* creativity or talent, however, may involve *aesthetic* creativity or talent *plus more*, since aesthetic properties are not the only significant properties of works of art. See section 4.1 of this chapter, and Chapter 5, sections 5 and 6.)[9]

Am I saying that art must be *original*? No. All we have is the thesis that art must have its origin in aesthetic insight. But insight need not be original. Given some insight, it is possible that someone else had a similar one a year earlier. Originality is a relational matter. It is a matter of the relation of ideas and works of art to other ideas and works of art. Originality is not an *aesthetic* quality of works of art, although it may be an *artistically* valuable quality of them. Of course, in many cases originality involves aesthetic qualities. But originality is then a second-order property; it is a property a work has in virtue of having aesthetic properties that stand in certain relations to the aesthetic properties of other works.

## 3.3 Insight and Ideas

We should distinguish aesthetic *insight* from aesthetic *ideas*. Insight is the psychological event or process of apprehending or grasping an aesthetic/nonaesthetic dependence relation without being prompted by some actual instantiation of the aesthetic property in combination with the nonaesthetic property. One forms *aesthetic ideas* on the basis of aesthetic insights. Insight is the personal acquisition of an idea. A person cannot share an insight with another person. But aesthetic ideas are public and sharable. So a person can share aesthetic ideas with another person. Ideas are public, insight is personal.[10]

Let us also stipulate that insight is *veridical*. Insight is a moment of acquiring *knowledge*. (It is somewhat like Ludwig Wittgenstein's

---

[8] Kant, *Critique of Judgement*, Oxford: Oxford University Press, 1928, section 48.

[9] Many psychological studies of artistic creativity operate with an impoverished conception of what it is they are investigating. There seems to be little appreciation of the fact that creative thought might have a *content* that matters. This explains the implausibility of the existing computational models of creative thought. See, for example, Philip Johnson-Laird's content-blind model in *Computers and the Mind*, London: Fontana, 1988, chapter 14.

[10] There are obviously Kantian overtones here with this talk of art in terms of "aesthetic ideas". But with a respectful nod in his direction, let us steer away from textual enquiries.

moment of knowing how to go on to extend a series to new cases.)[11] We must know that the envisaged aesthetic properties really would depend on the nonaesthetic properties. Let us say that an aesthetic *thought* is what we have when we *believe* that certain nonaesthetic properties would depend on certain aesthetic properties. If, in addition, they would, and one's aesthetic thought was non-accidentally correct, we can say that the thought was an aesthetic *insight*.[12]

## 3.4 Phases

According to the Aesthetic Creation Theory, the production of a particular work of art has three, in principle, separable phases: first, there is the insight that by creating certain nonaesthetic properties, certain aesthetic properties will be realized; second, there is the intention to realize the aesthetic properties in the nonaesthetic properties, as envisaged in the insight; and, third, there is the more or less successful action of realizing the aesthetic properties in the nonaesthetic properties, as envisaged in the insight and intention.

The insight into the aesthetic/nonaesthetic dependence is *in principle* separable from the intention to execute that idea by realizing the aesthetic property in the nonaesthetic property. This is obvious in cases where aesthetic ideas are not executed. For example, many architectural designs are never built. Some academic architects have even made their careers as 'paper architects'. However, in many cases there is no time-lapse between insight and execution. One might have ideas *as* one makes. One can improvise visually as one can improvise in music. It is not as if one always sets up some kind of blueprint in one's mind, which one then mechanically realizes. One can think *in* acting and making.[13] In such cases one acts intentionally without a previously formed intention. But that does not mean that in such unreflective intentional action, an intention is not a cause of the action.[14] Tinkering and experimenting are often part of the artistic process. Insight and execution usually flow into each other and affect each other. It is rare that a work of art stems

---

[11] Ludwig Wittgenstein, *Philosophical Investigations*, Oxford: Blackwell, 1953, sections 151 and 179.

[12] I here espouse 'externalism' about the epistemology of insight. That is, one need not have justification for one's insight. See further section 5 of this chapter.

[13] See Andrew Harrison, *Making and Thinking*, Indianapolis: Hackett, 1978.

[14] Donald Davidson, "Intending", in *Essays on Actions and Events*, Oxford: Clarendon, 1980.

from just one solitary insight. Usually matters are more complex, and many efficacious insights are affected by the evolution of the work as it is constructed. (See Chapter 6 section 5.) However, the point remains that aesthetic insight and intention are different psychological states that are separable in principle.

## 3.5 Art, Insight and Origin

We can now return to the problem of the studio assistant and factory worker. In these cases, there is a causal relation between an insight and an intention; it is just that the person with the aesthetic intention is not the same person as the person who had the aesthetic insight. In many cases they are the same. Artists might have an idea and then execute it themselves. Or they may leave much of the execution to someone else—the studio assistant or factory worker. The studio assistant or factory worker may have the aesthetic *idea,* but it derived from someone else—the person who had the *insight.* That person is the artist. However, in both cases there is a causal relation between insight and execution; and in both cases what is produced is a work of art. It is just that in one case the causal chain goes via another person.[15]

There can be aesthetic intentions that do not have their origin in aesthetic insight. The person who grows potted plants or who casts replica shells does so because they intend to realize the beauty of the plant or shell. The products of such intentions lack art status (if that is all there is to it). The plant and replica are not works of art. By contrast, where an aesthetic intention implements somebody else's aesthetic insight, that does yield a work of art.

# 4 COMMENTS, CAVEATS AND MINOR OBJECTIONS

## 4.1 Other Functions?

One surprisingly common objection to any aesthetic theory of art is that works of art cannot have essential aesthetic roles because works of

---

[15] Suppose that a creative but lazy artist has an insight into an aesthetic/nonaesthetic dependency but fails even to intend to realize the aesthetic/nonaesthetic property combination. Suppose also that another person somehow gains access to the insight and realizes the combination. In that case, the resulting work of art has essential origins both in the insight of the lazy artist and in the intentions of the enterprising second person.

art are often created with other purposes, such as religious, economic or propaganda purposes. Despite the frequency with which this objection is put to aesthetic theories, it commits an obvious non-sequitur. To be sure, works of art are often created with religious, moral, economic or propaganda purposes, just as works of architecture are often created to keep the rain out. But for the Aesthetic Creation Theory, it is only necessary that aesthetic considerations had *some* impact on the design of a thing. There must be aesthetic intentions. What we can call the 'some–all fallacy' is committed by someone who argues that there are many nonaesthetic pressures on the production of works of art, *so* there is no need to appeal to aesthetic factors to explain art. Of course, people often have many *other* aims in making works of art. Works of art serve all sorts of nonaesthetic functions. The aesthetic function may be just *one* of the functions that a work of art has. The aesthetic function need not even be the primary or most important function.[16] But it must be a significant factor. We can cast this in counterfactual terms. It must be the case that had the person not had aesthetic intentions, then, other things being equal, the object or event would have been different in nonaesthetic respects. (The 'other things being equal' clause serves to deal with the rare case where the result is overdetermined by aesthetic and nonaesthetic considerations.) There are three ways that nonaesthetic functions can figure. (A) The nonaesthetic aims might sit alongside the aesthetic aims. For example, one might make a work of art to be beautiful and also to worship God, or to make money, or to inspire moral or political improvement. One might kill two birds with one artistic stone. (B) The nonaesthetic aims might be *prior* to the aesthetic aims. For example, one might create something beautiful *in order* to worship God or *in order* to make money or *in order to* inspire moral improvement. The work of art serves its theological, financial or moral purpose *by* serving its aesthetic purpose. (C) The aesthetic aims might be prior to the nonaesthetic aims. Something might be beautiful as something that serves a certain purpose. For example, music might be beautiful *as* music for marching or praying or dancing (but not I think for shopping). Kant called this 'dependent beauty'.[17]

---

[16] Stephen Davies put forward the suggestion that ". . . the aesthetic character [of art] must be relevant to its serving the main purpose at which it is aimed" (*Southern Journal of Philosophy*, XXXV, 1997, p. 29). This is an interesting suggestion, but I fear it may be over-strict. The aesthetic purpose might be important but not bound up with the most important purpose.

[17] Kant, *Critique of Judgement*, section 16. See also chapter 4 of *Metaphysics of Beauty*.

## 4.2 Dead Author Discourse?

The Aesthetic Creation Theory makes free use of the notion of intention. But has this not been discredited? Are we not supposed to have learned that 'the author is dead'?[18] Three points: first, those who engage in Dead Author Discourse often conflate *constitutive* and *epistemological* questions. Giving a constitutive role to intention in determining what it is to be art, and what it is to be a specific work of art, does not imply that the best way to *find out* about the aesthetic properties of a work of art is by investigating the author's intentions without reference to the work. We are not committed to a methodology of rooting around in biography. It could be that the best way to know about the author's aesthetic intention is to consider the work itself. The author's intention may be *manifest in* the work of art.[19] Take Cycladic sculptures. We have little idea of their nonaesthetic role. We do not know their religious function, assuming they had one.[20] How do we know that they are works of art? Surely we can know pretty much by looking at Cycladic sculptures that they were designed with aesthetic intentions (among others). For Cycladic sculptures have great aesthetic value, and it is obviously no accident that they do. (By contrast, it *is* an accident when surgical instruments or railway signals have valuable aesthetic qualities.) Second, the claim is not that the artist's intentions determine the aesthetic properties of the work of art. Whether a work of art *succeeds* in having the aesthetic properties the artist intended it to have is an open question. That is something that we must judge. The work may fail in many respects. An artist might intend that a work will have aesthetic value in virtue of substantive aesthetic properties which it does not in fact possess. On the other hand, it is unlikely that a work will actually possess aesthetic value in virtue of substantive aesthetic properties that were not at all intended. Third, *sometimes* Dead Author Discourse is interpretable as an outright rejection of any role for the artist's intention in the essence of art. But we never see any argument for that.

---

[18] This issue is usually one about the representational and semantic properties of works of art; but to make it relevant to the Aesthetic Creation Theory, I assume that it applies to aesthetic intentions as well as semantic and representational intentions.

[19] Note also that artists have no privileged access to their aesthetic intentions: their intentions are one thing; their views about them is another.

[20] Prehistoric archaeologists sometimes seem to operate with a principle of *uncharity* in interpretation, when they assume that every representational thing they find has a religious or magical function.

## 4.3 Aesthetic Thought and Talk?

Although I have referred to the various particular aesthetic properties that someone might want to realize in a work of art, there is also its *total aesthetic character*. This is the conjunction of *all* the aesthetic properties that it possesses. It is a *maximal* aesthetic property. This property will be more complex than merely being graceful or dumpy. Perhaps, in more interesting cases, it is not expressible in language. There is an inexhaustibility to our aesthetic description of anything moderately interesting. This means that the makers of works of art have thoughts with very complex and elusive contents. There is no reason to think that this is particularly problematic. (Life is complex and elusive.) However, we might worry about the possibility of a radical mismatch between legitimate aesthetic descriptions of a work of art and what passed through the mind of the artist. Obviously, the artist need not have mastered a critic's sophisticated vocabulary. We are interested in aesthetic *thought* not *talk*. But, except where aspects of a work have failed, legitimate descriptions cannot come as a complete surprise to the artist. The artist must think, "Well, I wouldn't have thought to put it like that, but, yes, that is a fair description of what I was trying to do." The linguistic description of aesthetic thought is relatively controversial because aesthetic thought is not itself linguistic.[21] There is room for imaginative metaphorical description. But apt linguistic descriptions of successful works of art cannot diverge greatly from the artist's non-linguistic intentions.[22]

## 4.4 Chance?

Am I implying that every aspect of a work of art is intentionally produced? No. Chance often plays a role, for example rather dramatically so in the paintings of Jackson Pollock. However, even in Pollock's paintings, chance played a role only within certain confined and intended parameters. How his paintings turned out was very far from being

---

[21] See *Metaphysics of Beauty*, chapter 10, part 3.

[22] Anthony Blunt writes ". . . parallels can be shown between paintings by Picasso and works which it is fairly certain he did not know" (*Guernica*, Oxford: Oxford University Press, 1969, p. 6). Although Picasso need not have been aware of the source of the borrowed style, and he need not remember the works by which the style reached him, he was surely aware of the immediate qualities of the style itself.

completely a matter of luck. There was always some result that was deliberately produced.

## 4.5 Contextualism?

Some aestheticians think that the aesthetic properties of an object depend on its intrinsic nonaesthetic properties *plus* facts about its artistic context. Does the Aesthetic Creation Theory ignore that context? No. We can say that the artistic intention is the intention that by creating nonaesthetic properties *in a wider context,* certain aesthetic properties will thereby be realized. Or alternatively, we can say that the nonaesthetic properties of works of art, on which its aesthetic properties depend, can include relations to artistic contexts as well as intrinsic nonaesthetic properties. We might or might not require that the artist is *aware* of the context and its determining role. But, at any rate, contextualism about aesthetic properties is compatible with the Aesthetic Creation Theory. I happen to have considerable sympathy for a moderate version of formalism that denies the importance of context in many cases. Nevertheless, the Aesthetic Creation Theory is compatible with both formalism and anti-formalism.

## 4.6 Art/Craft?

On the Aesthetic Creation Theory, is there a distinction between 'art' and 'craft'? No. For the Aesthetic Creation Theory, art is a sub-class of craft: it is aesthetic craft. If craft were defined as having no aesthetic aspiration, then an art/craft distinction would be acceptable as a stipulation. But much that would normally be included as craft has an aesthetic function. I am happy to include this as art. I will comment on this inclusiveness in the next chapter and in the Appendix to Chapter 6.

## 4.7 High/Low?

A distinction is sometimes drawn between Art-with-a-capital-'A', or Fine art, on the one hand, and decorative art, on the other. This sort of distinction also goes by various other names: we have 'high-brow' versus 'low-brow', 'high-culture' versus what plebs, proletarians and peasants like, and sometimes 'art' versus 'craft'. The Aesthetic Creation Theory does not at all depend on these distinctions. Both fine art and decorative art, both high-brow art and low-brow art, and both high-culture art and what plebs, proletarians and peasants like, have and are intended to have aesthetic qualities. So there is no philosophically interesting distinction here. We need not be against a sociological account of this sort of distinction *within* the aesthetic.[23] Maybe it is true that different social classes make different judgements of taste. However, that does not begin to show what many sociological writers say it shows—for example, that Kant was wrong, or that the idea of a faculty of taste is a bourgeois illusion, and so on.[24] Nevertheless, there *is* some justice in the complaints of the sociologically minded that such groupings are evaluatively and politically loaded.[25] What is deemed 'high' or 'fine' art is thereby given a higher value than what is excluded. As will be clear at many points in this book, I firmly reject reductionist sociological approaches to *general* theorizing about art (see Chapters 2, 6 and 7). But I agree that these sociological theorists are *sometimes* right about those distinctions. The sociologist's mistake is not to see that the philosophy of art can carry on without those distinctions. The Aesthetic Creation Theory can embrace both 'high' or 'fine' art as well as the more lowly sorts of art. In my view, the general theory of art should be blind to the high-art/low-art distinction.

## 4.8 Metaphysics?

Does the Aesthetic Creation Theory beg any questions about the metaphysical status of aesthetic properties? No. The account of art proposed here presupposes that we have *some* respectable notion of an aesthetic property. It might turn out that the best theory of aesthetic properties is realism, projectivism or an aspect theory. The Aesthetic Creation Theory need not commit itself on this controversial matter. It can remain neutral on it.[26]

## 4.9 Other Aesthetic Definitions?

The Aesthetic Creation Theory differs from the usual sort of aesthetic account of art which appeals to the aesthetic *experiences* of people who

[23] See Peter Kivy, "Is Music an Art?", *Journal of Philosophy*, 1993, reprinted in *The Fine Art of Repetition*, Cambridge: Cambridge University Press, 1993.
[24] See chapter 12 of *Metaphysics of Beauty*.
[25] See Pierre Bourdieu, *Distinction*, London: Routledge & Kegan Paul, 1984.
[26] See *Metaphysics of Beauty* and "Aesthetic Realism", in (ed.) Jerrold Levinson, *Oxford Companion to Aesthetics*, Oxford University Press, 2003.

perceive works of art. Monroe Beardsley gave an account of this sort in his paper "An Aesthetic Definition of Art".[27] I have much sympathy with Beardsley's account. Like the Aesthetic Creation Theory, Beardsley's aesthetic account is intention-based, and it deploys the notion of the aesthetic. However, instead of appealing to the intention to realize aesthetic properties, Beardsley appeals to the intention to endow an object with a capacity to satisfy an 'aesthetic interest'. Readers who prefer aesthetic experience accounts, such as Beardsley's, may want to translate my account into theirs by substituting "capacity to satisfy an aesthetic interest" or "disposition to provoke an aesthetic experience" where I write "aesthetic property". Quite a lot of the discussion could go ahead in these terms. I shall not now give a proper argument against this rival sort of aesthetic theory. I give a quite general argument against all audience theories in Chapter 6. However, I will note here that it seems to me that Beardsley's notion of an aesthetic interest is not easy to grasp. More importantly, even if this were not a difficulty, we can ask: *in virtue of what* does a thing have the capacity to satisfy an aesthetic interest? The Aesthetic Creation Theory can answer that question with ease since it invokes aesthetic properties. But without aesthetic properties, the capacity that Beardsley invokes is surely too vague. For in a sense *everything* has a *capacity* to satisfy an aesthetic interest (if we are generous enough about the possible circumstances in which the capacity is exercised). So there is an important gap in Beardsley's account. In Chapter 6, I will object to all audience theories that artists often do not care about the effects of what they create, either on others or on themselves. Beardsley's theory seems to be as vulnerable as any audience theory to this objection. I feel bad about turning against my ally. I go a long way with Beardsley. But, sadly, there is a point where we must part.

## 4.10 Ontological Quandaries?

The Aesthetic Creation Theory sheds some light on a difficulty in the ontology of art. We want to think two things are in tension. We want to think of some works of art, such as sculptures and paintings, as *particular objects or events*, existing at a particular place and time. But we also want to think that works of art are *types*—agreeing with P. F. Strawson that the tendency to think otherwise in the case of paintings and

---

[27] Monroe Beardsley, "The Aesthetic Definition of Art", in (ed.) Hugh Curtler, *What is Art?*, New York: Haven, 1983.

sculptures arises only from the contingent limitations of present day reproductive techniques.[28] But a work of art cannot be both a token and a type. The Aesthetic Creation Theory explains this tension. The intuition that a work of art is a token, derives from the condition that a work of art is the end product of a causal process which begins with certain psychological states. As an item in the causal nexus, it seems that a work of art must be a particular. The intuition that a work of art is a type derives from the condition that a work of art's aesthetic properties depend on its nonaesthetic properties. So something else could realize the same aesthetic properties if it were nonaesthetically the same. Since these aesthetic properties are essential to the work of art, it seems that a work of art must be a type. We are pulled both ways; and the Aesthetic Creation Theory explains this.

## 4.11 Concepts or Reality?

The Aesthetic Creation Theory is an account of what art is and not of the concept of art. The aim is to provide something more like a 'real definition' rather than conceptual analysis. The aim is to describe and explain a phenomenon, not a word or a concept. But it would not matter much if it turned out that the essence of art is built into some concept of art. However, the more sophisticated the theory of the essence of art becomes, the less likely it is that ordinary folk grasp that essence in their thought about art.

## 5 THE SOCIOLOGY OF GENIUS

### 5.1 Genius, Mysticism, History

It will be objected that I am committing myself to an implausibly romantic, mystical and ahistorical notion of creativity.

My reply is, yes—I am happy to embrace a romantic and mystical view of creativity—but, no—it is not ahistorical.

The classic romantic mystic about this subject was Plato in his dialogue the *Ion*. There is a lot to be said for the view that Plato expresses there. The view is that the origin of art lies in divine inspiration—insight comes from the *muse*. Plato's vision of art in the *Ion* is in many respects

---

[28] P. F. Strawson, *Individuals*, London: Methuen, 1959, p. 231.

congenial to the Aesthetic Creation Theory.[29] Like magnetic charge, an aesthetic idea can be that which is transmitted from muse to poet to rhapsode to audience. And aesthetic insight is what transpires during possession by the muse. Perhaps, sadly, it is no longer possible literally to believe in the muse. But Plato's picture of art as the product of divine inspiration is a fruitful one.[30]

Such a picture is anathema to the contemporary sociology of art. For example, Janet Wolff writes that she is against

. . . the romantic idea of art as the creation of 'genius', transcending existence, society and time, . . . it is rather the complex construction of a number of real, historical factors.

She thinks that

. . . art and literature have to be seen as historical, situated and produced, and not as descending as a divine inspiration to people of innate genius.[31]

But this is a false opposition. Why cannot genius and insight be historically conditioned? We can say that a genius can only have certain muse-inspired insights given a certain state of the artistic culture and given a stylistic heritage.[32] As Vaughan Williams wrote:

The other fallacy is that the genius springs from nowhere, defies all rules, acknowledges no musical ancestry and is beholden to no tradition. . . . Is not the mighty river of Wagner but a confluence of the smaller streams of Weber, Marschner, and Liszt?[33]

Maybe there is something mysterious about how a great artist arrives at novel aesthetic ideas. But, as Williams sees, this is compatible with saying

---

[29] There is no need to assume that the *Ion* involves a view of art as mimesis or as that which produces emotional effects, as some commentators have thought. One should not read doctrines of Plato's later works back into the *Ion*. Eva Schaper makes this mistake in *Prelude to Aesthetics*, London: Allen and Unwin, 1968, pp. 29–30.

[30] See also *Exodus*, 31.1–4.

[31] The *Social Production of Art*, London: Macmillan, 1981, p. 1.

[32] Wolff never questions the assumption that historical situatedness and genius are incompatible. The rest of her book contains very little argument apart from appeals to supposedly desirable political associations of her view, on the one hand, and an entirely *a priori* Marxist analysis, on the other. The notion of genius has become politically charged and the debate has suffered. Peter Kivy's book *The Possessor and the Possessed* (Yale University Press, 2001) is a welcome exception.

[33] "Should Music be National?", *National Music*, Oxford: Oxford University Press, 1987, p. 3. He continues:

I would define genius as being the right man [sic] in the right place at the right time. We know, of course, too many instances of the time being ripe but the place being vacant that the artist could not have arrived at those novel ideas if there had not been a previous artistic tradition on which to draw. Historical and social context is *necessary*. But it is not *sufficient* for insight. The rest—the magical elixir of creativity—is something individual. The romantic and perhaps mystical emphasis on creative genius is compatible with the historical embeddedness of the exercise of that creative capacity. There seems to be a strange blindness to this point among sociological writers on art.[34]

I take genius to be the property of being very creative, which I take to be the capacity to have valuable aesthetic insights. But if such a capacity is to manifest itself and yield interesting aesthetic ideas, then it needs good insights. And to have these, even genius construed as a capacity, is not enough. It needs inspiration—perhaps by the muse. Great artistic achievement requires the capacity, which is genius, plus its manifestation, in an episode of creative inspiration. The existence of both genius and inspiration, however, can be contingent on previous artistic tradition and on non-artistic social factors.

## 5.2 Autonomy, Individualism, Innateness

Sociological writers on art tend to attack the *autonomy* of art practice. The idea under attack is that the reason artists do what they do is to some degree internal to the work of art in question or to that work of art plus other works of art. Marxists and feminists and post-modernists may be right to insist that art is not *completely* autonomous. But they are wrong—and deeply wrong—when they deny *any* autonomous aspect to art. This is only possible if a completely untenable amount of false consciousness is attributed to artists and their audiences.[35] While art is

---

and no man to fill it. But we shall never know the numbers of 'mute and inglorious Miltons' who failed because the place and time were not ready for them.

See also "What are the Social Foundations of Music?", in *National Music*, pp. 232–233.

[34] There have also been many feminist critiques of the idea of genius (e.g. Christine Battersby, *Gender and Genius*, Indiana University Press, 1989). The usual strategy is to unearth some particularly odd statements that various hapless (male) theorists have made about genius, and from that conclude that the notion of genius is defective and that the phenomenon is a myth. But this is a bizarre form of argument. From the fact that people have said odd or implausible things about water or perception it would be hasty to infer that there is no water or perception or that we should dispense with the notions of water or perception.

[35] See further Chapter 7 on these issues.

no doubt subjected to external pressures, it also has its own point and trajectory. Ignore that and we ignore something fundamental.

However, let us not over-do things. Some fair points may be excavated from the anti-genius 'discourse'.

First, it is true that the production of art can be viewed too individualistically. Most obviously, the production of art is often a co-operative or collaborative venture, for example in the performance of plays and symphonies and in making films.[36] But it is also true that even when it takes only one person to construct the work out of given materials, that lone artist is part of a community in which there are many aesthetic and nonaesthetic assumptions and expectations. These constrain the individual in many ways. The potential genius needs training and opportunity—the right social conditions. And perhaps only in a sympathetic artistic milieu can genius emerge, or only when the artistic time is ripe. On the other hand, maybe artists can transcend the narrow bounds of their age and cultural setting. There are difficult issues, which parallel deep issues in moral and political philosophy. Some 'communitarians' say, in Hegelian spirit, that we do not possess a Kantian ahistorical self, and that we are essentially situated in a certain cultural milieu. Similarly, it might be said, for the artistic self. On the other hand, others defend the Kantian self as a self able to reflect freely, rationally and critically on its cultural and psychological inheritance from an independent standpoint. And, perhaps, similarly for the artistic self. This is an interesting issue.

Second, we should not think that a small group of people have the quality of genius to a high degree while others lack it altogether. But it is undeniable that some are more creative than others. There is surely an innate factor in how creative a person can become. According to Kant, genius is

. . . bestowed directly from the hand of nature upon each individual, and so with him it dies, awaiting the day when nature once again endows another in the same way . . .[37]

Whether this creative potential is realized depends on historical circumstances. But it is a fact of life that some are endowed with more potential

---

[36] Sally Price explodes the Western myth that only in Western society do we celebrate individual artistic creativity, and that in small-scale non-Western society, art is viewed as the product of a communal tradition in which the artist remains anonymous. See her *Primitive Art in Civilized Places*, Chicago: Chicago University Press, 2001.

[37] Kant, *Critique of Judgement*, p. 170.

to have higher-quality insights than others. If this is thought to be 'elitist', then so be it. But maybe I can do penance by noting that people who are not classified as artists are sometimes more creative than those who are classified as artists. Certainly, this is true of fine art in the narrow sense: consider, for example, the excellent British propaganda poster art of the Second World War. And today, advertising often surpasses gallery art. If genius is—as parodied—a mystical divine inspiration which is present in great artists, then there may be a touch of the divine in everyone.[38]

\* \* \*

## SUMMARY STATEMENT OF THE THEORY

According to the Aesthetic Creation Theory, there are three, in principle separable, stages to the creative process. First, an aesthetic idea is acquired in an aesthetic insight. Second, this idea is translated into an aesthetic intention. And, third, this intention is acted on, bringing into existence the work of art.

So an object or event is a work of art because and only because:

(A) Someone has the insight that certain aesthetic properties depend on certain nonaesthetic properties, and thus comes to believe that if certain nonaesthetic properties were produced then certain aesthetic properties would be realized in those nonaesthetic properties.

(B) Someone intends to realize those aesthetic properties in the object or event by realizing the nonaesthetic properties of the object or event.

(C) The intention was caused in the right way by the insight.

(D) Some proportion of the aesthetic properties of the object or event does in fact depend on the nonaesthetic properties in the object or event as envisaged in the insight.

(E) Those aesthetic properties of the object were caused in the right way by the person who intended to realize them by realizing the nonaesthetic properties.

---

[38] Wittgenstein interestingly connects genius with *character* (in *Culture and Value*, Oxford: Blackwell, 1980, pp. 35, 38, 65). The idea seems to be that the virtues that artists display in their work are a manifestation of more general traits of character.

The *elements* of the Aesthetic Creation Theory are three: dependence, mental states and causality. In particular, the elements are: the dependence of particular aesthetic properties on particular nonaesthetic properties; the insight into this dependence and the intention to manifest the dependence relation; and the causal relations between insight and intention, and between intention and work of art. The three elements contain three dependence relations: the dependence between particular aesthetic and nonaesthetic properties; the believed and intended dependence between particular aesthetic and particular nonaesthetic properties; and the causal dependence between insight and intention and between intention and the actual realization of the aesthetic properties in nonaesthetic properties.

# 3

# Are There Counterexamples to Aesthetic Theories of Art?

## 1 THE AVANT GARDE REJECTION OF THE AESTHETIC?

### 1.1 Extensional Adequacy; Avant Garde Counterexamples?

Do all works of art have an *aesthetic* purpose? It is not particularly controversial to say that *many* works of art have an aesthetic purpose; what will be disputed is whether they *all* do. Aestheticians, art-historians, critics and to a lesser extent artists often complain that aesthetic considerations do not play a particularly significant role in the production of many works of art, especially the more experimental products of the twentieth century.[1] This is the most common objection to any aesthetic account of art.[2] Are aesthetic theories overly conservative?

Those who put forward this criticism tend to prefer more sociological theories of art, such as institutional or historical theories. The Aesthetic Creation Theory is a *traditional* account, most of all in its employment of the notion of the *aesthetic*. But many aestheticians think that no definition of art that appeals to the aesthetic can be satisfactory because such a theory will go wrong in what it says about twentieth century art. More than a few artists of the twentieth century have claimed to eschew any interest in the aesthetic. And many art historians, critics and philosophers have echoed them. Many artists, we are told, deny having any interest in the aesthetic. So it will be said that this shows

---

[1] For example, see the writings of Arthur Danto, George Dickie and others.

[2] See, for example, the writings of Arthur Danto and George Dickie, among others. See Danto's "The Artworld", *Journal of Philosophy*, 1964; and *The Transfiguration of the Commonplace*, Cambridge, MA: Harvard University Press, 1981. See also Dickie's *Aesthetics*, Bobbs-Merrill, 1971; *Art and the Aesthetic*, Ithaca: Cornell, 1974; and *The Art Circle*, New York: Haven, 1984.

that we cannot define art in terms of aesthetic properties, or in terms of the intention to produce aesthetic properties. Are aesthetic theories out of touch with the avant garde? Are these theories a hangover from a past era, when perhaps they were true of most or all art? Are aesthetic theories of art now out of date?

An advantage of aesthetic theories of art is that they allow that fine art, high art or artworld art (whatever we call it) lies on a continuum with everyday artistic activities. The art of galleries and concert halls and the like is a refinement or extension of the artistic activities of everyday life.[3] High artworld art is a refinement or extension of 'folk art'. Hence we can be generously open-minded about *including* in aesthetic theories of art much that is *outside* the artworld. If cake-decoration, tattooing and fireworks fall out as cases of art, that's fine for the aesthetic theorist. However, the present objection is that aesthetic theories *exclude* much that is *inside* the artworld. It seems that an aesthetic theory is in danger of being faulted for extensional inadequacy by what it fails to include.

## 1.2 Minorities and Majorities

Before I deal with the main thrust of this objection, I want to point out that even if it were correct, it could only have a restricted significance. I want to pour cold water over the evangelical ambitions of those who appeal to the avant garde in order to make a general point about art. It is important not to be bullied into discussing the favoured examples without first raising the issue of why those cases are thought to be so important, whatever we say about them.

One thing which is objectionable in this style of argument is the emphasis placed on *twentieth century* art in achieving a general under-standing of art. Some aestheticians write as if it is obvious that the most important ambition for a theory of art is to account for the recent art-scene.[4] But if we are concerned with extensional adequacy, it is difficult to see why we should be especially concerned with tailoring the philosophy of art to the art of the present and recent past. Why should contemporary art be more important than the art of centuries ago? This is a kind of unjustified prejudice in favour of the present and recent past. The art of past ages is no less art because it existed back

---

[3] See Yuriko Saito, *Everyday Aesthetics*, Oxford: Oxford University Press, 2007.
[4] An example would be Cynthia Freeland, *But is it Art?*, Oxford: Oxford University Press, 2001. She is a follower of Danto.

then. It is difficult to see why fitting the contemporary art-scene should have special weight in constructing a theory of art. Furthermore, the argument also tacitly assumes that we are most interested in Western art. It is hard to see how that could be justified.

Even if we turn to the twentieth century, and we also restrict the focus to Western art,[5] it is far from clear that there is a general rejection of aesthetic properties. Aesthetic properties not only include properties such as beauty and ugliness but also properties such as daintiness, elegance, sadness, delicacy, power, movement and balance. These *substantive* aesthetic properties may more obviously play a role. Some twentieth century Western artists may claim that they eschew *beauty*. But they also certainly talk freely about their concern with substantive aesthetic properties. If we listen carefully to what artists say and if we carefully consider their works, we do not find a rejection of the substantive aesthetic properties. Quite the opposite. And anyway, what they mean by 'beauty' is usually something like 'prettiness'. It is a substantive aesthetic concept rather than one that denotes pure aesthetic merit.[6]

Exactly how much twentieth century Western art was produced by artists who affected to reject the aesthetic in the broader sense that includes both verdictive and substantive properties? The answer is: not as much as we have been led to believe. Most twentieth century Western art was not 'cutting edge' experimental avant garde art. If an art critic, theorist or aestheticians says that nevertheless the *significant* work was the 'cutting edge' experimental avant garde art, then that claim needs to be justified. Many aestheticians blow this phenomenon out of all proportion. In fact, the only artists in the current Western visual artworld, at the turn of the twenty-first century, who *say* they reject the aesthetic are a somewhat dated minority. Almost the entire contemporary Western artworld is very much concerned with the aesthetic properties of art—alongside other sorts of properties. (This is easily confirmed.) Recall again that we can admit that other sorts of properties are sometimes more important to the artist than aesthetic ones, so long as we allow that aesthetic properties play a significant role; and recall also that aesthetic properties may include substantive ones.

---

[5] For discussion of this issue see Stephen Davies, "Non-Western Art and Art's Definition", in (ed.) Noel Carroll, *Theories of Art Today*, University of Wisconsin Press, 2000.

[6] See further chapter 1, section 1.3 of *Metaphysics of Beauty*.

Thus we should strive to avoid concentrating too much on recent art in our theorizing about art. And even if we look carefully at the contemporary Western art-scene, we will not find much that is problematic for an aesthetic theory. The apparent rejection of the aesthetic is a minuscule phenomenon. It is absurd to make the whole of the philosophy of art turn on the antics of a minute minority. The role that such aberrant works have been given in recent art theory is wholly disproportionate to their numbers and importance.[7]

## 1.3 Uncrude Aesthetic Theories

However, let us put to one side this general complaint about the over-emphasis on twentieth century Western avant garde art in the general theory of art, and return to consider these cases of art and whether they really are counterexamples to aesthetic theories.

We should first make sure that the aesthetic theory under considera-tion is not a straw man.

Aesthetic theories easily can concede that works of art have important nonaesthetic purposes. For example, works of art often have important religious or political purposes. Aesthetic theories hold that having *some* aesthetic function is a *necessary* and *sufficient* condition for something to be a work of art. But having a specific aesthetic function may only be a *necessary* condition for being some *particular* work of art, and there may be *other* nonaesthetic necessary conditions for being a particular work. So works of art with religious and political dimensions are easily accommodated.

It will be argued that this concession does not save aesthetic theories because the aesthetic should not even be among the *necessary* conditions for being a work of art. Many works, it will be said, have absolutely *no* aesthetic purpose. But the idea that some works of art have absolutely no aesthetic purpose is quite another matter from admitting that many works of art have important nonaesthetic purposes. Theorists often slide too easily from the latter claim to the former. We should be circumspect about the thesis that a great many works of art have no aesthetic point at all. This is often a mythology. One source of this mythology is that people take too seriously artists' 'manifestos'—which often should be taken no more seriously than any other piece of advertising! The

---

[7] The idea that the philosophy of art should turn on such uninteresting artists as Claus Oldenberg or Robert Rauschenberg is surely absurd.

works themselves often belie the anti-aesthetic description. For instance, almost all conceptual art has significant aesthetic aspirations. Even if the aesthetic is not the *most* important aspect of the work, it is still important and indeed essential that the 'concepts' in question are embodied in aesthetically significant ways. There is room for scepticism about how much conceptual art is purely conceptual.

It is true that many works of art are not supposed to be 'beautiful' in some narrow sense; but they *are* supposed to possess 'substantive' aesthetic properties such as daintiness, dumpiness, elegance, delicacy, balance, power or serenity. The same critics and artists who affect to reject talk of beauty, ugliness and aesthetic merit talk liberally of substantive aesthetic properties. The aesthetic theorist can claim that it is the function of sustaining *these* aesthetic properties that is essential to works of art. But the appeal to these aesthetic properties only makes sense if they are thought of as making the work beautiful or aesthetically valuable.

Moreover, contrary to some art theorists, the tendency of some visual artists to pursue 'non-objectual' works of art, such as installations or earthworks, has nothing to do with a rejection of the aesthetic. For example, Robert Smithson's "Spiral Jetty" has plenty of formal aesthetic values.

The foregoing obvious points serve to ensure that the aesthetic theory that is the target of putative counterexamples is not needlessly and implausibly strict.

However, it will be insisted that in at least *some* cases, such as Duchamp's famous urinal *Fountain* and his *L.H.O.O.Q.* (*L.H.O.O.Q.* is a reproduction of the *Mona Lisa* with a moustache added.), we have a complete rejection of *all* aesthetic properties—including substantive aesthetic properties. There are also some other cases, in particular *some* performances and conceptual art, where the artists do not so much reject the aesthetic as have nothing to do with it. Aesthetic theories seem not to apply to such works. There remain some other residual problematic phenomena. Let us consider various strategies that the aesthetic theorist can deploy with respect to these kinds of cases.

## 1.4 Tactical Retreat and Aestheticization Strategies

One strategy is to say that it is perfectly acceptable for the small number of avant garde works not to fit aesthetic theories of art. Perhaps we can be content to concede that aesthetic theories exclude such works of art, since the theory comfortably applies to so many other works of art. All art before the twentieth century conforms to this model, and the overwhelming majority of art since then also conforms. This strategy, which might be viewed as somewhat defeatist, is to restrict the range of aesthetic theories of art. The thesis could be restricted to the vast majority of works of art that have an aesthetic point. So aesthetic theories of art hold only of those works of art that *were* created in part for aesthetic reasons. Such a theory covers most works of art, and perhaps we need not worry too much about the minority of works that do not fit. We could say that it is only a minor quirk with no great significance.[8]

The claim would be that *if* something is a work of art *and* it has an aesthetic function *then* it is essential that it has it, rather than the claim that *if* something is a work of art *then* it has some aesthetic function that is essential to it. The former claim, unlike the latter, allows that some works of art have no aesthetic dimension at all. Those works of art—if there are any—that lack aesthetic functions, obviously do not have aesthetic functions essentially; but it is still the case that those works of art that *have* aesthetic functions have them essentially. This is the 'tactical retreat' strategy.[9]

However, although the tactical retreat strategy is an option—and I shall later explore what it involves in more depth—it is not clear that it should be applied monolithically to all avant garde art. Given some artistic phenomena that are a potential problem for aesthetic theories of art, there are two options: we can admit that the definition fails to cover them, or we can try to incorporate them into an aesthetic theory. That is, we can either try to brazen it out and say that the account excludes them, or else we can try to sneak them in. Perhaps we should retreat and leave some avant garde phenomena outside the fold. But in the case of *some* avant garde phenomena, I think it is better to try to sneak them in. I say this not out of fear of counterexamples but rather out of a desire to do justice to the works in question. In particular, we shall see that ready-mades and other appropriated works can and should be accommodated. Thus Monroe Beardsley goes the wrong way on ready-mades when he writes:

The fuss that has been made about Duchamp's *Fountain* has long amazed me. It does not seem that in submitting that object to the art show and getting it

---

[8] Suppose someone says "Yesterday I thought about elephants for five seconds and that was a work of art". We need not be worried about such cases. It is not a shortcoming in an aesthetic theory that it fails to include them.

[9] The claim might also be that those works of art that *lack* aesthetic functions do so essentially.

more or less hidden from view, Duchamp or anyone else thought of it either as art or as having an aesthetic capacity.[10]

Although I sympathize with the complaint about the fuss, I do not agree with Beardsley here. However, there is one kind of argument against Beardsley on this point that I do not endorse. A naive appeal to 'common sense' would be to say that *Fountain* is now classified as a work of art, even if, in some moods, Duchamp described it as 'anti-art'. One can read about *Fountain* in art history books, for example. And most people (in the West) do or would classify *Fountain* as a work of art. So, the argument goes that, unless we have a special reason to suppose that there is a widespread illusion on this matter, we should accept the common verdict. But this kind of argument is very problematic, as we shall see in part 2 of this chapter. My strategy is different both from Beardsley's rejectionism and from naive common sense conceptual conservativism. I think that we should concede art status to ready-mades and embrace them in an aesthetic theory given their nature, and not given what people say about them. But how exactly should we do this?

One thing we might say is that if we look carefully even at the most radical 'performance art', 'conceptual art' and the like, we find that there *is* in fact some aesthetic concern. We should not believe everything that artists say about their work. It is safer to look at what artists *do*. We can ask: if conceptual art is so conceptual, why do we need to be provided with anything to look at at all? Why can't it all be done with concepts? The truth, it might be said, is that the art is not entirely conceptual. What about 'happenings'? In any area you might choose—aesthetic, intellectual or political—happenings tend to be mind-bendingly uninteresting. But perhaps there is a certain minimal drama or atmosphere which has a little aesthetic worth. Or take monochrome painted canvasses: it might be suggested that these have a certain pleasing texture and reassuring regularity. The idea is not that such progressive experimental works achieve nothing aesthetically, just that they achieve very little. So perhaps some minimal aesthetic concern can after all be found in such works. This is the 'aestheticization strategy'.

Arthur Danto was complaining about this sort of move when, speaking of Duchamp's *Fountain,* he wrote:

But certainly the work itself has properties that urinals themselves lack: it is daring, impudent, irreverent, witty, and clever. What would have provoked

---

[10] "The Aesthetic Definition of Art", p. 25.

Duchamp to madness or murder, I should think, would be the sight of aesthetes mooning over the gleaming surfaces of the porcelain object he had man-handled into exhibition space . . . [11]

This is somewhat over-dramatic, but it is true that it is not clear that the point of avant garde works like *Fountain* can plausibly be described as 'aesthetic'. Danto says that *Fountain* was "daring, impudent, irreverent, witty, and clever". But those are surely not *aesthetic* qualities, although they are artistic properties. Perhaps the aesthetic has to do with what can be appreciated in perception, as the name suggests. Either it is rooted in the direct perception of the intrinsic properties of the object, or perhaps perception can be informed by knowledge of contextual matters. If so, we see a work of art differently when we see it in context, and our appreciation is combined with a contextually informed perception. But either way, it may be doubted that the point of some works is a matter of the aesthetic appreciation of what is perceived in either the narrow or broad sense. So—the argument will go—these works have no aesthetic point, and this means that the Aesthetic Theory of Art fails to do them justice.[12]

The aesthetic theory seems to exclude these works of art, and thus looks extensionally inadequate. How can this challenge be met?

## 1.5 Appropriation

The aestheticization strategy does not work; or at least it does not work in many cases. But there is more to be said about some avant garde works—in particular about appropriation. Let us put conceptual and performance art on hold for a while and consider in more depth what to say about artistic *appropriation*—including ready-mades and some pop-art. Can aesthetic theories cope with the fact that members of the artworld sometimes appropriate ordinary manufactured objects? Can it cope with 'ready-mades' such as Duchamp's *Fountain* or the appropriation of Andy Warhol's *Brillo Box*? When we look carefully at these phenomena we will see that they can be tamed.

One way to try to do this would be to say that if we are dealing with appropriated manufactured items, then there is a sense in which

---

[11] "Aesthetics and the Work of Art", *The Transfiguration of the Commonplace*, pp. 93–94.

[12] Duchamp often said that the point of *Fountain* was to make something with no aesthetic value.

they were art *before* appropriation. Ordinary manufactured items are usually designed with considerable attention to aesthetic considerations even if they also have to do something else as a priority.[13] What Beardsley calls 'aesthetic interest' is available in modest quantities from the pre-appropriated urinal. The urinal was an object designed with some regard for aesthetic considerations, in addition to functional considerations. George Dickie often compares Duchamp's presentation of his urinal to a plumber displaying his or her wares.[14] But some urinals are visually dull and others are visually interesting, and they were intended to be so. Some urinals can be appreciated more than others. Some are a pleasure to use! So perhaps there is not a significant difference *of kind* between Duchamp's urinal and that of a plumber. Both urinals have aesthetic merits, just as both are goods which can be bought and sold for practical use as well as for appreciation. (The same goes for Andy Warhol's *Brillo Box*.) So appropriation is rather like Columbus discovering America—there were already people there. Ready-mades were aesthetic works of art all along. Call this 'the Columbus Strategy'.

This is one way to try to sneak appropriated objects into an aesthetic theory. Does it work? It is true that *Fountain* has a kind of 'meaning' that a pre-appropriated urinal does not. How so? Appropriation *did* turn the relatively unassuming object into a piece of high-artworld art and gave it a special meaning in virtue of it being placed in a specific art-history *context*.[15] Only because of this can it be "daring, impudent, irreverent, witty, and clever", as Danto says. But perhaps all that shows is that *Fountain* has extra aesthetic properties not possessed by an indistinguishable unappropriated urinal. By itself, it does not establish that the pre-appropriated urinal was not a work of art. (Danto seems to admit that the ordinary urinal has aesthetic properties when he talks of ". . . aesthetes mooning over the gleaming surfaces . . .".) The fact that *Fountain* has a context-dependent meaning does not show that an indistinguishable object has *no claim at all* to being a work of art. Danto is right that the two objects have many different properties. They have different properties in virtue of their different contexts. But no direct inference can be drawn from there

---

[13] See further the Appendix to Chapter 6.

[14] *Aesthetics*, p. 103; *Art and the Aesthetic*, p. 38.

[15] Kendall Walton emphasizes the importance of art-historical context in his "Categories of Art".

regarding matters of art status. It is indisputable that appropriation *did* make *Fountain* an item of *high-artworld art,* which it was not before; but it *is* disputable whether appropriation turned the urinal into a piece of aesthetic art, for it may be that it was one already. Duchamp placed the object incongruously into a high-artworld context. And this is why the appropriated urinal came to have properties which others lack. But this does not mean that the two objects differ in art status, since it may be that the unappropriated object was an artwork of a more humble sort. If so, we can deny that there is the earth-shattering metaphysical divide that Danto and his followers see between urinals or Brillo boxes that have been appropriated by the artworld and those which have not.

That is one point that needs to be made. But more needs to be said. For it *could* be that an act of appropriation into a high artworld context *did* confer art status, even if this is not how it was with Duchamp's urinal. The Columbus strategy says that appropriation confers *high*-art status, not simply art status. But consider what we might say about appropriated *natural* objects which are not altered—such as driftwood. And consider what we might say about appropriated manufactured items that were made with no aesthetic ambitions at all—for example, surgical instruments or railway signals. Perhaps the urinal is a bad example since there was insufficiently drastic appropriation. Perhaps Duchamp's snow shovel (called *In Advance of the Broken Arm*) is a better example, assuming that the shovel was a purely functionally designed object. The Columbus strategy does not cover some cases.

Let us focus even more closely on appropriation. If driftwood, surgical instruments, railway signals or shovels were exhibited purely for their pre-appropriated aesthetic merits, then such exhibiting would not confer art status. It would just be an act of exhibiting aesthetically interesting non-art. But I take it that such exhibiting would not amount to *appropriation*, properly so called. It would not have the aim of making a 'statement', as Danto would say. That is, it would not involve an intention that the thing should be seen in the context of a certain tradition. It does not, as it were, 'refer' to other works of art, in the sense that it is intended to be seen in the light of, or juxtaposed to, those other works of art. Appropriation is necessarily self-conscious about art-historical context, and understanding appropriation involves understanding that. The mere exhibiting of non-art for its aesthetic qualities involves no such intention.[16] But when non-art is exhibited with such a contextual intention, then that is 'appropriation' properly so called: appropriation makes a self-conscious reference to art-historical context. And this is why appropriation can be metaphysically efficacious. Appropriation *can* and sometimes *does* make something art without altering it in intrinsic respects. This is the 'contextual' approach.

However, we should be careful where we go from the admission that appropriation *can* confer art status. We should not lose sight of the fact that works of art themselves are often appropriated. If something is *already* art, then appropriation cannot *make* it art, since one cannot make something what it already is. Appropriation sometimes *enhances* art status—taking something from regular art to high-artworld art. And Duchamp's *L.H.O.O.Q.* appropriates something which is already high-artworld art.[17] Here art status is *altered* rather than *conferred* or *enhanced*. What appropriation does in all these cases is to place an object in an unfamiliar art-history context. This is what appropriation does essentially. This *explains why* art status is conferred, enhanced or altered. The crossing of the non-art/art divide is *not* what is essential to appropriation. That is a side-effect not the core of the matter. So Danto is mistaken about the nature and importance of appropriation.

### 1.6 Intrinsic and Derived Art Status: The Second-Order Strategy

Where does that leave the Aesthetic Theory of Art? An Aesthetic Theory of Art might try to deal with appropriation, by taking the Columbus strategy. If so, there is no huge metaphysical divide between urinals or Brillo boxes that have been appropriated by the artworld and those that have not. On that approach, the idea that appropriation creates art status is a mistake, even if it can confer extra aesthetic properties. On the contextual strategy, we admit that appropriation into an unusual context *can* turn an ordinary thing into art. In such a case, presentation in an unusual artworld context *is* the creative act by which it comes to have new aesthetic properties. Appropriation can make something art, just as it can enhance or alter it, in both cases, by aesthetic augmentation.

---

[16] This means that the contextual view of appropriation is not in danger of deeming newspaper art reviews to be art, for writing a review of an art-show in a newspaper does not involve such a contextual intention.

[17] Another example is Robert Rauschenberg's *Erased De Kooning* drawing.

However, although the Columbus strategy or contextual strategies can account for many of the facts of appropriation, they cannot account for all. For both strategies assume that appropriation has an *aesthetic* point. It will be argued that this fails to take on board the extent to which the aesthetic has been rejected in the twentieth century.

In response, I suggest that the contextual account of appropriation put forward in the last section can be combined with another strategy to tame cases of appropriation. On this view, the Aesthetic Theory of Art should allow that the art status of some works is *derived*. Let us then suppose that A, B and C are works of art because they have the features which an Aesthetic Theory of Art specifies, and that D is a purely reflexive work. It has no aesthetic purpose, but it aims to make some kind of 'comment' on A, B and C. So D is a contextual work: it cannot be understood except in the context of A, B ad C. Then I propose that we *grant* art status to D, but call it *derived* rather than *intrinsic* art status. John Searle used these terms in his book, *Intentionality*.[18] For Searle, *intrinsic* intentionality attaches to mental states; but *derived* intentionality attaches to spoken language, symbols and pictures. The latter only have intentionality by depending on the former. It can be similar with art: *intrinsic art status* attaches to works with aesthetic endowments or ambitions. But *derived art status*—of appropriation, conceptual art, and the like—is dependent upon the intrinsic art status of artworks which have an aesthetic point.

Works such as *Fountain* and *L.H.O.O.Q. indirectly* involve aesthetic functions. Although such works have no immediate aesthetic function, their point lies in the fact that they are meant to be seen in the context of, and by contrast with, traditional works of art. They indirectly involve the aesthetic functions of those other works. It couldn't be the case that *all* works are like *Fountain* and *L.H.O.O.Q.* The point of such works depends on the viewer being someone who has knowledge of conventional works of art. Duchamp wanted *Fountain* to have no aesthetic point only because he wanted it to contrast with those works of art that did. The point of *L.H.O.O.Q.* would be lost on someone who did not know the *Mona Lisa*. Duchamp's *Fountain* and *L.H.O.O.Q.* are *second-order* works; and second-order works require first-order works. Nonaesthetic works are second-order works that make no sense except in the context of other works. They are parasitic works; and they are parasitic on aesthetic works of art. Although *Fountain* and *L.H.O.O.Q.*

---

[18] John Searle, *Intentionality*, Cambridge: Cambridge University Press, 1983.

have no aesthetic functions themselves, their functions involve the aesthetic functions of the works in the context in which they are meant to be considered. In this respect they are like forgeries. The aesthetic functions of other works are essential to the functions of the parasitic works. This is the 'second-order' strategy.

This may have particular plausibility because some of the works in question—such as Duchamp's *Fountain* and *L.H.O.O.Q.*—seem to involve a conscious *rejection* of the aesthetic. They are *anti-aesthetic* works. So it is not merely that it is essential to such works that they *lack* an aesthetic function, rather they have a *negative* aesthetic function. The point of such works is to lack positive aesthetic properties. This is historically appropriate if we consider the irony that one of the failings of *Fountain*, from Duchamp's point of view, was that quite a few people came to admire its sculpted curves and gleaming surface, and so missed the point—or so Duchamp said. Although Duchamp may have been irritated by this reaction, the urinal invited it. Perhaps he should have presented something more aesthetically neutral. Saying that works of art have negative aesthetic functions still involves conceding that some works have no positive aesthetic function. So in that respect the strategy is tactical retreat; nevertheless, what it is to be that work of art is not independent of aesthetic functions—the aesthetic functions of other works.

This gives something to both sides. Aesthetic theories are basically right. Those who would abandon them for the sake of a handful of clever flourishes are misguided. But purely contextual art with no aesthetic point is also rightly classified as art. This art comprises purely second-order works of art. But then such art only makes sense in the context of a set of works which are conventional, aesthetic works of art. Works can have either intrinsic or derived art status. Purely contextual art, ironically, does not refute traditional aesthetic theories as its devotees have urged. Quite the opposite. It demonstrates its dependence on conventional aesthetic art.

## 1.7 Duane Hanson and the Second-Order Strategy

There are, however, some works that are difficult to interpret according to this second-order strategy. One interesting artist in this respect is Duane Hanson. His 'hyper-realist' sculptures neither seem to have a negative point, nor do they seem to be second-order, like Duchamp's appropriations. Hanson's sculpture seems to be an extreme case of works that only have meanings, without any aesthetic aspiration, or even anti-aesthetic aspiration. Hanson's sculptures are disturbing, while offering a kind of dignity to his subjects. But it is hard to see how they have an *aesthetic* point. Moreover, Hanson's work does not seem to be second-order, like Duchamp's appropriations. In this respect, Hanson was more radical than Duchamp. Hanson does not seem to be rejecting the aesthetic, but he does seem to be doing something different.

A reply, which has some plausibility, is that Hanson's works belong to the category of *sculpture*, and as such are an instance of a *sort* of thing that has an essential aesthetic function. Hanson's sculptures are meant to be seen *as* sculptures. But sculptures generally *do* have essential aesthetic functions even if Hanson's unusual sculptures do not. Just as a work of art need not succeed in performing its aesthetic functions, so not all instances of an *art-form* need share the usual functions of works of that art-form. Consider, for example, that few would think that the waxworks at Madame Tussaud's are works of art. But how are these different from Hanson's sculptures? It seems to be important that Hanson's figures are intended for exhibition in the contexts where we normally see sculptures. They are *deviant* sculptures, or *extreme* cases of sculptures of a certain sort, and we are meant to see them as such.[19] So, as with Duchamp's *Fountain* and *L.H.O.O.Q.*, it is only because there are other works of art that have aesthetic functions that Hanson's sculptures can lack them. So Hanson's sculptures are second-order works after all. (Ironically, the appeal to indiscernible counterparts in this case *helps* the aesthetic theorist.)

I am not entirely sure about how effective all these defensive strategies are. Much of the time I find them convincing—but I can imagine other people not being convinced. Nevertheless, given the irritatingly dogmatic and simple-minded way that many aestheticians assert that avant garde works are unproblematic refutations of aesthetic theories of art, I would be showing great self-restraint if I merely replied that it is not obvious that such theories cannot defend themselves against this charge. It is in fact absolutely certain that such works do not provide an absolutely certain refutation of aesthetic theories of art, as is so often alleged. Moreover the negative and second-order accounts of many of these aberrant works do more justice to their actual nature than to the

---

[19] On deviant properties of works within an established art form, see Kendall Walton, "Categories of Art", *Philosophical Review*, 1970. He calls such properties 'contra-standard' properties. I critique Walton's essay in chapter 5 of *Metaphysics of Beauty*.

account given by those who seek to conscript them willy-nilly in the service of their ideological campaign against aesthetic theories of art.[20]

## 2 METHODOLOGICAL REFLECTIONS

### 2.1 The Narrative Arts

However, there is a much more troublesome and obvious range of counterexamples. What about narrative arts, such as novels, plays and films? Poems have some aspects that are of aesthetic significance. The precise words used can be aesthetically important, either as pure sound or as the aesthetically apt expression of a certain meaning.[21] But it is not plausible that novels, plays and films always have significant aesthetic aspects. There is often a purely visual aesthetic in films and performances of plays, but its importance is often not central.[22] And even if there are some films and performances of plays that have significant visual aesthetic virtues (Passolini's wonderful films *Medea* and *Oedipus Rex*, for example), there are many others in which such aesthetic aspects are insignificant. It is the same with the poetic qualities of the language used in play and films. In some plays and films the lanuage is aesthetically important. The use of language may be beautiful or elegant. But in others, this is not so. There are plays and films in which what we see and hear is only *dramatically* important; it is not beautiful or elegant as pure form or as the aesthetically apt embodiment of a certain narrative meaning. (Ordinary horror movies are examples.) Therefore, it seems that there are arts of pure narrative meaning, where what is important is the story.

---

[20] Artworld and institutional theorists often present themselves as being particularly open-minded about what counts as art and therefore they are, in principle, receptive and sympathetic to new artistic ventures in novel media. But it is not at all clear that this is a true picture. For example, there was once a debate about whether photography is 'art'. But there could never have been a serious debate about whether it was art in an aesthetic sense. Therefore (as with the association of relativism with toleration) I would reverse the association of artworld and institutional theorists with open-mindedness to new artistic media. Aesthetic theories of art are in fact less likely to be conservative than artworld and institutional theorists in this respect, since in those theories what is accepted in the artworld at that time constrains what can be art at that time.

[21] See chapter 4, section 4, of *Metaphysics of Beauty*.

[22] The film, *The English Patient*, for example, had some visual virtues, but it was flawed in so many other respects that its purely visual aesthetic virtues did little to redeem it.

So if we say that works of art are essentially things that have an aesthetic point, then it seems that some narrative works will fall outside the bounds of art. Similarly, although much performance and conceptual art has aesthetic ambitions, *some* performance and conceptual art may fall into the class of works with meaning but no aesthetic point. That is, they have no ambition to have an aesthetically interesting visual or aural aspect, and neither are they meant to be seen as aberrant works of another sort that have an aesthetic point. Of course, in such cases, the *visual* or *aural* presentation of meaning is important. The narrative content must be realized in visually or aurally significant ways. But perhaps the significance of the visual or aural presentation of content is not always of *aesthetic* significance. To recall, I take aesthetic significance to be either a matter of beauty and ugliness or of features such as daintiness, dumpiness and elegance that make a thing beautiful or ugly. This is perhaps a rather restrictive notion of the aesthetic. But I think that we need such a notion if the aesthetic is not to become a vacuous notion and the interesting issues dissipated. Given such a non-vacuous notion of the aesthetic, it does seem that there are *some* works of art that have no aesthetic functions.[23]

Moreover there are some conceptual or performance works that seem not to be tameable by the second-order contextual strategy. Some avant garde works may have a positive aesthetic function, others may have a second-order aesthetic function, but it does seem that some conceptual and performance works are not concerned to *reject* the aesthetic but to do something else that has nothing to do with the aesthetic.

It is only when there are narrative meanings without an aesthetic point that there is trouble for aesthetic theories of art. When there are aesthetic purposes *as well as* meanings, then the works are not works of pure meaning, and there is no problem. In these cases, either the aesthetic and narrative purposes are separate or they are mingled together. In the latter case, we cannot disentangle the meaning from the aesthetic aspect; so we cannot separate two independent sources of the value of the work with no connection to each other. But whether or not the aesthetic and narrative purposes are entangled in this way, aesthetic theories of art are secure so long as there are some aesthetic purposes

[23] See further chapter 6 of *Metaphysics of Beauty*). It might be argued that the narrative arts possess *substantive* aesthetic properties, such as power, balance, elegance or delicacy. But in that chapter I argue that such descriptions may not be aesthetic descriptions, and that when they deploy typically aesthetic words (such as "elegance" or "beauty"), their use may be metaphorical.

in play. The problematic cases with only narrative content are not like this. They have no aesthetic point at all, which seems to be bad news for aesthetic theorists. Given the existence of purely narrative works, what then is left of a *general* aesthetic theory of art?

## 2.2 Concepts of Art and Fine Art

At this point we need to reflect on our goals in the philosophy of art, and on our mode of achieving those goals. Aesthetic theories of art succeed in capturing the essential truth about a large range of the objects and events in the category of art. But they seem not to capture the truth about them all. How should we react to this? In my view, it is not obvious that we must say that aesthetic theories are false because they suffer counterexamples. We are not forced to react to the purely narrative arts in this way.

Another reaction would be to say that the 'folk' category of art has an error built into it. Stephen Stich argued that we might find out that although Folk Psychology presupposes that there is one kind of state underlying a variety of kinds of behaviour, in fact it turns out that there are two or more distinct kinds of underlying state.[24] And Hilary Putnam says that our notion of jade in fact picks out two superficially similar but different natural kinds. Jade is a disjunction of jadite and nephrite.[25] So we need an error theory of our folk concept of jade. Jade is not a unified natural kind as folk geology presumes. Similarly, maybe there is an error built into the folk concept of art because falling under that concept there are two different kinds of phenomena (with an overlap)—things that have aesthetic functions, and things that have narrative functions. Maybe art is like jade. Perhaps art is a disjunctive kind: works of art either have an aesthetic point or a narrative point (or some combination of the two). Or perhaps there is more of a continuum—with absolute music and abstract painting at one end, representational paintings and operas in the middle, then poetry, with novels, plays and films at the other end.

The possibility that 'art' is like 'jade' is not merely an abstract possibility. Peter Kivy has drawn attention to the fact that our concept of 'Fine

[24] Stephen Stich, *From Folk Psychology to Cognitive Science*, Cambridge, MA: MIT Press, 1983, p. 231.
[25] Hilary Putnam, "The Meaning of Meaning", in *Philosophical Papers*, vol. 2, Cambridge: Cambridge University Press, 1975, p. 241.

Art' has its origin in the 'Modern System of the Arts', which canonised certain art forms in the eighteenth century.[26] At that time, a number of artistic activities were for the first time conceptually grouped together and deemed the 'Fine Arts' or simply 'The Arts'—these were painting, sculpture, architecture, poetry and music. That concept had a certain extension. It included both the aesthetic and the narrative arts. That concept is the one that is deployed in contemporary philosophy (in courses and textbooks). But need we have our hands tied by that concept?

In ancient Greece and in the Renaissance the 'arts' were grouped completely differently: music was grouped with mathematics; and poetry was grouped with linguistics and grammar.[27] And in Japan, there is a high art category—'the road'—which includes calligraphy, some martial arts, flower arranging, incense and the tea ceremony. This variability of groupings means that we cannot take for granted the usefulness or appropriateness of the groupings that are enshrined in some local and perhaps parochial concept of art that we happen to deploy. Even if we have been lucky and we deploy a healthy concept, this is not something we can take for granted.

## 2.3 What Ordinary Notion?

If we are not to use the concept of Fine Art, then we might wonder what other concept we should use. Perhaps we should use a more everyday concept of art, which contrasts with the notion of Fine Art. The trouble is that it is not obvious what our ordinary folk notion is. It is not obvious that there is such a folk notion.

One common use of "art" means a skill—but the philosopher's use is more restrictive than that. Another common use of "art" means *visual* art—but the philosopher's use is more general than that. Some, but not all, dictionaries list the high-fallutin philosophical use of "the arts", which includes literature, music and the visual arts. But that high-fallutin concept is not a common concept deployed by many ordinary folk. That concept is one deployed by those who accept the theory implicitly

---

[26] Peter Kivy, *Philosophies of the Arts: An Essay in Differences*, Cambridge: Cambridge University Press, 1997.

[27] See Paul Kristeller, "The Modern System of the Arts", in *Renaissance Thought and the Arts*, New York: Harper and Row, 1965. (A shortened version of this essay can be found in Susan Feagin and Patrick Maynard (eds.), *Aesthetics*, Oxford: Oxford University Press, 1997.) This makes salutary reading.

embodied in the Modern System of the Arts, and those who deploy that concept may buy into the values that that concept presupposes.[28]

The disconcerting fact is that there is *no* common folk concept of art that we must respect. It is simply not true that English-speaking folk use the English word "art" to pick out the arts that were selected in the Modern System of the Arts or those arts that tend to be covered in philosophy of art courses and textbooks. Many dictionaries list no such usage. (Philosophers' opinions about what the folk think is often an expedient mythology.) Gilbert Harman notes the way philosophy instructors have to *teach* students to make the analytic/synthetic distinction. It doesn't come naturally to them. And that is because they are being taught a piece of theory, not something they knew all along.[29] It is the same with the notion of 'art' in aesthetics courses. There is no pre-theoretic notion that students are recollecting or making explicit. Instead they are imbibing and internalizing the ideology of the Modern System of the Arts, which is embodied in the notion of Fine Art. The idea that students are drawing on a neutral folk concept which they already possess, and which can be analysed at leisure, is an illusion. Instead, the students are being subtly indoctrinated. (Conceptual analysis as ideology.)

We might call the highfalutin concept of Fine Art, the 'bourgeois' concept of art (which I do not take to have pejorative overtones). If the bourgeois concept of art is not the most common folk concept of art, there is no reason for us to contemplate an error theory about most of the folk because of the diversity of things that fall under the bourgeois concept. And if the bourgeois concept is not the most common folk concept, we do not have to worry about counterexamples to aesthetic theories of art that stem from the fact that there are things that are art according to the bourgeois concept that are not art according to aesthetic

---

[28] Francis Sparshott describes the way that dance came to be thought of as one of the Fine Arts when it was not previously so classified (in *Off the Ground*, Princeton: Princeton University Press, 1988). He also thinks that some dance is 'art' and some is not. He addresses the question of what marks this distinction (ibid., p. 269). The general account he offers is in terms of "appreciation" (ibid., p. 274). In his view this means that he cannot avoid blurring the boundaries between dance and other activities rarely considered 'art', such as rituals, ceremonies, martial arts, many kinds of sport, bull-fighting, cheerleading and parades. This blurring is a good thing, in my view. Mara Miller describes the fall of the garden from Fine Art status (in *The Garden as an Art*, Albany: SUNY Press, 1993). She also addresses the 'art' status of gardens, and finds the notion of Fine Art wanting.

[29] Gilbert Harman, *Reasoning, Meaning and Mind*, Clarendon: Oxford, 1999, p. 142.

theories. Of course, the bourgeoisie are themselves folk. (I am one of them.) But the bourgeois concept of art is not very widespread. We *should* hold an error theory about the bourgeois concept of art because the things it groups together have no common nature. But this error theory is modest and restricted. The folk, or at least most of the English-speaking folk, are not in error. I am not sure about the extent to which speakers of other languages have words that select all and only those arts (in the skill sense) that are canonized in the Modern System of the Arts.[30] If they do, perhaps the folk who use those words in those languages *are* in systematic error when they deploy those words, and my error theory would then be less modest and restricted than it is in respect of English-speaking folk. I leave this as an open question, although I must admit to some default scepticism about whether very many of those folk have such a concept.

## 2.4 Methodological Moral

In all this it is crucial to remember that what we are interested in when we reflect on art is not a *concept* but a range of puzzling *objects* and *events* and a range of puzzling *attitudes* to those objects and events.[31] We need to understand these phenomena. It is an open question how much in common there will be in some grouping of these phenomena. The eighteenth century Modern System of the Arts does violence to the nature of the things that it classifies together. The items on the list of the Modern System of the Arts should be viewed as more heterogeneous than has been thought. So a theory of art that applies to many but not all of the items on the list may be unobjectionable.

Furthermore, in my view we need a theory of art that includes items that the Modern System of Arts excludes. For example, I am keen to have a notion that includes painting, music, architecture and some literature, and which also includes everyday creative activities such as industrial design, advertising, weaving, whistling, cake-decorating, arranging and decorating rooms, religious rituals and fireworks displays.[32] The fact that the items that the aesthetic theory includes and excludes do not

---

[30] Perhaps the German word "*kunst*" expresses such a notion. Ancient Greek and Latin had no such word. It is silly to say that Plato held the view that all art is mimetic or representational.

[31] See further Chapter 1.

[32] For discussion of the status of 'non-Western' art, see Stephen Davies, "Non-Western Art and Art's Definition", and Denis Dutton, ' "But They Don't have Our

coincide with the items that the Modern System of the Arts includes and excludes is of little consequence.

Am I flagrantly committing what is known as the "No True Scotsman" fallacy (someone offers the generalization that all Scotsmen wear kilts; someone else points out Hamish, who is Scottish but who seems not to be wearing a kilt; to this the original person replies that Hamish is "no true Scotsman", thus apparently saving the generalization)? Am I just dismissing counterexamples to aesthetic theories of art in an ad hoc way merely to save my theory? But the analogy is somewhat illuminating. I have tried to 'problematize' the notion of art. The concept of a Scot is also problematic. Who is a Scot, and in what does being a Scot consist? Must one have been born in Scotland? Brought up in Scotland? Educated in Scotland? Identify in some way with Scotland? For all but the blindest nationalist, the notion is problematic. Similarly, the notion of art is problematic for all but the blindest adherent of the Modern System of the Arts. Maybe the folk notion of a Scot is over-simplistic or even based on an error. (According to Anthony Smith, all national identities are based on myths about the past.)[33] There may even be different and incompatible folk notions of Scottishness. The real question is: which notion *should* we deploy? (This issue has recently come to the fore now that there are different funding rules for Scottish and English students.) Those who would rest with conceptual analysis are complacent here as they are elsewhere. Perhaps there could be reasons to cultivate a notion of a Scotsman so that it *does* turn out that all Scotsmen wear kilts! That might be a useful notion of a Scotsman for other reasons. Similarly, given the virtues of the aesthetic theory of art, a 'No True Scotsman' style of argument may on balance be a good move.

What we are in search of is a good theory of the *nature* of art. This issue does not concern the word "art" or the category or the concept of art. We want to know about a range of objects and events, not about the words or concepts that we use to talk about those things. We are interested in objects, not concepts—the world not words. We are doing metaphysics, not linguistic or conceptual analysis. Indeed, the task of *defining art*, so popular for so long—and enshrined in many a textbook

Concept of Art" ', both in (ed.) Noel Carroll, *Theories of Art Today*, Maddison, Wisconsin: University of Wisconsin Press, 2000.

[33] See, for example, Anthony Smith, *The Ethnic Origins of Nations*, Blackwell: Oxford, 1986.

and anthology—is clearly a category mistake, unless "defining" is meant in the sense of 'real definition'. (In any ordinary sense of definition, we might try to define "art" but not art.) I suspect that many aestheticians hanker after the project of conceptual analysis. However, if we need to refashion concepts in order to understand things, then so be it. We want to understand the nature of a range of things, and not just gaze at our own conceptual navels!

Someone might object, saying: how are we to know *which* things are the things we want a theory of? Surely, it will be argued, at this point we have to think about words or concepts, for we are interested in the nature of those things that we typically pick out with the word "art" or to which we usually apply the concept of art. However, a warning light should go on when philosophers use the word "we" in this way. It is a reliable indicator of a rhetorical move. The objection assumes that there is some universally shared concept and some kind of consensus in its application. But there is no such universally shared concept and no such consensus. Furthermore, even if there were, the question is not what concept or concepts of art we *have*, but what concept or concepts we *need*, given the natures of a wide range of human artefacts. Those artefacts have natures independent of our conceptualization, and our job as theorists is to track those natures in our theories and concepts. Common folk concepts or more erudite concepts that are already in circulation may or may not be what we need.[34]

It seems that what counts as the *target* for explanation in the theory of art is somewhat shifting. To some extent, we must set up a target and then shoot at it. So long as the aesthetic theory succeeds in presenting the essence of a great many art forms, I do not think that we should worry too neurotically about whether it is applicable to every item in the

---

[34] Walter Gropius writes:

There is a widespread heresy that art is just a useless luxury. This is one of our fatal legacies from a generation which arbitrarily elevated some of its branches above the rest as the 'Fine Arts', and in so doing robbed all of their basic identity and common life. . . . By depriving handicrafts and industry of the informing services of the artist the academies drained them of their vitality, and brought about the artist's complete isolation from the community.

(Walter Gropius, *The New Architecture and the Bauhaus*, Cambridge, MA: MIT Press, 1965, pp. 57–58.)

Gropius is someone who contests the notion of Fine Art. See also Miller, *The Garden as an Art*, chapter 4.

Modern System of the Arts. I maintain that if we draw a circle around most of the traditional arts (painting, sculpture, architecture, music and poetry), together with the sort of everyday creative activities that I mentioned, we get an interesting grouping. We get a class of things with an interesting unifying principle—that provided by an aesthetic theory. On the other hand, if we retain the traditional five arts in the Modern System of the Arts, exclude the everyday cases, and add those novels, plays and films that are purely narrative, then the aesthetic is no longer a unifying principle, and there is no other, so far as I can see.[35]

I am sceptical about the possibility and desirability of providing an entirely general theory of the nature of art in the sense of providing a theory of the nature of all and only the items in the Modern System of the Arts. I don't think that this is something we should aspire to do. However, we should not lurch from one extreme to the other. Some recent writers in the philosophy of art, such as Kivy, have been concerned to proselytize in favour of the quest for differences among the arts. They resist any attempt to impose a unified theory of the nature and value of art. They worry that such a theory will not be able to do justice to the differences among the arts. While I think that there is something to be said for this view, I also think it can be taken too far. Down that path lies a kind of anarchy of the individual case that precludes the understanding that finding something in common yields. The aesthetic theory of art does provide us with an understanding of a wide range of things. It provides an account of the nature of those things, as well as providing the basis for an explanation of our interest in those things, and of the actions and institutions that sustain them. We should not allow pessimism about general theories to derail such a theory. If there is an aesthetic theory close to hand that captures a nature common to a great many things, why not reach out for it?

---

[35] It might be suggested that Kant's idea of pleasures of imagination might be a mental act that is the appropriate response to all and only the items in the Modern System of the Arts. But this is a vain hope, for that mental act is also appropriately exercised in response to the everyday creative activities I listed.

# 4

# Art Essence, Identity and Survival

Do works of art have their aesthetic properties essentially? Let us call a theory that says that they do, 'Aesthetic Essentialism'. In this chapter, I will consider a particularly straightforward aesthetic essentialist view of art. I explore its consequences for the survival of works of art over time. I critically compare the Aesthetic Essentialist view with a view that appeals to essential material origins, which is very different from the aesthetic essentialist view. I conclude by arguing against both theories. Neither theory will do, despite the attractions of both. But valuable lessons will have been learned about what the correct theory must be like.

## 1 ESSENTIALISM AND AESTHETIC PROPERTIES

Let us begin by rehearsing some familiar considerations about aesthetic properties and about the identity of works of art. I shall draw on these considerations when I state, refine and defend different versions of Aesthetic Essentialism.

(A) *Aesthetic and Nonaesthetic Properties.* In the class of aesthetic properties, I include the following: 'verdictive' properties, such as beauty or aesthetic merit; 'substantive' aesthetic properties, such as grace, daintiness and elegance; and metaphorically described aesthetic properties, such as delicacy and melancholy. I use 'nonaesthetic' as a blanket term to cover physical properties, sensory properties, representational properties and perhaps more. Let us not worry here about what it is that unites the members of the list of aesthetic properties. That is a topic for extended investigation. There is much to be said about the distinction between aesthetic and nonaesthetic properties, but let us assume that the distinction is in good order.[1]

---

[1] See chapters 1 and 2 of *Metaphysics of Beauty*, Ithaca: Cornell University Press, 2001.

(B) *Aesthetic Dependence and Supervenience.* Given the distinction between aesthetic and nonaesthetic properties, we should accept the thesis that aesthetic properties *depend* on nonaesthetic properties. This implies a strong supervenience thesis to the effect that if something has an aesthetic property, then it has some nonaesthetic properties, such that if there is anything, at any time that has the nonaesthetic properties, then it must also have the aesthetic property.[2] This strong version of supervenience entails the more usual versions according to which there can be no aesthetic difference between two things without a nonaesthetic difference between them, or according to which there can be no aesthetic change in a thing without a nonaesthetic change in it.

(C) *Anti-formalism.* Aesthetic/nonaesthetic dependence is a plausible principle even though we might want to reject the principle that the aesthetic properties of an object or event depends on just its *intrinsic* nonaesthetic properties. Anti-formalists hold that *relational* nonaesthetic properties of a work of art are also important. In particular, they hold that facts concerning the relation of a work of art to other works of art, or to the circumstances of its history of production, are part of the dependence base of a work of art's aesthetic properties. The context in which a work of art is created may count aesthetically. So sameness of intrinsic nonaesthetic properties may not suffice for sameness of aesthetic properties. Kendall Walton argued this in his paper "Categories of Art", although he did not put it in these terms.[3] Walton's anti-formalist thesis does not mean that we cannot believe in dependence and supervenience relations between aesthetic and nonaesthetic properties; but it does mean that we must be careful about the extent of the nonaesthetic bases. If Walton is right, the dependence and subvening bases include historical nonaesthetic properties.

(D) *Indiscernible Duplicates.* Many aestheticians have thought that a great deal turned on the fact that different works of art can be intrinsically indistinguishable, or that only one of two intrinsically

---

[2] See Jaegwon Kim, "Concepts of Supervenience", *Philosophy and Phenomenological Research*, 1984, also reprinted in his *Supervenience and Mind*, Cambridge: Cambridge University Press, 1993. On aesthetic-nonaesthetic dependence see Frank Sibley, "Aesthetic/Nonaesthetic", *Philosophical Review*, 1965.
[3] Kendall Walton, "Categories of Art", *Philosophical Review*, 1970.

indistinguishable objects might be a work of art.[4] They think that this encourages a theory of art that essentially locates a work of art in a social context. But this inference is a non-sequitur. All it shows is that having certain intrinsic properties is not sufficient for being a particular work of art, or even for being a work of art rather than an ordinary object.

## 2 INITIAL STATEMENT OF AESTHETIC ESSENTIALISM

We are now in a position to state a preliminary version of Aesthetic Essentialism. So far I have introduced the distinction between aesthetic and nonaesthetic properties, stated aesthetic/nonaesthetic dependence and supervenience, and noted a sophistication that we may have to embrace when thinking about these relations. But none of those observations directly concerns questions about the essence of works of art, even though, as we shall see, they have an indirect bearing on such questions. I then raised a negative point concerning the relation of intrinsic nonaesthetic properties to the essence of works of art. So we had some observations on the relation between the aesthetic and the nonaesthetic, and then a point about the nonaesthetic and the identity conditions of works of art. But that leaves open a third possible combination. There might be a relation between aesthetic properties and the essence of works of art.

Consider the following modal claims:

If the antelope fresco from prehistoric Santorini is elegant, then it could not have failed to be elegant.
If the Alhambra is a beautiful work of architecture, then a building that is ugly could not possibly be the Alhambra.
If Bach's Sonatas and Partitas are excellent pieces of music, then they could not have failed to be excellent.[5]

Many find modal claims like these claims to be intuitive. They encourage the essentialist view:

AE Works of art have their aesthetic properties essentially.

---

[4] See, for example, Arthur Danto, *The Transfiguration of the Commonplace*, Cambridge, MA: Harvard University Press, 1981.
[5] Were we thinking about *genres* rather than works of art in particular, we might consider the claim that there cannot be delicate heavy metal music.

This essentialist claim implies that possessing certain aesthetic properties is *necessary* for being a certain work of art; something with different aesthetic properties *cannot* be that work of art.[6]

Concerning particular works of art—the modal claim is that a painting or a sculpture could not have different aesthetic properties from those that it actually possesses. And—concerning multi-instantiable works of art—the modal claim is that a novel or a symphony could not have different aesthetic properties from those which it actually possesses.[7]

As a first approximation, we might sharpen such a modal thesis so that we arrive at the following claim:

A work of art must possess the aesthetic properties that it actually possesses; that is, a work of art that possesses certain aesthetic properties must possess those aesthetic properties. So it cannot possess different aesthetic properties; an aesthetically different thing would not be that work of art.

And we might also embrace a cross-time formulation—that is, a 'diachronic' as well as a 'synchronic' formulation.

If something remains the same work of art, then it must remain unchanged in aesthetic respects; it cannot possess different aesthetic properties at a later time. So if something changes in aesthetic respects, it must cease to be the same work of art.

Let us now take on board a modification that the view requires.


## 3 VAGUE ESSENCE

For simplicity, I have introduced the Aesthetic Essentialist claims and its modal consequences in too strong a form. Consider another essentialist claim: a table has its composition essentially. This should not be taken to imply that it could not differ in some *minor* way while remaining the same table. But it does imply that it could not be entirely or mostly composed of something quite different. We can say something similar about art. Had Turner added a few extra thick brush strokes to one of his

---

[6] For such a view, see Peter Lamarque, "Aesthetic Essentialism", in (eds.) Emily Brady and Jerrold Levinson, *Aesthetic Concepts: Sibley and After*, Oxford University Press, 2001.

[7] This is not the claim that two objects or events cannot be *instances* or *performances* of the same work of art if they have quite different aesthetic properties. See further section 4.7 of this chapter.

impressionistic seascapes, it might not have had quite the same ethereal luminosity, but it might have been the same work of art nonetheless. But had he painted, on the same canvas and at the same time, an interior of quite different colours, it would have had quite different aesthetic properties and it would have been a different work of art. But, brush-stroke for brush-stroke, the difference between the two is a matter of degree.

So we do better not to assert the strong claim that it is not possible for a work of art to have aesthetic properties other than all those it actually possesses. We do better to say that it is not possible for a certain work of art to have *very different* aesthetic properties from those which it actually possesses. The vagueness of 'very different' is a virtue not a vice, since questions about the identity of works of art are in fact vague. There is a point between the few extra brush strokes on the seascape and the painting of an interior where we do not and should not know what to say.

The vagueness should surface in our formulation of the modal consequences of Aesthetic Essentialism. We should modify our earlier formulations as follows:

A work of art must possess most of the aesthetic properties that it actually possesses; that is, a work of art which actually possesses certain aesthetic properties must possess roughly similar aesthetic properties. So it cannot possess very different aesthetic properties; an aesthetically very different thing would not be that work of art.

If something remains the same work of art, then it must remain roughly unchanged in aesthetic respects; it cannot possess very different aesthetic properties at the later time. So if something changes drastically in aesthetic respects, it must cease to be the same work of art.

Pictures can fade slightly, sculptures can be slightly damaged, texts can be imperfectly transcribed. But they remain more or less the same work of art even though, due to a slight change in nonaesthetic properties, their aesthetic properties have slightly changed. The matter is a vague one. A minute amount of damage will not jeopardize many of the aesthetic properties that the work of art possessed when it was in pristine condition. So works of art may survive a little damage. But if the nonaesthetic dependence base of a work of art's original aesthetic properties is mostly destroyed, then the work of art has not survived. For example, if what was once a gleaming statue of a discus thrower is now just a heap of marble chunks, the work has not survived because those chunks do not sustain most of the aesthetic properties of the original.

Artwork survival is a matter of degree.[8] Similarly, we can imagine a work of art with slightly different aesthetic properties due to slightly different subvening nonaesthetic properties. But if we imagine very different aesthetic properties, we are not imagining the same work.

## 4 REMARKS, RAMIFICATIONS, COROLLARIES, AND MINOR PROBLEMS

### 4.1 The Metaphysics of Aesthetic Properties

The aesthetic essentialist thesis we are considering is neutral about the metaphysical status of aesthetic properties. It just says that aesthetic properties, *whatever they are*, are essential to works of art. This leaves open whether the correct theory of aesthetic properties is realist, response-dependent or even sentimentalist. That said, however, it may well turn out that the truth of Aesthetic Essentialism is best *explained* by aesthetic realism. Perhaps Aesthetic Essentialism can be used as the premise of an argument for aesthetic realism. All that Aesthetic Essentialism definitely assumes is that there is a right answer to the question of whether or not an aesthetic description correctly applies to a work of art. Perhaps only a realist can say that; or perhaps non-realists can argue that they can also say it. However, this is a controversial issue that we need not address here.

### 4.2 Comparison with Essentialism about Aesthetic Properties

It is worth contrasting the Aesthetic Essentialism view of *artwork identity* with the idea of an essentialist theory of *aesthetic properties*. The possibility—not to speak of the actuality—of the varied or multiple realization of aesthetic properties in nonaesthetic properties means that aesthetic properties have no nonaesthetic essence. Things are graceful in all sorts of different ways. There is no nonaesthetic property common to all graceful things (poems, pieces of music, trees).[9] So grace

---

[8] Note that some works of art involve change (for instance, plays and music) such that the work of art's aesthetic properties at one phase of their rendition are different from the properties at another phase within the same work of art. The cross-time essentialist claim only applies to a work of art considered as a whole.

[9] I do not think that there is a plausible dispositional account according to which there are, after all, dispositional similarities between apparently dissimilar graceful things.

has no nonaesthetic essence. Essentialism about aesthetic properties is implausible. But such essentialism is obviously different from the view advanced here, which implies that a work of art cannot possess quite different aesthetic properties from those it actually possesses, and it cannot radically change in aesthetic respects.

## 4.3 Indiscernible Duplicates Again

From the fact that aesthetic properties are essential to art identity, and aesthetic properties depend on certain nonaesthetic properties, it does *not* follow that whatever has nonaesthetic properties is the same work of art. So the present doctrine does not conflict with the possibility of there being intrinsic duplicates that are different works of art. The two determination relations flow the wrong way with respect to each other. Art identity determines aesthetic properties; and nonaesthetic properties determine aesthetic properties. That is: the same work of art implies the same aesthetic properties; and the same nonaesthetic properties imply the same aesthetic properties. But that does not mean that the same nonaesthetic properties imply the same work of art.

## 4.4 Anti-formalism Again

Anti-formalists can happily agree with Aesthetic Essentialism. What anti-formalists deny is that the aesthetic properties of a thing supervene only on its *intrinsic* nonaesthetic properties. This is compatible with admitting that once the aesthetic properties are determined—however they are determined—they are essential to the work of art to which they belong.[10] We should be circumspect about the indiscernibles and anti-formalism points. They may be right, but there is much that they do not entail. In particular, they do not have the anti-essentialist consequences that they are often supposed to have.

## 4.5 Necessity and Sufficiency

Aesthetic Essentialism is not committed to the thesis that aesthetic properties *determine* the identity of works of art. That would be

[10] Contrast Gregory Currie, "Supervenience, Essentialism and Aesthetic Properties", *Philosophical Studies* 58, 1990, pp. 243–257. Currie denies that works of art have essential aesthetic properties on the grounds that aesthetic properties are determined contextually.

the wrong way round. The view is not that aesthetic properties are *sufficient* for art identity, rather that they are *necessary*—that art identity determines the aesthetic properties that an artwork has. If a work of art instantiates certain aesthetic properties, then it does so essentially and necessarily. This leaves open an important possibility. The fact that something has certain essential properties does not imply that it has no others. As Arnauld said in reply to Descartes in the "Fourth Objections and Replies" in the *Meditations*, we might be essentially thinking beings, but we might be essentially material beings too. Similarly, works of art might have *other* essential properties beside aesthetic properties. Perhaps certain other properties are needed, in conjunction with the aesthetic properties, in order to have *sufficient* conditions for being a particular work of art. For example—as we shall see in a moment—it is plausible that works of art have essential *origins*. These essential origins might be certain social institutions, creative thought process or hunks of matter. Aesthetic Essentialism is compatible with institutional, creative or material origin theories of art if those theories propose merely *necessary* conditions of being art.

## 4.6 Anti-aesthetic Art

What about works of art which allegedly lack aesthetic properties, such as Duchamp's *Fountain*, and other avant garde works of visual art? Assume that it is indeed true that such works lack aesthetic properties. That creates no difficulty for Aesthetic Essentialism, for we can say that it is part of the point of these works to *lack* aesthetic properties. This very lack is essential to them. So perhaps it is essential that they possess negative aesthetic properties. Moreover, since Aesthetic Essentialism only claims that aesthetic properties are *necessary* conditions of art-identity, when the aesthetic properties in question are all negative, *other* essential properties (whatever they are) can play a more dominant role in determining identity.

## 4.7 Performing Arts

Plays and composed pieces of music are types that are meant to be performed. But they may be performed badly. A performance of a work of art may be so poor that it fails to possess many of the aesthetic properties that the type possesses. For example, a performance of *King Lear* may be comic instead of tragic, and thus it might lack the dramatic tension of

the type *King Lear*. Since a performance might lack the aesthetic properties that the type work of art possesses, it might be argued that those
aesthetic properties are not essential to the work of art. In responding to
this objection, we can avoid begging any large questions about universals
and particulars in the ontology of art. We can either consider types or
performances. Begin with types. It is true that the aesthetic properties of
*King Lear* might be *lost* in a certain performance. Different performances
have different aesthetic properties. But the fact that a *performance* of
*King Lear* does not have the aesthetic properties of the *type King Lear*
would not show that it is not essential to the *type King Lear* to have
its aesthetic properties. It does not show that it is possible that the *type
King Lear* has different properties from those that it actually possesses.
There might be other reasons for denying that type works of art have
essential aesthetic properties, but this is not one of them. Now consider
*performances* of *King Lear*. It is plausible that Aesthetic Essentialism also
holds of *performances* of the play. Intuitively, it could not be *that* performance if it possessed quite different aesthetic properties. So we have
a benign dilemma. If we consider types, bad performances fail to show
that the type does not possess its aesthetic properties essentially. And
if we consider individual performances, Aesthetic Essentialism holds of
those performances. Thus whether we consider types or performances,
the Aesthetic Essentialist claim can be maintained.


## 5 COMPOSITIONAL ORIGIN ESSENTIALISM AND CONJUNCTIVE ESSENTIALISM

So far we have seen that Aesthetic Essentialism has quite a lot going for
it. Now Aesthetic Essentialism leaves open the material composition of a
work of art. It allows that a work can change its material composition so
long as its aesthetic properties continue to be sustained. By contrast, let
us now introduce a view in which composition plays a more fundamental
role. On this view, it is essential to a work of art that it is composed
of whatever it was originally composed. So a work of art must have its
origin in the physical hunk of matter that it was originally composed
of, and a work of art survives only if its material descendant survives.
Call this view *Compositional Origin Essentialism*—"COE" for short.[11]

---

[11] For an example of such a view, see Jerrold Levinson, "Zemach on Paintings",
*British Journal of Aesthetics*, 1987.

COE is a certain kind of origin essentialism. The view contrasts with versions of origin essentialism that say that a work of art has essential origins in a certain institution or creative intention. It also contrasts with the view that a work has an essential composition, rather like a natural kind, so that a work at any one time is necessarily composed of whatever it is actually composed of at that time. This would imply, implausibly, that a work cannot alter in composition over time. But COE allows that it can.

Note that by 'material composition', I do not mean to restrict COE to the claim that all works of art are composed of brute physical matter. That would pose problems for the inclusion of literature and music. I take the 'material' of music to be sounds, and that of literature to be words. Sounds and words are themselves elusive entities; but we can bracket off the general difficulties they raise, for they do not turn specifically on considerations arising from aesthetic properties or works of art.

Both Aesthetic Essentialism (='AE' for short). and COE are attractive, so maybe we can have both. Let us consider *conjoining* AE with COE. Let us call the view that AE and COE are both true *Conjunctive Essentialism*—'CE' for short.

Now CE allows that survival can be a matter of degree. The view is structurally like a psychological continuity theory of personal identity according to which personal survival from one time to another consists in retaining a similar psychological profile (narrowly construed) plus the right causal connections.[12] Similarly, for CE, artwork survival consists in retaining a similar aesthetic profile plus the right causal history. But then, by analogy with the psychological continuity theory of personal identity, art survival might be a matter of degree rather than an all or nothing matter. A slight aesthetic change might not threaten artwork survival. But a succession of slight changes might mean that one work of art gradually evolves into another. Works of art can be the descendants of other works of art. Of course, most works of art are not like this. Most are finally and definitively completed, and their fate is then either survival as that same work of art or else a gradual or sudden return to the dust, as it were—restoration perhaps arresting that final fate for a while. In this respect most actual works of art are like most actual people.

[12] See Sydney Shoemaker, "Personal Identity: A Materialist's Account", in (eds.) Sydney Shoemaker and Richard Swinburne, *Personal Identity*, Oxford: Blackwell, 1984.

Furthermore, in principle CE allows that it is possible that works of art are subject to fission and fusion. Works of art might divide and unite. Consider works of art which are co-operative ventures and which do not clearly begin or cease to exist at a particular moment. For example, a cathedral or a bridge may be augmented or diminished over the centuries. Such works of art evolve and mutate. And one cathedral or bridge could become two, or two could become one. (This should seem relatively unproblematic, unless one is encumbered with dogmas concerning identity over time that are imported from notions of strict identity that are usual in logic and mathematics. But if someone insisted on those dogmas, we could talk of "persistence" or "survival" rather than 'identity'.)

## 6 TWO OBJECTIONS

It might be argued that CE has difficulty in accommodating the dynamic process of making a work of art. Typically there is no finished blueprint in the mind of the artist that is then realized without modification. Usually the thing is fashioned and coaxed into its final form, undergoing many mutations along the way. (There is a film of the progress of one of Picasso's paintings that makes fascinating viewing in this respect.) It seems that, as with a cathedral or bridge that is built over many generations, we have a mutation of forms, which ceases at a certain point. What remains is then deemed *the* work of art. But in many ways, the point at which an artist stops modifying a work is rather arbitrary. The objection to CE is that previous 'art-stages' (by analogy with 'person-stages' in psychological continuity theory) in the causal history of the final work of art may have had quite different aesthetic properties. Imagine a work of art that an artist worked on for one hundred hours and which turned out to be a tremendous success due to an inspired decision taken in the last five minutes. Or alternatively, imagine that the work was going tremendously well until an unfortunate and disastrous decision taken in the last five minutes. It might be suggested that this shows that this very work of art could have had very different aesthetic properties. And that would be a problem for AE and thus for CE too. Surely—we might be tempted to think—anything that partakes of this causal history is this work of art regardless of its aesthetic properties. Why not scrap AE and CE and just go with COE?

The reply to this objection is that if a different decision had been taken in the last five minutes, it would not have been the work of art that it actually turned out to be. There was a particularly important art-changing last minute decision—one that made all the difference to its identity. It is not that *this work of art* was nearly much worse (or better) than it was, but that *this physical thing* was nearly a different work of art that was very much worse (or better). The *physical object* that the artist was making might indeed have had very different aesthetic properties. That is, the *lump of stuff* might have been aesthetically very different. But then it would have been a different work of art. CE can overcome this problem.

A slightly more difficult case is that of an artist who never manages to finish some work. Consider one of the sculptures of slaves that Michelangelo never finished. Call some such sculpture *Slave*. The figure in this work looks as if it is emerging from the rock, or is half buried in it. What about its aesthetic properties? *Slave* possesses many different aesthetic properties from those that the finished work would have possessed if Michelangelo had finished the job. For example, *Slave* possesses the aesthetic property, eeriness, which the finished work would not have possessed. How then can eeriness be essential to *Slave*? One line would be to say that *Slave is* essentially eerie, but it is not the same work that it would have evolved into if Michelangelo had kept going. Alternatively we could say that since eeriness was not intentionally achieved, unlike other aesthetic properties of the work, we should distinguish those aesthetic properties which are essential to the work from those which are not, by saying that those which are there by design are essential while those which are there by accident are not. Either way, the problem dissolves.

## 7 THE PROBLEM WITH AESTHETIC ESSENTIALISM: DYSFUNCTIONALITY

Let us now turn to the major problem for AE. If the objection is good—as I think it is—then AE is false, which also means that CE is false.

Consider a case in which the original hunk of matter of a painting or sculpture is preserved, by and large, but with an alteration that means that most of its original aesthetic properties are lost. There is a *modest* divergence in material composition that *drastically* alters the work of

art's original aesthetic qualities. For example, slight physical damage to
a painting or sculpture of a face may utterly ruin its aesthetic impact.
But the painting or sculpture persists nonetheless. So a work of art may
survive without most of its original aesthetic qualities. And it seems
that we are forced to accept that the persistence of the original hunk of
matter is what counts. It is not just *necessary* for artwork survival, as CE
concedes, but it is also *sufficient*. If hunk persistence is compatible with
drastic aesthetic change, then aesthetic persistence is not necessary for
artwork survival. This is the problem of *aesthetically dysfunctional* works
of art; it is the fundamental difficulty for AE, and the usual reaction is
to embrace COE.

This sort of argument is effective only in so far as it applies to works
of art such as paintings or sculptures. It is doubtful whether it can
be extended to literature and composed music. Consider the situation
where the words of a piece of literature are mostly preserved but with
a slight alteration, say of the ending. Would *King Lear* have survived if
someone had substituted a happy ending in all copies without this being
known? Suppose Lear and Cordelia both come back to life due to a magic
spell and live happily ever after. Has Shakespeare's original play *King
Lear* survived, with such a radical change? Some would be inclined to say
not, or that it has survived to a reduced degree. The same goes for similar
musical examples. Suppose that someone intersperses ludicrously out
of character short passages throughout a great symphony. That would
intuitively threaten the survival of the musical work. In the cases of
literature and music, we think that slight changes in composition that
have drastic aesthetic consequences *do* threaten artwork survival. Our
intuition in favour of COE and against AE seems to be stronger in the
cases of painting and sculpture than in the cases of literature and music.

So let us remain with painting and sculpture where AE clearly fails. In
those cases, our ordinary modal intuition that there can be dysfunctional
art makes serious trouble for AE.


## 8 THE PROBLEM WITH COE: SELECTING
## CONTINUANTS

Should this problem encourage philosophers to rush into the arms
of COE? I think not. Although COE can indeed explain our intuitions concerning the possibility of aesthetically dysfunctional works, it

might not be the only theory that can do so. Moreover, COE has its own problems.

Begin with the following unsuccessful argument against COE. Take some ugly lump of rock, B, that was once some elegant sculpture, A. The ugly lump is the physical continuant of A. But most or all of A's aesthetic properties are not possessed by B. The question is: does B stand in the same work of art relation to A? Consider the counterfactual situation in which the artist who originally made A, instead made sculpture C out of the same block, which is a physical duplicate of B. And imagine that C also possesses the same aesthetic properties as B. In this situation, would C be the same work of art as A? We have a clear intuition that it would not. But this might seem a rum thing. How can B stand in the same work of art relation to A, if C does not? Why does this relation hold across time but not across possibilities? This seems mysterious. But the argument is not effective; for the defender of COE might just *insist* that art-identity is a question of causal origin—and this is why it holds across time but not across possibilities. Assume that this is what the defender of COE will say. The following problem swiftly ensues: surely not *anything* causally continuous with a thing is its survivor. For example, the present conjunction of the atoms that originally composed a statue of Athena in the Acropolis is not the same healthily surviving statue of Athena. The material that composed that statue could now be collected and refashioned into a different statue or over one just like the original Athena. The question COE must face is: *which causal continuants are survivors?* The fact is that COE by itself cannot answer this question.

Someone might reply that what counts is the persistence of a hunk of matter *in something like its original form or shape*. But then a whole lot of unexplained work is being done by the extra clause. That clause is usually inserted in order to exclude cases where the matter is intact, although its parts are ordered differently. Those who favour COE sometimes add such a clause as a casual afterthought. But that is to sneak in a consideration of certain significant properties beside compositional origins. And then an explanation needs to be given of why *those* properties of the hunk are selected but not others.

So by itself, COE is crucially incomplete. It is at exactly this point that AE has an answer: only those causal continuants which preserve most of the original aesthetic properties are survivors of the original work of art. AE has an answer to the problem of selecting among causal continuants, but we saw that it ran into trouble with our ordinary modal intuitions over aesthetically dysfunctional works.

## 9 ONTOLOGICAL ANTINOMY?

We arrive at an apparent antinomy. COE by itself will not do—because of the problem of selecting among causal continuants. But the failings of COE cannot be made good by adding AE, yielding CE, for CE is stuck with the same problem as AE—the problem of artwork persistence without aesthetic persistence. The *dysfunction* objection to AE encourages COE; but the *selection* objection to COE encourages AE.

Neither AE nor COE will do; and a conjunction of them won't do either. We need a different theory, but not one that is a million miles away. The difficulties faced by AE and COE do not warrant altogether abandoning the search for the essence of art, or reaching for some completely alien sociological account of art. We are in a strange situation: both COE and AE have virtues and faults, and what is more, the virtues of one are the faults of the other. Any completely alien theory will fail to capture the virtues of each theory—those virtues that made it preferable to its rival. What we need is some way of combining the two theories so that we retain the virtues and exclude the vices. CE, of course, could not do that, just because the combination was mere conjunction. And a disjunctive theory would be too arbitrary. If we are to give a satisfactory account of the essence of art, what we need is some subtler mode of combination of certain aspects of the two theories, but not others. At least we now know what sort of animal we are looking for.[13]

---

[13] To look beyond this chapter, to the next: the intuition behind CE was right; we need to combine the aesthetic approach with the origin approach. In my view, what we need to do is to factor the aesthetic properties into the origins of the work. This can be done either by saying that a work must have its origin in a thing with certain aesthetic properties, but it can also be done by saying that aesthetic properties figure in the intentional or creative origins of the work. The latter approach is what I think we need. We then arrive at an origin-essentialist view, but not one that appeals to material origins. I develop such a theory in the next chapter.

# 5

# Aesthetic Functionalism

I am old-fashioned about art. I think that we must understand it in terms of beauty and other aesthetic properties. In this chapter, I propose a metaphysics of art to accompany the Aesthetic Creation Theory that I introduced in Chapter 2. I focus on what the theory should say about the persistence or survival of works of art over time and about the essential properties of works of art. The view proposed builds on the negative lessons of the last chapter.

I shall here leave aside questions about whether the theory is extensionally adequate, having addressed that in Chapter 3. The theory certainly applies to a great many works of art (for example, it applies to most paintings and most music). It may or may not apply to all works of art. If it does not, then I can be taken to be providing a theory of the metaphysics of those works that have aesthetic aspirations. To have given an account of their nature would be success enough.

Furthermore, I will not here attempt to supply a reason for holding the Aesthetic Creation Theory beyond showing that it has intuitively satisfactory metaphysical consequences. As should by now be familiar, the reason for embracing it is that it enters into a convincing explanation of the fact that we produce and consume works of art. But I shall concentrate here on developing and defending the metaphysical aspects of a theory that I assume to be well motivated.

In section 1, I outline the metaphysical view of art that I call 'Aesthetic Functionalism'. In section 2, I consider its normative consequences. In section 3, I consider the composition and persistence of functional things of all sorts. In section 4, I explore the composition and persistence of works of art, given Aesthetic Functionalism. In section 5, I consider what Aesthetic Functionalism can say about the nonaesthetic functions of art. Lastly, in section 6, I discuss the metaphysics of appropriation.

# 1 FUNCTIONAL ART

## 1.1 Artefactuality

I begin with a simple and familiar point: works of art are *artefacts*. This means that they fall into the class of *functional* objects and events.[1] The point seems to be a modest one, but in fact it has far-reaching consequences.[2]

Consider a functional kind, such as *clock* or *heart*. Having such a function is a *relational* property. In particular, it is a *historical* property. A thing is a functional thing of a certain sort partly in virtue of its standing in a causal relation either to an *intention* or to an *evolutionary mechanism* that caused its existence.[3] The functional (or 'teleological') properties of natural objects derive from the blind hand of natural selection. And the functional properties of artefacts derive from intentions. Since a thing's functional properties depend in part on its history, there can be two intrinsically identical things, with the same causal powers, which have different functional properties. For example, something just like a table that materializes after lightning strikes a swamp is not a table. There can be no 'swamp tables'. A table has an essential origin in intentional activity.

If works of art are artefacts, then they are intentionally made in order to have certain properties. The immediate consequence of this is that we must not hold a view of art with two quite independent conjuncts, which say (1) works of art are artefacts, and (2) that they have certain significant properties—as if these two features of art are unconnected. (George Dickie's institutional theories are explicitly of this form.)[4] We need a theory that *connects* the two conjuncts. We need a theory of the *kind* of functions that works of art have. What functions works of art have is controversial, but that they have functions is uncontroversial. Some aestheticians have denied that works of art are always artefacts because of the possibility of the artistic appropriation of found natural

---

[1] For simplicity, I shall ignore *events* in what follows; events can have functions just like enduring objects. As in chapter 1, section 8, I take "artefact" in a broad sense.

[2] It is sometimes said that works of arts have no purpose, but what is intended is that works of art are merely for the purpose of contemplation, and not for some other more practical purpose.

[3] See Ruth Millikan, *White Queen Psychology*, Cambridge, MA: MIT Press, 1993.

[4] See, for instance, his *Art and the Aesthetic*, Ithaca: Cornell University Press, 1971.

objects, but we can return to this issue when we are clearer about what artefacts and functions are.

## 1.2 Aesthetic Functionalism

I shall explore the view that works of art have *aesthetic functions*. This means that, just as hearts have the function of pumping blood, and spades have the function of enabling us to dig, so works of art have the function of embodying or sustaining aesthetic properties such as beauty, elegance, delicacy, daintiness and dumpiness. That's the basic idea.

Someone might think this implies that works of art have the purpose of being for human use and experience. But this does not follow. Not all artefacts are for human use. For example, we might build a dam in a stream. The dam has the function of stopping water. Its function does not involve human beings even though it was given that function by a human being.[5]

The aesthetic functionalist thesis is one about the *nature* of art. The general functionalist claim is:

Being a functional thing is essential to being a work of art.

And the claim of *Aesthetic Functionalism* is:

AF (1) Being a work of art is having an aesthetic function; and (2) each work of art has some specific aesthetic function that is essential to its being the particular work of art that it is.

For example, a painting of Mondrian's mature period has the aesthetic function of having the aesthetic properties of elegance and boldness in virtue of a certain arrangement of black, white and primary coloured rectilinear shapes.[6]

## 1.3 Further Remarks

(A) In characterizing Aesthetic Functionalism, I have made heavy use of the notion of an *aesthetic property*. For the purposes of this chapter I

---

[5] See Chapter 6 for the idea that an aesthetic theory of art need not make essential reference to an audience.

[6] The fact that only one function need be an aesthetic function has the consequence that many ordinary household things gain art status. This does not worry me. Someone might propose that the 'primary' function of a work of art is its aesthetic function, but I think that such a thesis would be hard to defend, and hard even to define. I would, however, be sympathetic to the suggestion that the greater the degree to which a thing is as it is because of an aesthetic concern, the greater the degree to which it attains art status.

shall characterize aesthetic properties by means of a list. By 'aesthetic' properties, I mean properties such as being beautiful, ugly, dainty, dumpy, elegant, powerful, garish, delicate, balanced, warm, passionate, brooding, awkward or sad. (I also assume that aesthetic value or merit is a kind of aesthetic property.) I assume here a workable distinction between aesthetic and nonaesthetic properties. Works of art have many other kinds of properties beside aesthetic properties, and those other properties may be relevant to the general *artistic* worth of the work. These nonaesthetic artistic properties may be essential to particular works of art. For example, *originality* is not usefully categorized as an aesthetic property. Originality is a property that bears on the *artistic* excellence of a work, but it is not a property that bears on its *aesthetic* excellence.

(B) I also assume that aesthetic properties *depend* on nonaesthetic properties. So if something has an aesthetic property then it is *because of* or *in virtue of* some nonaesthetic property. Such a dependence thesis is compatible with the idea that the aesthetic properties of a work depend in part on its context, so that the aesthetic properties of an object have a wide dependence base that reaches beyond its intrinsic nonaesthetic properties, and includes relational facts about its history or cultural context. I have defended these assumptions elsewhere.[7]

(C) The artist's intention is not merely that the thing will have certain aesthetic properties *and* that it will also have certain nonaesthetic properties, but that it will have the aesthetic properties *because* it will have the nonaesthetic properties. Mondrian intended that his painting would have the aesthetic properties (elegance and boldness) *in virtue of* the nonaesthetic properties (a certain arrangement of black, white and primary coloured rectilinear shapes) that he produced on the canvas. Moreover, he was successful in executing his intentions.

---

[7] As elsewhere in this book, I depend on the notion of an aesthetic property and aesthetic-nonaesthetic dependence, which I defend in *Metaphysics of Beauty* (Ithaca: Cornell University Press, 2001). For a discussion of aesthetic supervenience, see Jerrold Levinson, "Aesthetic Supervenience", in his *Music, Art and Metaphysics* (Ithaca: Cornell, 1990.) The idea of dependence without laws can be found in Frank Sibley's early papers some time before the same combination became popular in the philosophy of mind. See Sibley, "Aesthetic Concepts", *Philosophical Review*, 1959, and "Aesthetic and Nonaesthetic", *Philosophical Review*, 1965.

(D) If a work of art has an aesthetic function then it is at least true that someone must have intended that it has certain aesthetic properties. It is also plausible that there must also be some success in realizing that intention. However, these two conditions seem not to be enough. Consider seeds that someone plants so that they will grow into beautiful flowers. Do these flowers have an aesthetic function? And if so, are they works of art? That seems problematic. We might say that planting seeds for certain purposes does not give them a function corresponding to that purpose because the seeds and flowers are not *artefacts*.[8] One *plants* a seed and *tends* it; one does not *make* it.

(E) We can express the Aesthetic Functionalist thesis by saying that to be a work of art *is* to have an aesthetic function. But that "is" does not indicate the notion of identity, but that of nature or essence. For the notion of identity is symmetrical unlike the notion of nature or essence. We need the idea that having an aesthetic function has metaphysical primacy over being a work of art; something is a work of art in virtue of having an aesthetic function, but something does not have an aesthetic function in virtue of being a work of art. Moreover, I have not thus far expressed claims about the nature or essence of art in terms of necessary and sufficient conditions, because the notions of nature and essence that we need are stronger than such modal claims.[9] But we can endorse modalized versions of the above theses. For example, we might assert

AF*    (1) Having an aesthetic function is necessary and sufficient for being a work of art; and (2) each work of art has some specific aesthetic function that is necessary for its being the particular work of art that it is.

However, the essentialist claims of AF are *stronger* than the modal claims of AF*, and thus would *explain* them. Furthermore, as we will see, many of our modal intuitions concerning works of art are explained by the fact that we grasp that 'art' is a functional kind.[10]

---

[8] Of course, many flowers, such as most roses, have been bred for their looks. Such cases cross the border from nature into art. Perhaps most roses are artefacts, or are artefacts to a degree. And if someone plants many seeds so that the resulting flowers form a harmonious pattern, then that arrangement of flowers also veers into being art. We do not need to draw a sharp line.

[9] See Kit Fine, "Essence and Modality", *Philosophical Perspectives*, vol. 8, 1994.

[10] On general issues about functional kinds and modal intuitions, see George Bealer, "The Limits of Scientific Essentialism", *Philosophical Perspectives*, vol. 1, 1987.

(F) Given Aesthetic Functionalism, it is natural to hold that there is no fundamental metaphysical difference between multi-instantiable works of art, such as novels, symphonies and prints, and particularistic arts, such as painting and sculpture. Peter Strawson was right to think that there is no difference of kind here, only a matter of current technological limitations.[11] This is because of the generality of the dependence relation. (Anything with the nonaesthetic properties has the aesthetic properties.) A perfect duplicate of the *Mona Lisa* found on Mars is not the same work of art as the *Mona Lisa* that hangs in the Louvre, since the Martian object has no connection with Leonardo Da Vinci. But if Leonardo had produced a perfect mechanical copy of the *Mona Lisa* at the time that he completed the original canvas, that would be a different matter. The two things would have the same aesthetic functions and the same origin. So they would have an equal claim to being the *Mona Lisa*. There would be no grounds for privileging one above the other. In a sense, a painter or sculptor makes a *recipe* for producing aesthetic properties from nonaesthetic properties just as much as a composer who writes musical notation on a stave; the only difference is that the painter or sculptor creates the recipe at the same time as making an instance of the work.

(G) One of the advantages of Aesthetic Functionalism is that it can easily explain our *concern* with the existence of art and its survival over time. We care about the existence of art and the survival of particular works because we care about the role that works of art are charged to perform. We care about works of art and their survival because we care about their aesthetic properties, especially aesthetic values.

## 2 NORMS AND FUNCTIONS

### 2.1 Aesthetic Essentialism and Normative Aesthetic Essentialism

Aesthetic Functionalism contrasts with *Aesthetic Essentialism*, which we met in the last chapter, but I shall put it a little differently here:

---

[11] See his *Freedom and Resentment and other Essays*, London: Methuen, 1963, pp. 183–184. Note that not all multi-instantiable works involve notation.

(1)   Having aesthetic properties is essential to being a work of art; and (2) each work of art has specific aesthetic properties that are essential to its being the particular work that it is.[12]

Although I have some sympathy with Aesthetic Essentialism, the thesis is not plausible, because it has the problematic consequence that a work of art cannot persist without its aesthetic properties—which it surely can. There can be aesthetically *dysfunctional* works of art. It is not in general true that functional things have the capacity to perform their functions. (That is, they might not have the properties they were intended or selected to have.) For example, a knife might become so blunt that it fails to have the capacity to cut; and not all hearts can pump blood. Equally, not all works of art can discharge their aesthetic functions. A painting might be damaged with such drastic aesthetic consequences that most of its original aesthetic properties are lost. As I argued in the last chapter, in that case, Aesthetic Essentialism has the consequence that the work of art has not survived. But that is counterintuitive.[13] The Aesthetic Functionalist, by contrast, says that the damaged painting without its aesthetic properties is like a heart that cannot pump blood. It has its aesthetic function even though it cannot perform it.[14]

The nature of functional things is not *actually* to perform their functions or even to have a disposition to perform them, since there can be defective functional things. But it seems that they *somehow* involve the actual performance of the function. A night-watchman has the *role* of keeping watch at night even if he is dead drunk and fast asleep. Actually keeping watch is what he is *supposed* to do. It is what he *should* do. Functional categories bring norms with them. So the view Aesthetic

---

[12] I have cast the initial claim here in terms of an essential property (and thus a necessary condition) rather than in terms of what being a work of art is (which would imply a necessary and sufficient condition), in order to avoid obvious falsification by beautiful natural things.

[13] See further Chapter 2. One would be in danger of committing oneself to Aesthetic Essentialism if one accepted what I called the 'success condition' in too strong a form.

[14] Do functions involve dispositions? Does a broken clock that does not actually show the time nevertheless have a *disposition* to show the time? It depends how generous we are with the notion of a disposition. Sperm have the function of fertilizing eggs. But do sperm have a disposition to fertilize eggs even though the probability of any one of them achieving this is tiny? (This is Millikan's example.) Of course we might specify suitable circumstances in such complete detail that sperm would in those circumstances have a high probability of executing their function. One could also specify other circumstances in which they would have a high probability of doing something else (for example, selecting a Lottery winning number). But which set of circumstances is relevant depends on historical facts.

Functionalism invites is *Normative Aesthetic Essentialism*. The thesis should not be that it is essential that works of art *have* their aesthetic properties, but that they *should* have them.[15] What we need is:

NAE (1) Being a work of art is being such that there are some aesthetic properties that it should have; and (2) it is essential to being each particular work that there are specific aesthetic properties that it should have.

Works of art have normative essences.[16] A work of art *should* sustain the aesthetic properties that it has the function of sustaining, just as hearts should pump blood, can-openers should open cans and night-watchmen should keep watch at night. The 'should' is a functional 'should'.[17]

NAE is explained by AF. The normative essence is consequential on the constitutive functional essence.[18]

## 2.2 Artistic Failure

The norms bearing on an artefactual functional thing ultimately derive from the original intentions with which it was made. But the relation between intentions and norms may not be straightforward where the thing in question falls short of its maker's intention. Things can go wrong in two ways: they might be *ill-designed* or *ill-constructed*. This goes for works of art just as much as other artefacts.

On the one hand, artists might successfully realize the nonaesthetic properties that they intended to realize, but contrary to their beliefs and hopes, they don't in fact realize the aesthetic properties that they had in mind. For example, a painter might intend to make a painting delicate

---

[15] This is parallel to what I think we should say about what is called 'functionalism' in the philosophy of mind: it is not essential that mental stakes stand in *dispositional* relations to other propositional attitudes, inputs and outputs, as is allegedly embodied in the platitudes of 'folk psychology', but it is essential that some mental states stand in *normative* relations to other mental states. See my "Direction of Fit and Normative Functionalism", *Philosophical Studies*, 91, 1998, and "The Normativity of the Mental", *Philosophical Explorations*, 2005.

[16] Compare Nicholas Wolterstorff, *Works and Worlds of Art*, Oxford: Oxford University Press, 1980, pp. 56–57.

[17] *Pristine* works of art are those works whose aesthetic functions are perfectly realized. Their aesthetic roles are fully discharged. But, as we shall see, the aesthetic properties of pristine works are not essential to their survival.

[18] Kit Fine makes the useful distinction between *constitutive* and *consequential* essence in his "Ontological Dependence", *Proceedings of the Aristotelian Society*, XCV, 1995, pp. 276–278.

in virtue of certain lines and colours, but in fact those lines and colours determine pallidness not delicacy. What are the norms here? It is not absolutely clear. But there is something attractive about the idea that it is essential to the work to have the function of being *pallid* (not delicate) in virtue of the lines and colours that the artist realized. Moreover, the work *should* be pallid. We should probably not say that the work should be better than it actually is, because that would be to say that it should be a different work. Perhaps the *painter* should have made a delicate painting, but the *painting* should be pallid. Similarly, consider a poet who writes a poem with unintentional spelling mistakes that affect its sense. Should the publisher correct them? It seems that no sin against the *poet* would have been committed. Quite the opposite. But the *poem* as published is not quite the same poem as the one the poet delivered to the publisher. *That* poem *has* been violated.

On the other hand, the artist might intend to realize certain aesthetic properties in virtue of certain nonaesthetic properties, but might fail to produce those nonaesthetic properties. For example, a painter might aim to make a painting delicate in virtue of certain lines and colours, but fail to make it delicate because of a failure to produce the delicate-making lines and colours which would have realized delicacy. Instead other lines and colours were produced that realize pallidness. What are the norms here? Again, it is not absolutely clear. In this sort of case, I feel some inclination to say that the maker's intention that the painting will be delicate sets the norms for the artefact, even if it turns out not to be delicate. So the work should be *delicate* (not pallid). However, there may be cases of artistic disaster where the thing falls so far short of being as intended in nonaesthetic respects that one would be more inclined to say that it fails to have the aesthetic function of being delicate. If so, it is not the case that it should be delicate. It is rather hard to know what to say about artefacts that are ill-formed in the first place, but the problem is a quite general one and does not only afflict works of art.[19]

[19] Someone might try to make an aeroplane but make it so badly that it is incapable of leaving the ground. The thing falls short with respect to its maker's original intention that it could and would fly. It is supposed to fly. But it can't. There are two possible reasons for this: on the one hand, it might be that if it had been constructed as intended (in physical terms) then it could fly; but, sadly, it was not properly constructed. On the other hand, it might have been ill-designed, so that even if it had been constructed as intended, it could not fly. In both cases, there are a range of such cases. Take cases of bad design. If someone misguidedly tries to make an aeroplane out of a television, what is made is not an aeroplane that doesn't work—it is not a aeroplane at all. But if someone tries to make an aeroplane, and makes one just like a normal aeroplane except

These two kinds of artistic failure are quite different from the kind of failure I discussed in the last section. In those cases, the work fell short of the way it should be because it did not discharge or could not discharge the aesthetic functions that were essential to it. By contrast, what I have explored in this section is the way the aesthetic functions of a work may depend not just on the artist's intentions but also on how the work in fact turns out. Fortunately, there is usually considerable convergence between the artist's intentions and the work itself, so that the work has many of the aesthetic properties it was intended to have. In practice, we do not have to worry too much about cases of artistic failure.

## 2.3  Norms and Performances

What is the relation between the aesthetic properties of works of art that are meant to be performed—such as plays, musical compositions and choreographed dances—and the aesthetic properties of performances of those works? This is a controversial matter. But it is clear that the relation is a normative one. The type, as it were, prescribes the performance. It is probably not necessary for Aesthetic Functionalism to be committed to a very exact position on this, but it is worth sketching the shape of the issue. The substantive question is: to what *extent* do properties of a work constrain properties of good performances of that work? On the one hand, do the properties of the work *Oedipus Rex* completely determine what good performances of *Oedipus Rex* must be like? Or, on the other hand, is the goodness of performances wholly unconstrained by the properties of the work? Or is there some moderate position between these two extremes? To put the issue another way: To what extent is what a playwright writes or what a composer composes capable of interpretation in performance? Does interpretation in performance have no limits, as an extreme liberal would say? Or is there one ideal performance as an extreme authoritarian would have it?

The extreme authoritarian view seems wrong. Two excellent performances of one work may be very different. They can have incommensurable values as performances. But that does not mean that the one work allows *any* interpretation, as the extreme liberal says. There

for the fact that the wings are upside-down (due to the maker not having understood Bernoulli's principle), then the thing probably is an aeroplane that cannot fly. But there doesn't seem to be a fundamental difference between the two cases. The difference is a matter of degree.

is considerable flexibility of interpretation. A moderate position is that this flexibility has certain limits, which derive from what the work is like. For example, good performances of *Oedipus Rex* must bring out its dramatic tension, even if they do this in very different ways. But if the performance is comic, it falls short as a performance of *Oedipus Rex*. Maybe part of what makes a play a great play is that it allows and invites very different excellent interpretations. That might be true without interpretation being entirely unconstrained. So the moderate stance is preferable.

This confirms the aesthetic functionalist viewpoint comfortably. A composer or choreographer who writes a manuscript is like the person who writes the instructions for building a model aircraft. The instructions and manuscript are *meta-functional*. They have the function of prescribing how the functional thing is to be brought into existence. But this prescription is indeterminate within certain limits, which makes room for creative interpretation. The manuscript prescribes, but not rigidly.

## 3 FUNCTION, IDENTITY AND COMPOSITION

### 3.1 Function, Identity, Causality and Stuff

There has been a complex discussion among metaphysicians about the relation between a statue and a lump of clay. Is the relation necessary or contingent? Is the relation identity or constitution?[20] I shall turn directly to Sydney Shoemaker's helpful causal account of cross-time identity.[21] For Shoemaker, the identity of a material object or person over time consists in the obtaining of the appropriate sort of causal relations

---

[20] One classic discussion is John Perry, "The Same *F*", *Philosophical Review*, 1970. For a more recent discussion, see Mark Johnston, "Constitution is not Identity", *Mind*, 1992. See also Stephen Yablo's "Identity, Essence and Indiscernibility", *Journal of Philosophy*, 1987; and Mark Della Rocca's "Essentialists and Essentialism", *Journal of Philosophy*, 1996, which includes a discussion of the *prima facie* implausibility of the widely drawn conclusion that a lump of clay and a statue are not distinct.

[21] Sydney Shoemaker, "Identity, Properties and Causality", *Identity, Cause and Mind*, Cambridge: Cambridge University Press, 1984. Shoemaker's causal account could not serve as an absolutely general account of identity. For one thing, it is at least not obvious how to extend the account to cover synchronic identity (of the Cicero=Tully sort). And for another, it would not apply to the identity of mathematical objects. But the causal account is attractive for diachronic, cross-time identity (or persistence) of material objects, artefacts and, maybe, persons.

among its stages.[22] On such a causal account, the persistence of one and
the same object (the identity of that object over time) consists in the
holding of certain causal relations among its stages, and—as Shoemaker
rightly emphasizes—this means the holding of causal relations between
the *properties* of its stages. But this is a very schematic principle, and it
applies in different ways to different kinds of things.

The difference between asserting the cross-time identity of a *non-
functional* thing and asserting the cross-time identity of a *functional*
thing is a matter of *which* properties are in question. If we ask whether
thing$_1$ at time t$_1$ is the same *rock* as thing$_2$ at time t$_2$ then what we
want to know is whether thing$_2$ at t$_2$ has a certain material composition
as a causal consequence of thing$_1$ at t$_1$ having a certain material
composition. (Radioactive decay might mean that the thing no longer
has exactly the same substance composition, but that doesn't matter
so long as the relevant causal relations between the phases hold.) By
contrast, if we ask whether thing$_1$ at t$_1$ is the same *clock* as thing$_2$ at t$_2$
then what we want to know is not whether they share a certain material
composition, but whether they share certain significant causal properties
and a certain history. The significant properties of a clock are properties
such as having a disposition to cause humans to form beliefs about
the time, or at least having properties that its maker believed would
give it a disposition to cause humans to form beliefs about the time.[23]
Of course, having a certain material composition also involves having
certain dispositional causal properties. However, one difference is that
the significant dispositional causal properties relevant to being a clock
are neutral about matters of substance. Causal roles, such as having
a disposition to cause humans to form beliefs about the time, can be
variably or multiply realized in different material substances. On some
views, the same goes for biological things, such as hearts, which have
the function of pumping blood. That is less clear than the artefactual
case.

This means that if we classify an object according to its function then
its cross-time identity conditions (the conditions of its being the same
functional thing) hinge on significant properties that are not specific
to its particular composition. Which those significant properties are

---

[22] They can only be *described* as 'stages' or 'phases' of one material object or person
given that the causal relations hold between the temporally circumscribed states of
affairs.

[23] I am trying to be neutral on the question of absolute vs. relative identity. Can
something be the same heart as an earlier thing, but not the same cells?

is historically determined. In referring to a thing as a clock, we are giving warning that we are interested in certain significant properties, a certain history, and their connection. We are not interested solely in what matter they are made of. The survival of clocks depends on the extent to which the significant properties are sustained so that the thing at another time possesses the significant properties as a direct causal consequence of the significant properties of the earlier phase.[24]

## 3.2 Function and Origin

Is this general view of cross-time identity for functional things incompatible with a doctrine of the essence of origin which says that the matter that originally composed a table is essential to it? Consider a functional kind with an old philosophical pedigree. A ship might set out to sea composed of wooden planks, and a sailor might gradually change them for aluminium ones, throwing the wooden planks overboard. In that case, the same ship returns, since the functions relevant to its being a ship are preserved in something spatio-temporally continuous with and causally 'downstream' from the original ship. It persists without its original stuff.

This might seem to create a problem for the idea that a functional thing's original matter is essential to it. But it does not. What is allowed is that a ship might originally have been differently composed from the way it comes to be composed at a later time: so long as the functional properties remain intact, and the later ship phase is spatio-temporally continuous with, and a consequence of, the earlier one, retaining or losing the original stuff does not matter. A Strong Compositional Origin Essentialist claim is that if a wooden ship is the same ship as some earlier ship then it must be composed of the same wood that composed the earlier ship. A survivor of the earlier ship must be made of the same wood. This is false. What is more likely to be true is a Weak Compositional Origin Essentialist claim that an aluminium ship, which *was* originally made of wood, could not originally have been made of something other than wood. Suppose that a wooden ship becomes fossilized. Then that stone ship must originally have been made of wood. Similarly, the aluminium ship must originally have been made of

---

[24] I am not sure what to say about waves and rivers, which are non-functional things and are constantly reconstituted. Millikan worries about such cases in the first two chapters of *White Queen Psychology*.

wood. The weak doctrine allows that a ship or table that is now made of wood can mutate so that it comes to be made of something else. Strong Compositional Origin Essentialism is surely false for artefacts, and maybe for people too.[25] (It might, however, be true for rocks and rivers; I make no judgement about non-functional categories.) On the other hand, Weak Compositional Origin Essentialism might still be true for artefacts: it might still be the case that an artefact must have its origin in a certain hunk of matter; so a ship or table must still be made of whatever it was originally made of. It is just that—contrary to Strong Compositional Origin Essentialism—the persistence of the artefact does not depend on the persistence of the original matter.

However, Weak Compositional Origin Essentialism can be challenged by someone who wants to push the point of origin back to an even earlier stage—to the *intentions* of the artisan who made it. Perhaps the intentions are essential but the artefact could have been composed of something different at the moment of its completion. Imagine that the intention of the artisan was a rather elaborate one, such as the intention to make a certain kind of sculpture of a mermaid for the figurehead of a boat. An assistant fetched pieces of wood from a big pile of wood in a shed, but could easily have chosen other similar pieces of wood, or even pieces made of a wood substitute. Looking at the resulting exquisitely carved and intricately constructed product, one might well think that if the assistant had fetched different pieces of wood, or some other similar material, it would still have been the very same artefact. So it seems that a figurehead, table or ship *could* originally have been made of something different. Similarly, a particular painting could have been painted using numerically different but qualitatively similar tubes of paint. It would have been the same painting. (I shall return to this issue.)

### 3.3  Pristine, Defective and Ex-Functional Things

Clocks are supposed to tell the time but not all of them do: some are defective. It is not that they used to be clocks but aren't any more. They are still clocks even though they don't work. Other things, however, are clocks no more. They are ex-clocks. An artefact is a thing that is

---

[25] Compare Saul Kripke, *Naming and Necessity*, Cambridge, MA: Harvard University Press, 1980, pp. 114–115, footnotes 56 and 57. William Carter objects to Saul Kripke's and Nathan Salmon's strong views on essential origins of artefacts in "Salmon on Artefact Origin and Lost Possibilities", *Philosophical Review*, 1983.

created with a certain intention, which is that the object will have certain significant properties. Moreover, the object must also have *some* of its properties as a result of the person acting on that intention. But there can be coffee-makers that fail to have a disposition to make coffee. On the other hand, *too* much failure to possess the dispositional causal role associated with coffee-makers means that at a certain point the thing is no longer properly classified as a coffee-maker at all. But then, what's the difference between a broken coffee-maker and an ex-coffee-maker? Some things are more than just broken. (As John Cleese once noted: there is a difference between a malingering parrot and an ex-parrot.)

In a pristine, well-functioning case of an artefact with function *F*, a thing has the significant property *F* (for instance, the capacity to make coffee) as a causal consequence of its being intended to have that property. But in a malfunctioning case of an artefact with the function *F*, the thing does not have the significant property, but it has properties that are related *in a certain way* to the significant property *F*. Thinking about that special way will enlighten us about the difference between a malfunctioning *F* and an ex-*F*.

A functional thing usually has a *mechanism*. A *well*-functioning functional thing is not a thing that merely has some one simple causal role. It is a *functional system*. It discharges its *overall* role by having a complex interlocking system of things with causal roles that together *realize* or *implement* the *overall* role. In a malfunctioning heart or coffee-maker, most of the sub-mechanisms are in place, but either some crucial part is missing or defective, or else some extrinsic factor intervenes, so that the whole no longer discharges the overall role that it was meant to discharge. (Simple functional things, such as doorstops and wastepaper baskets, do not involve a mechanism in the sense of an *inner* mechanism, but they do involve a structured range of causal properties.)

Suppose that there is an intention to make a thing do F. One possibility is that it never works at all. Could a thing be a coffee-maker if it *never* had the capacity to make coffee? I am not sure about this. But suppose that it works for a while, but then ceases to work, and eventually completely falls to pieces. This would be because, initially, the implementing mechanism satisfactorily realized the overall role, but then some parts of the overall mechanism failed or else something extrinsic intervened so that it could no longer discharge that role. Finally, either the parts of the mechanism ceased to exist or else none of them were connected in the requisite way to discharge any of the sub-roles. If we break a fragile watch by stamping on it, it is still a watch even if it is beyond repair. But if we then grind it into metallic dust, it is no longer a watch at all, despite the persistence of the original material. In a broken watch, some of the sub-mechanisms that realized its overall time-displaying properties are intact, but not enough to make it work. In a hand-full of dust, not even they remain.

# 4 ART IDENTITY AND COMPOSITION

## 4.1 Stuff Survival

What are the consequences of the foregoing for the identity and composition of works of art? Knowing that works of art are functional things, and that 'art' is a functional category, immediately yields a negative metaphysical result. We know that the persistence of a work of art does not depend on its retaining the same matter. Stuff identity and art identity can diverge, at least diachronically. The same is true of watches, bridges and all artefactual functional things. Some think that this is also true of hearts and eyes. If so, a whole organism and a part of an organism can survive the complete replacement of its original matter. This is not obvious. But it is clearer that an artefact like a ship can survive the complete replacement of its original matter. And if art is an artefactual, functional kind, the same is true of art.

A work of art's persistence through time depends on the causal relations between its phases. But which causal relations are in question for a particular work of art depends on the specific aesthetic functions of that work. If something has an aesthetic function, then someone must have intended it to have aesthetic properties in virtue of nonaesthetic properties, and its persistence conditions depend on that intention. (I assume for simplicity that we are not dealing with failed works.) The cross-time identity of a work of art depends on the persistence of most of the nonaesthetic properties that realize the aesthetic properties that were envisaged in the artist's intentions. However, those aesthetic properties can be realized by different stuff at different times, so long as the different stuff realizes most of the same aesthetic properties as a causal consequence (of the right kind) of earlier phases.[26]

---

[26] I want to be neutral on the exact relation between a statue and a lump of clay. It may be contingent identity or it may be what is called 'constitution'. The crucial thing is that the statue can continue to exist without its original matter, and that it could have existed without its actual matter. And we can say that in either genre.

Pristine works of art are those that persist in having all the envisaged aesthetic properties in virtue of the nonaesthetic properties they have at a later time. They fulfil their aesthetic functions perfectly. But a descendant of a pristine work may not be pristine. It may have many but not all the nonaesthetic properties that were supposed to realize the aesthetic properties—in which case the work may lack the aesthetic properties even though it retains its aesthetic function.

Material survival is not *necessary* for art survival. Moreover, material survival is not *sufficient* for art survival—a scrambled pile of rubble could be an ex-sculpture of a discus thrower: the sculpture has not survived even though its remnants have. And we can make a different sculpture out of the stuff of an old one. So we cannot say that once a work of art exists its material descendants are that same work of art, regardless of whether the material descendants have preserved the earlier work of art's original aesthetic function.

Does Aesthetic Functionalism imply Weak Compositional Origin Essentialism, so that a work of art must have had whatever composition it originally had, even though it need not retain that composition? Aesthetic Functionalism is *compatible* with insisting on essential material origins. But it is not clear that we should insist on them. Perhaps a work of art could originally have been differently composed, as in the mermaid figurehead example of section 3.2 of this chapter. However, I do want to insist that the original *intentions* are essential. A work must have its origin in the intention to make a thing with certain aesthetic properties in virtue of certain nonaesthetic properties. And a work of art must also have its origin in the creative insight that produced the intention. This origin essentialism is part of Aesthetic Functionalism, and the Aesthetic Creation Theory requires it.

## 4.2 Restoration and Function

Aesthetic Functionalism has a certain consequence for issues about the restoration of works of art. Some aestheticians say that if we restore a damaged work of art to a state superficially perceptually indistinguishable from its original state, but out of entirely different materials, we have not preserved but destroyed the original work of art.[27] But such aestheticians believe falsely that retaining the original hunk of matter is essential for

---

[27] See Mark Sagoff, "On Restoring and Reproducing Art", *Journal of Philosophy*, 1978.

the persistence of the work, and this is because they have overlooked the functional nature of art. If we restore a work of art to its original physical arrangement out of perceptually indistinguishable but different physical stuff, then we will have restored the bulk of its original aesthetic properties and functions (given aesthetic/nonaesthetic dependence and supervenience). This is necessary and sufficient for restoring the work of art, since the work will once again perform its original functions as envisaged by the artist and as a consequence of earlier phases. It is just that the latest phase of the transmission of the aesthetic properties from one phase to another was rather unusual in that it involved a restorer. Strictly speaking, this means that in such a case, the aesthetic properties of one phase of a work of art are not *entirely* causally dependent on the aesthetic properties of previous phases, since the restorer intervened from outside. But then, it still depends *in part* on those properties. Some degree of spatio-temporal continuity is also necessary.[28] We might replace the motor of a vacuum cleaner without destroying it. We replace the motor of the vacuum cleaner so that it can do the job it used to do and was supposed to do. Similarly, it is crucial that the intention of the art restorer involve *fidelity* to the earlier intentions of the artist—those that gave the work its function.

At this point someone might protest: would Michelangelo's *David* really survive if it came to be made of plastic? Surely that would be a *copy* of *David*; it would not *be David*. It will help to distinguish different cases. In one case—the Controversial Replacement Case—we imagine someone gradually replacing the stone of the original *David* with plastic that looks (and feels) like the original stone. Eventually there is no stone left and we have an entirely plastic sculpture. The question then arises: Is the statue still Michelangelo's *David*? Put this Controversial Replacement Case on one side for a while. Consider the following case. Imagine there is something special about the stone that Michelangelo used (a property that he may or may not have known about). Over a period of 500 years, the stone gradually turns into plastic which looks (and feels) exactly like the original stone. Is the plastic sculpture, 500 years later, Michelangelo's *David*? Surely it is. (A wooden sculpture that has become fossilized would be a similar case.) We would not rudely throw away the plastic descendant and declare *David* a lost work. So it cannot be the change in material in

---

[28] Hence a plastic David cast from a rubber mould taken from the original is not *David*.

the Controversial Replacement Case that is problematic. It might be thought that it is the alien physical intrusion that is worrying. But imagine that there is something strange about the particular stone that Michelangelo used so that the stone interacts with the molecules in the air which emanate from a local Florence plastics factory. The stone gradually absorbs the plastic from the air and that somehow causes the stone to decay or excrete itself. This is just what this kind of stone naturally does when it comes in contact with plastic vapour. Eventually, the statue comes to be entirely composed of plastic that looks (and feels) exactly like the original stone as a result of alien intrusion rather than inner mutation. Is it still Michelangelo's *David*? I think it is. It is not the alien physical intrusion that is worrying. What worries people in the Controversial Replacement Case is the trespassing of the alien *intentions* of the restorer. But so long as the alien intentions involve the aim of fidelity to Michelangelo's intentions, and the alien intentions succeed in their aims, there is nothing to fear.

Works of art have essential origins in intentions. And if Weak Compositional Origin Essentialism is true, they also have essential material origins. But Strong Compositional Origin Essentialism is false since the persistence of original matter is not necessary for survival. That would only be the case if works of art were not functional things.

## 4.3 Specific Material Intentions?

It follows from the previous discussion that there is no rationale for a kind of 'stuff fetishist' view according to which art survival requires stuff survival.[29] Art survival does not require material persistence, although that is one way, and perhaps the easiest way, to ensure continuity of the relevant aesthetic functions. In practice, however, it may be that a work must be composed of what it is in fact composed of, because no other available material would have been quite the same. Consider a sculpture made from a piece of wood with a particular grain. It might be that only that material will look a certain way. But this is contingent. It is a contingency that creates the illusion that material composition is essential, even though a work can in fact survive without its original matter.

---

[29] For opposition to 'stuff fetishism', see Eddy Zemach, "No Identity Without Evaluation", *British Journal of Aesthetics*, 1986.

It might be objected that there seem to be works that depend on being composed of a certain kind of stuff. Surely an artist might intend that we know what the material is and what it is not, in which case the matter would seem to be essential to such works. For example, in many contemporary works, a point is being made by the use of certain specific materials. The force of Duane Hanson's very lifelike cast sculptures of people depends on their *not* being real flesh-and-blood people, although they look just like real people. And the force of living sculptures depends on the reverse being true; they look like lifeless sculptures, but in fact they are real people. It seems that artists do sometimes think that the material composition of their work matters. It is part of their intention in making a work that it is composed of a particular sort of stuff. But if aesthetic functionalism were true, why would artists have such intentions? Surely they wouldn't, unless they were confused. So what is going on in cases where the matter seems to matter?

What really does matter, and is of concern to artists, I think, is not the fact that the works *are* composed as they are, but merely that they *seem* to be. Imagine that an artist could not afford a certain expensive material but could make it seem *as if* the work is made of the expensive material by using a cheaper alternative that looked the same. Then surely the work would be just as effective as it would be if it really were composed of the expensive material, so long as no one else knew. The trouble, again, is the contingent fact that different materials tend to look different. The material composition of a work might contribute to inducing certain thoughts in an audience about its material composition, but that does not mean that those thoughts have to be correct. A title might also induce those thoughts. What is important is merely that the work *seems* to have a certain material composition, or that the audience *believes* it does, not that it actually has it. If artists have a material-specific intention, it is only because they think that it is the best way to make a thing *look* as if it were made of a certain material. At some point, it becomes obvious to viewers that Hanson's sculptures are not real people and that living sculptures are real people. If no one ever became aware of this—if people remained fooled—the point of such works would be lost.[30]

---

[30] The artist's intentions concerning a work are not always so straightforward. He might intend that audience to have false beliefs about a work's material composition. Or he might merely intend that the audience see the work as composed of what it is not composed of. The Minoans made clay pots that looked like leather, and they sculpted shells out of stone. So it might be argued that it was important that the pot was clay and

Consider a visual artist who works with a particular hunk of material—a particular piece of marble or wood or tube of paint. It is true that their thoughts are directed to that particular material ('*de re*' as philosophers say). But the question is: which *properties* of that particular stuff preoccupy the artist? The plausible answer is that they are properties that can be seen, such as spatial or sensory properties. But such properties are properties that are not material-specific properties. They can be variably realized in very different materials. Therefore when artists intend to realize such properties, and perhaps have some degree of success, they endow the work with functional properties.

A Harold Rosenberg might say that it is essential to Jackson Pollock's paintings that the paint was actually splashed on the canvas. It is essentially 'action painting' in the sense that it is essential to a particular painting that it is the result of a particular action of applying paint. But I think a Clement Greenberg would be right to insist that what is important is that the paint looks *as if* it were splashed on, not that it actually was. That appearance generates the formal energy that Greenberg celebrates. It looks as if it is the result of action painting, but it need not actually *be* action painting. Similarly, what *is* essential to *David* is not the persistence of the stone that was chiselled by Michaelangelo, but the persistence of material that looks *as if* it is chiselled stone. A plastic *David* can pass that test. Both stone and plastic can look as if they are chiselled stone, just as a fossilized sculpture that was originally carved wood can look like carved wood.

So the alleged phenomenon of material-specific intentions needs to be reinterpreted, and when it is, it does not show that material composition is necessary for art identity.

## 5 NONAESTHETIC FUNCTIONS OF ART

### 5.1 Multi-functional Art

So far I have been operating with a somewhat oversimplified picture in which there are only aesthetic functions. Let us now examine the more complex scenario in which works of art have nonaesthetic functions *as well as* aesthetic functions. (As I mentioned at the beginning

---

not leather and that the sculpted shell was stone and not a real shell from the sea. But at some point, it must become obvious that the pot is clay and not leather, and that the shell is stone and not from the sea.

of this chapter, I shall not be concerned with examining the scenario—which some think important—where works of art seem *only* to have nonaesthetic functions and *no* aesthetic functions.)

The thesis of Aesthetic Functionalism is that works of art *have* aesthetic functions that are essential to them; it is not that their aesthetic functions are their *only* functions. A work can also have *nonaesthetic* functions that are essential for its being the work of art that it is. For example, a work of art might have the nonaesthetic functions of representing a tree, protesting against injustice, yielding insight into human motivation, provoking emotional reactions, and so on. What the Aesthetic Functionalist claims is that if a work of art has a range of functions, then it is essential that at least *one* of them is that of embodying aesthetic properties. Works of art can have many different functions, and the Aesthetic Functionalist should concede that in many cases only one of them need be the aesthetic function. (This was the point of the aesthetic function merely being an essential property in the second clauses of AF and NAE, rather than a stronger relation, which would imply a necessary and sufficient condition.) So it is possible that a continuant of a work discharges some or all of its nonaesthetic functions even though it fails to discharge its aesthetic function. In such a case, the work of art has survived without its original aesthetic properties. (As we have seen, the latter is not a problem for Aesthetic Functionalism. Indeed, it is a point in its favour.)

What is going on where we have nonaesthetic functions as well as aesthetic functions? In some works, the aesthetic functions may sit side by side with the nonaesthetic functions, in which case the functions are *independent*. But some works involve the aesthetically appropriate *expression* or *realization* of nonaesthetic functions. For example, music can be for marching, praying or dancing, and buildings can be made to look as if they are stations, libraries or schools. In these cases, one cannot separate the aesthetic from the nonaesthetic functions. This is a special kind of multi-functionality. In these cases there is a *double* aesthetic functionality. The aesthetic function emerges from the nonaesthetic function so that a new overall aesthetic function of the work is realized. This is 'dependent beauty', in Kant's sense.[31] In these cases, aesthetic and nonaesthetic functions are interwoven or intermingled in the work.

---

[31] See Kant, *Critique of Judgement*, trans. Meredith, Oxford: Oxford University Press, 1928, section 16. I reconstruct and apply this idea in chapter 4 of *The Metaphysics of Beauty*.

The beauty is dependent on the nonaesthetic function, whereas in simpler cases they are independent.

Let me put the point in modal terms, for ease of exposition: the Aesthetic Functionalist's claim is that having *some* aesthetic function is *necessary and sufficient* for being a work of art. Moreover, *particular* aesthetic functions are *necessary* for being a *particular* work of art. Some works of art also have nonaesthetic functions that are necessary for being those works. Those cases divide into two classes. Where the aesthetic and nonaesthetic functions are independent, having the aesthetic function is *necessary but not sufficient* for being a particular work of art. However, as we just noted, in some works, the aesthetic and nonaesthetic functions are mutually dependent and intermingled. The aesthetic function involves the nonaesthetic function in that the aesthetic and nonaesthetic functions are appropriate to each other. Each fits the other. The aesthetic function is the aesthetically apt realization of the nonaesthetic function. In such cases, the aesthetic function is *both necessary and sufficient* for being a particular work.

## 5.2 Essential Matter

Since Aesthetic Functionalism allows that works of art have nonaesthetic functions that are essential to their being the particular works they are, it seems to allow that a particular hunk of matter could after all be essential for the persistence of the work of art if the original matter were essential for the *nonaesthetic* functions that are essential for the work. But in fact, I don't think we can tell a plausible story according to which an artist has a material-specific nonaesthetic intention, as opposed to an intention that the material sustains certain (higher-order) properties that the artist is concerned with. For example, if meanings are embodied in certain material forms, then the matter does not matter in itself, it only matters that it should discharge its meaning-function. In general, if works of art have other functions beside aesthetic functions, it does not help the thesis that there are material conditions of persistence. For in *no* case does the survival of a (artefactual) functional thing depend on material persistence. General principles concerning the identity or survival of functional things dictate that functional things can survive without material persistence. So if some works have nonaesthetic functions as well as aesthetic functions (or even instead of them), material persistence is still not essential for their survival.

## 5.3 Forgery

A particularly unusual case of nonaesthetic function is that of forgeries. A forgery of a work of art has the nonaesthetic function of deceiving people. To do that successfully it has to mimic the aesthetic functions of a particular work or of some type of work. But in order to do that it must instantiate certain aesthetic functions. (The functions will be either the same or closely related to those possessed by the original work or an original of the type of work that is being forged.) A forgery of a particular work has some different functions from the original. It also has different origins. But on the Aesthetic Functionalist view, forgeries are works of art because they have an aesthetic function. It is just that the aesthetic function is a means to an end, not an end in itself.

## 5.4 Aesthetic Functional Disaster

Suppose a work of art has five functions only one of which is aesthetic. And suppose that the work of art is subject to damage, such that not only are its aesthetic *properties* lost but its aesthetic *functions* are also lost because the realizing system that the aesthetic function depends on is destroyed. Suppose also that the nonaesthetic functions are intact. This case seems to create a problem for Aesthetic Functionalism. The conditions of identity of such a work of art form a cluster that derives from the cluster of its original functions—and aesthetic functions are not privileged. So when the nonaesthetic functions are intact but the aesthetic function is lost, we must say that the work of art survives. The Aesthetic Functionalist position is that works of art must have an aesthetic function even though they might also have other essential functions. But our damaged multi-functional work seems to be a counterexample. Aesthetic Functionalism privileges the aesthetic function, so that without that function, a work of art would not be *that* work of art, or even *a* work of art. But how can the aesthetic function be privileged if a work can survive the loss of its aesthetic function?

I suggest two tactics.

(A) First, suppose we categorize something as a *painting* or *poem*. Given a cluster theory, the Aesthetic Functionalist might concede that the persistence of enough of the original functions makes for the survival of the painting or the poem. Whether a work, such as a painting or a philosophical, political or religious poem, survives depends on the persistence of its original functions. So if one out of five functions is lost then the work—the painting or poem—survives to a proportionately diminished extent. This is a non-hierarchical cluster theory since all the members of the cluster have equal weight. So when the aesthetic function is lost, a painting or poem can survive to a diminished extent in virtue of its nonaesthetic functions. But the Aesthetic Functionalist might say that the *art status* of the painting or poem is dependent on the persistence of the aesthetic function. For example, suppose we have a clumsy translation of what was originally a beautifully written philosophical, political or religious tract, and the original is lost. We can say that the *tract* has partly survived but not *as art*. On this approach, the terms 'painting' or 'poem' indicate that survival as a thing of that kind depends on a cluster of the thing's original functions. Paintings and poems are multi-dimensional and multi-functional things. But they are not necessarily art. When we ask whether something is the *same work of art*, we give warning that we are interested in one specific dimension or function—its aesthetic function. To some extent this is an arbitrary stipulation. I doubt that our concepts are fine-tuned enough to deal with this unusual kind of case. But it is a stipulation that does no great violence to how we think.[32]

(B) The second strategy is simpler. It is to concede that works of art may lose their aesthetic function but insist that anything that is a work of art must *originally* have had an aesthetic function. A certain kind of origin essentialism is thus envisaged. A work of art must have its origin in something that at one time had an aesthetic function, even if that function may be lost with the passage of time.

One or other of these strategies will deal with the imagined examples of isolated aesthetic functional disaster.

## 6 APPROPRIATION

### 6.1 Multi-functionality and Appropriating Functions

What is the difference between a large flannel and a small towel?[33] The difference cannot be solely one of composition since there could be two

---

[32] Given this strategy, we may need to deny that the work of art *is* the painting.
[33] Apparently 'flannel' translates into American English as 'wash-cloth'.

physically indiscernible things where one is a towel and not a flannel and the other is a flannel and not a towel. Flannels and towels have different functions: flannels are for washing whereas towels are for drying. (Even a towel that cannot absorb any water might still be a towel—just a bad one. It is a towel that fails to dry as opposed to something that fails to be a towel.) Suppose that lightning were to strike in a swamp and produce something molecularly indistinguishable from a flannel or a towel. Call the result 'Swamp-fabric'. Swamp-fabric is neither flannel nor towel. If tourists in the swamp come across Swamp-fabric and take it to be either a flannel or a towel, they would make a mistake. Whether some fabric is a flannel or towel, or neither, depends on its origins.[34]

The simplest kind of artefact is one that has just one function. We can call that the *uni-functional* case. But there might be a number of original intentions. Then we have a *multi-functional* case. Those original intentions might be more or less simultaneous. At some time, one or more people might intend that thing will do a number of different things. But the function-determining intentions might be spread out in time, such that the thing acquires different functional properties at different times.

One such case is when a manufacturer's purpose is overridden and something that is intended to be a towel is used a flannel. In such a case the philosophical conundrum over which the world holds its breath is: Is it a towel or a flannel? Or both? My intuition is that it is both. We might take two physically indiscernible pieces of absorbent material and designate one for washing and the other for drying. The intention in part *makes* the thing a flannel or a towel. But we can also do this to something that already has some other function. Consider the category of an 'offensive weapon'. By law, if someone carries a baseball bat with a certain intention it takes on the extra function of being an offensive weapon. A gun is an offensive weapon because of its *initial* function; but when someone carries a baseball bat as an offensive weapon, that is an *appropriated* function. But it is still a baseball bat.[35] There seem to be other cases where we are not quite so generous. If someone uses a sculpture as a doorstop, some will say that it does not *become* a doorstop

---

[34] We are familiar with the mind/body problem and the fact/value problem—but we also have the flannel/towel problem!

[35] A thing might be made to fulfil many initial functions, which would be a case of 'synchronic multi-functionality'. In such a case, there is no difficulty, and all the original purposes are uncontroversially on a par with each other. So why should we privilege the earlier or later intentions in the case of 'diachronic multi-functionality'?

even though it is *used as* a doorstop. Perhaps it *performs* a function that it doesn't *have*. If so, appropriation does not mean that the thing *becomes* a thing of the novel functional kind. I am not sure what the difference is between this case and the flannel and baseball bat cases. Anyway, in both cases, a thing retains its original function—the one for which it was created—unless it undergoes a radical break-up of the causal systems that implement that original function. A baseball bat that has been an offensive weapon can cease to be an offensive weapon, but it can never cease to be a baseball bat so long as it retains its physical integrity.

## 6.2 Appropriating Driftwood

What about apparently non-artefactual works of art? I mentioned earlier that some aestheticians have argued that pieces of driftwood that are appropriated by the artworld can become works of art even though they are not artefacts. However, given the above account of function, we can see that even though a piece of driftwood may not be an *artefact* in a narrow sense, it can nevertheless *perform* a function. Things can be *conscripted* to perform new functions. For example, a suitably shaped unworked stone or a cable drum can be used as a table. It takes on the table function. It is intended for use as a table, and it comes to be used as a table. I am not sure whether it thereby *becomes* a table because it is not an object that was constructed or altered so as to perform that function. Perhaps something needs to be constructed or altered if it is actually to *be* a table. I am not sure. But an unworked stone or cable drum can certainly *perform* whatever function tables have. They can have that functional *role*. Similarly, the artistic appropriation of driftwood or urinals (as opposed to their merely being displayed as interesting natural things or as plumbing artefacts), conscripts something with no function, or with an ordinary function, to perform a new and unusual artistic function—perhaps that of making a certain ironic gesture about other works of art. It is intended that the conscripted thing should perform the new function. If successful, the thing *takes on* or at least *performs* the new function, like the baseball bat that is used as a weapon. Once we are clear what functions are, such cases of appropriated driftwood are not counterexamples to the thesis that all works of art are functional things or, at least, that they are intended to perform functions. Appropriated driftwood may have an artistic functional role.

## 6.3 Appropriating Art and Identity

Duchamp's *L.H.O.O.Q.* was a replica of the *Mona Lisa* with a moustache added. However, suppose that Duchamp had got hold of the real *Mona Lisa* and added a moustache to it. Call that *Moustached Mona Lisa*. The *Mona Lisa* would have survived, although it would have been damaged, with aesthetic consequences. The question arises: Would there then be two works which happen to occupy roughly the same region of space (though not of course of space-time)? Alternatively, suppose that Duchamp had exhibited the real *Mona Lisa* unaltered without the added moustache, with the title *Non-Moustached Mona Lisa*. Then it would have been like the case of using a baseball bat as an offensive weapon, since the original thing was not changed. Again, there is the question: is *Non-Moustached Mona Lisa* distinct from the *Mona Lisa*? Both occupy exactly the same region of space.[36] But they have different temporal and modal properties.

One possibility would be to say that the *Mona Lisa* existed before *Non-Moustached Mona Lisa* but some time later they came to be identical. That would make it a case of contingent identity. If we allow contingent identities, then we will say that things that are identical must share all their *actual* properties, but they need not share all their *possible* properties. Since temporal properties are actual properties, the view would have to be that *Non-Moustached Mona Lisa* is contingently identical with a certain *phase* in the life of the *Mona Lisa*. On the other hand, if we don't like contingent identity, we can say more or less the same thing using the word 'constitution'. We can say that *Non-Moustached Mona Lisa* is constituted in part by *Mona Lisa*. I doubt that it matters very much how we put it. Either we assert contingent identity or we deny it and assert constitution. We can describe what happens in artistic appropriation in either mode.

## 6.4 Aesthetic Appropriation

An appropriated functional thing retains its original functions, and acquires a new one in addition. In the case of most twentieth-century

---

[36] Note that they are both subsumed under the same so-called 'sortal'—*work of art*. I am sceptical about whether the 'sortal' jargon helps much, unless it just serves to alert us to a thing's functional properties. Those who discussed identity in those terms in the late 1960s and 1970s reached for examples of artefactual and biological kinds.

appropriation of works of art, this means that even though the act of appropriation itself may not have an *aesthetic* point, appropriated works retain the original aesthetic functions of the works that are appropriated. Just as a baseball bat used as an offensive weapon is still a baseball bat, so an appropriated *Mona Lisa* retains whatever aesthetic functions the *Mona Lisa* had, even though it may no longer discharge those functions because it has been altered. (Appropriated works become parts or constituents of new works.) So from the point of view of Aesthetic Functionalism, the art status of appropriated aesthetic works of art is not in doubt. Aesthetic Functionalism can easily take such works on board.

More problematic are cases of artistic appropriation where non-art is appropriated. Someone might appropriate human artefacts or natural things that have no aesthetic purpose (such as medical equipment or driftwood). This raises the issues about the extensional adequacy of Aesthetic Functionalism that I am avoiding in this chapter. But in such cases, the trouble, if such it is, does not come from appropriation itself, since many other cases of appropriation are unproblematically works of art. The apparent difficulty comes from the fact that neither what was appropriated nor the act of appropriation had an aesthetic point. I argued in Chapter 3 that these marginal cases need not greatly concern us. This is not the place to comfort those aestheticians who are over-anxious about such phenomena.[37]

## CODA

Aesthetic Functionalism is a metaphysically healthy doctrine. It is a good partner for the Aesthetic Creation Theory. Aesthetic Functionalism can draw on general principles concerning functional things in order to

---

[37] In this discussion of the persistence of works of art over time I have appealed to intuitions. However, in Chapter 3, I expressed some scepticism about the appeal to intuitions about which things are art, since it seemed to stem from an over-sanguine reliance on the concept of art. However, the appeal to intuitions concerning the persistence of works of art derives from the idea that works of art are artefacts and from our understanding of what it is to be a particular work of art or some kind of work of art. The intuitions are not about whether or not something counts as art. Whether or not a tattoo is a work of art is problematic. But, apart from puzzle cases, whether the tattoo on John's arm is the same tattoo as the one that was there yesterday is not problematic. We have more reliable intuitions about the persistence conditions of tattoos than about whether they are art.

deliver a satisfactory understanding of the persistence of works of art through time. On this account works of art can survive while altering their material constitution. What is essential for survival are properties that are related in the right way to the maker's original intentions. The functionalist account privileges aesthetic intentions. But the basic account was extended to deal with cases where works also have nonaesthetic functions and where works are appropriated. We encountered no insurmountable difficulties for the Aesthetic Functionalist view, and we gathered considerable support along the way.

# 6

# Art and Audience

## 1 AUDIENCE THEORIES AND INITIAL DIFFICULTIES

Do works of art essentially involve a relation to an audience? Many otherwise very different theories of art agree that they do. So, according to such theories, the question "What is art?" has to be answered at least in part by describing that relation. I shall argue to the contrary that a theory of what art is should not invoke any essential relation to an audience. Art has nothing essential to do with an audience.

### 1.1 Audience Theories

The following are very rough statements of some diverse audience-based theories. According to Monroe Beardsley, a work of art is intentionally endowed with a disposition to produce aesthetic experiences (in an audience). For an expression theory of art such as that of Tolstoy, a work of art expresses emotions and has a disposition to elicit similar emotions (from an audience), or the artist intends that it expresses and has a disposition to elicit emotions (from an audience). According to Nelson Goodman, a work of art imparts a kind of understanding (to an audience). For Arthur Danto, a work of art makes a 'statement' to the artworld (a particular audience). In George Dickie's earlier institutional account, a work of art is deemed by someone to be a candidate for appreciation (by an audience). And in his later account, a work of art is intentionally presented to the artworld (a particular audience). According to Jerrold Levinson's historical account, a work of art is intended to be regarded (by an audience), in ways similar to the ways that past works of art were regarded (by their audiences).[1] In

---

[1] Monroe Beardsley, "An Aesthetic Definition of Art", in (ed.) Hugh Curtler, *What is Art?*, New York: Haven, 1983; Leo Tolstoy, *What is Art?*, Oxford: Oxford University

fact, most theories of art make some kind of essential reference to an audience.

Different kinds of audience theories emerge, given various distinctions. First, an audience might figure as the relatum of some real relation in which the work of art stands or an audience might figure as the object of the artist's intentions. Second, the relation to an audience might be an actual or dispositional relation. Third, different features of an audience might be important: perceptual experience, understanding, pleasure or emotion. Fourth, different audiences might be in question; the audience might be some select group, such as the 'artworld', or it might be the whole of humanity.

I shall come back to some of these distinctions, although I shall try to leave open exactly what form an audience theory should take. But we might as well note straight away that any plausible theory must involve *some* reference to an artist's intention, because surely: no intention, no work of art. Clouds can be experienced and appreciated by an audience or have a disposition to be experienced and appreciated by an audience even though they have no claim to art status. A *pure* audience theory would be left with no way of distinguishing works of art from appreciable non-art (such as clouds and industrial machines). Without reference to an artist's intention, it will be impossible to make that distinction. So the view that works of art involve actual or dispositional relations to an audience, but no intention that they do, is implausible. Let us ignore such a pure audience theory. An audience theorist might still maintain that it is essential that a work of art bears an actual or dispositional relation to an audience, but that needs to be conjoined with some role for the artist's intentions. However, so far, we have no reason to think that the content of an artist's intentions must involve an audience.

Having said this much, let us leave any further consideration of which version of audience theory is most plausible until it is necessary to consider it.

I shall argue that *all* such accounts are flawed. There should be *no* reference to an audience in a theory of the essential nature of art.

Press, 1955; Nelson Goodman, *Languages of Art*, Oxford: Oxford University Press, 1968; Arthur Danto, "The Artworld", *Journal of Philosophy*, 1964, and *The Transfiguration of the Commonplace*, Cambridge, MA: Harvard University Press, 1981; George Dickie, *Art and the Aesthetic*, Ithaca: Cornell University Press, 1974, and *The Art Circle*, New York: Haven, 1984: Jerrold Levinson, *Music, Art, and Metaphysics*, Ithaca: Cornell University Press, 1990.

## 1.2 Counterexamples

The initial problem for audience theories is that they seem to be subject to counterexamples. Although *many* works of art involve an audience, or are intended to do so, it seems that *some* works of art bear no actual or intended relation to an audience.

Jerrold Levinson has discussed the case of Kafka's novels *The Castle* and *The Trial*.[2] Kafka wanted these destroyed after his death. So we might think that these novels bore no intended relation to an audience. In response, Levinson suggested various possibilities. Perhaps Kafka did intend these for an audience when he wrote them, but he later changed his mind. Or perhaps he wanted them burned for quite different reasons as well as writing them in order for them to be read. Or perhaps he intended them for some imaginary ideal audience, but the actual audience fell disappointingly short of that ideal. These accounts are certainly possible. Daniel Kolak has disputed whether these suggestions do justice to the historical facts about Kafka's novels.[3] But it is difficult to know who is right. So it is not clear whether Kafka's novels are genuine counterexamples to audience theories.

Another source of counterexamples to audience theories might be sculptures that were made for burial with the dead. This again is another uncertain example. For it might be replied that the sculptors think that the gods, or the souls of the departed, will appreciate the sculptures. So there is an intended audience; it is just that it is a netherworldly audience.

These two examples are not clear-cut because they involve speculation about unknown intentions. However, there are two other cases which are more decisive in this respect.

The first example is that of private poetry. This is not intended for any audience. The vast majority of such poetry is never intended to be read by anyone except the person who wrote it.

The second example is that of working sketches which are made in the course of preparing works of art which *are* intended for presentation to an audience. Working sketches are usually made with no intention that they themselves will be exhibited. More often than not they are

---

[2] "Refining Art Historically," in his *Music, Art and Metaphysics*, Cornell: Cornell University Press, 1990, pp. 56–58; and "A Refiner's Fire: Reply to Sartwell and Kolak," *Journal of Aesthetic and Art Criticism*, 1990.

[3] Daniel Kolak, "Art and Intentionality," *Journal of Aesthetic and Art Criticism*, 1990.

destroyed. But they are surely works of art in their own right, although not the same works that they were studies for. Some of the working sketches of famous artists have been saved and exhibited and appreciated. They are considered to be works of art in themselves. But there are many other working sketches which have never been exhibited and which have not survived. These were works of art which bore no actual or intended relation to an audience.

So we have here two potential counterexamples to any audience account. It is a virtue of these two examples that they are not peripheral, unusual or controversial, as is the case with Kafka's two novels and burial sculptures.

## 1.3  Responses to the Counterexamples: Dispositional and Functional Theories

If we accept that these are genuine counterexamples, then it seems to create a problem for audience theories.

However, an audience theorist might try to include working sketches and private poetry in a *modified* audience account.

One line of thought would be that the connection between art and audience is sometimes *indirect*. Perhaps *either* a work of art is itself presented or intended for presentation to an audience *or* it is connected with some other work of art that is presented or that is intended for presentation to an audience. It might be said that it could not be the case that people *only* ever write private poetry or *make* working sketches. *Sometimes* people must write public poetry or produce finished paintings, *someone* must do these things for real. Perhaps that is what we should say about private poetry and working sketches. The idea is that private poetry and working sketches are derivative or parasitic cases. Working sketches are not the same work of art as the work of art that they were made in aid of. On the present suggestion, they only have art status because the other work was planned. So works of art divide into two classes—those which have *basic* art status, and those which have *derivative* art status.

This means that the art status of private poetry and working sketches is dependent on something else, or on projected works of art. But this is implausible. Maybe their existence is *causally* dependent on other projected works of art, but given that they exist, their art status is surely independent of those other projected works. Moreover, we now seem to be embracing a disjunctive conception of art according to which a work of art is either a basic or a derivative case of art. But that would give us an odd and unnatural conception? The theory seems to be ad hoc.

The audience theorist does better to shift tack. One alternative would be to appeal to a *disposition* to be experienced by an audience. On such a view, someone must intend that a work of art has a disposition to be experienced in a certain way by an audience. So a work of art need not be something which is intended *actually* to be experienced by an audience. Another theory—which may amount to the same thing as the intended disposition theory—would be a theory according to which works of art have the *function* of being experienced by an audience. But artworks need not fulfil their functions, just as there can be hearts that do not and cannot pump blood. To have a function, a thing must have an actual history, certain current dispositions, and the right relation between them.[4] On the functional audience theory, an audience must figure in the artist's actual historical intentions which, if things go well, cause later dispositions to affect an audience.

These alternative theories seem to rescue Kafka's doomed novels, burial sculptures, working sketches and private poetry, which, even though they do not *actually* involve an intended audience, are intended to have a dispositional relation to an audience, or have the function of being for an audience. It is just that in some cases the disposition is manifested while in others it is not—or some cases the function is fulfilled while in others it is not. These theories have the virtue of being unified theories and not ad hoc disjunctive theories.

In order to tackle these more subtle theories, we need to raise some more theoretical questions. Only after having done so will we be in a position to assess dispositional and functionalist audience theories. So let us put these theories on hold for a while.

## 1.4 Methodological Difficulties

There is another motive for turning to more theoretical questions. We need to move away from considering examples because there is an alternative dialectical scenario that we have so far ignored: an audience theorist might simply *deny* that the alleged counterexamples to audience theories *are* works of art. If they are not works of art, then it is acceptable that an audience theory excludes them. Now *I* find this move counterintuitive; but the stubborn audience theorist

[4] See Ruth Millikan, *White Queen Psychology*, Cambridge, MA: MIT Press, 1993.

might not be very concerned with my intuitions. The real trouble with counterexamples—as we know from philosophical experience—is that those who are theoretically committed are often prepared to deny them in order to save their theory. Given the possibility of such a dialectical stand-off, it would be nice to have something more principled than a simple appeal to cases.

However, finding a principled way of approaching the issue is not easy. In general, how do we decide whether a certain relation is essential for something to belong to a certain kind? Consider the property of being an uncle. If somebody is an uncle, then it is essential that he stands in a sibling relation to someone who has a child. A person can become or cease to be an uncle while remaining unchanged in intrinsic respects. Perhaps being a work of art is like being an uncle. The fact that one can stay the same in intrinsic respects while one gains or loses some kinship property obviously does not show that that kinship property is the property of being an uncle. It might be the property of being a grandmother. However, many recent aestheticians have been impressed by the fact that two intrinsically similar things can have a different art status, or that something can change its art status while remaining intrinsically unchanged.[5] But this only shows that being a work of art essentially involves *some* relational property. It does not show that an audience is the relatum of the relation which partly constitutes being a work of art. What we want to know is how to tell when a property is *not* a particular relational property. Being an uncle, for example, does *not* essentially involve a relation to a sibling's spouse. What is the epistemology of these negated relations? Presumably we need to see whether the existence and non-existence of a sibling's spouse affects someone's status as an uncle. The trouble is that this may be just as controversial as a theory of what an uncle is. In the case of art, we want to know whether art status can be sustained without an audience. But it seems that we will need to consider various actual and imaginary examples in order to test our intuitions. And we are then

---

[5] See, for instance, Arthur Danto, "The Artworld", *Journal of Philosophy*, 1964. The tendency to appeal to indiscernible counterparts has its roots in the Hegelian view that the history of art forms a *story* in which works of art, and the artist's aspirations in making them, only have significance in virtue of their place in that story. This idea probably entered the English-speaking academic world though Aby Warburg, who was schooled in Hegel. Erwin Panofsky, Ernst Gombrich and Michael Baxandall follow in this tradition. Gombrich presents an example of indiscernible counterparts in *Art and Illusion*, London: Phaidon, 1959, p. 313. I discuss this in *Metaphysics of Beauty*, chapter 5.

back to thrashing out Kafka cases—a procedure which may have *some* dialectical efficacy, but which may not work against an aesthetician who chooses to have very stubborn intuitions about cases. An argument of principle would be better.

## 2 RATIONAL ARTISTIC ACTIVITY

### 2.1 Intentional Transparency

Whether or not art-audience relations are *essential* for being art, some such relations undoubtedly hold. This relation, presumably, is not irreducible and inexplicable. The relation between a work of art and its audience must hold because of further properties of the work of art and of the audience. The question then is: what, exactly, are these properties? I shall argue that the prospects for an audience theory look unpromising when we try to specify these properties. The problem I want to develop is not generated merely by the fact that being a work of art is a relational property. For we need to take seriously the view that a work of art is something which has, or is intended to have, a disposition to affect human beings in certain ways, or that has the function of affecting human beings in certain ways. (I shall henceforth highlight the dispositional view and sideline the functional view, since I presume that functional properties of works of art derive from the intention that they have certain dispositions.) At first sight, there seems to be nothing, *in principle*, wrong with a dispositional audience view. The problem for such a view derives from the fact that there is something special about one of the relata, which precludes an illuminating relational account of art.

The peculiarity is on the audience side of the relation. We are not just concerned with the mere impact on the physical surface of the audience, which is caused by the physical presence of works of art. The content of the audience's experiences is crucial. Let us assume, for simplicity, that the dispositional audience account is that a work of art is something that has (or is intended to have) a disposition to produce certain experiences in certain circumstances. The question is: what is the content of the audience's experiences? (Parallel questions arise if a work of art is supposed to offer us understanding or emotion or pleasure.) The audience's experience is *of* the object or event which is a work of art. And these experiences are mental states that represent the object as having certain properties. So the relevant properties of the audience must indirectly involve certain properties of the works of art. Thus if we want to give an account of the relation between art and audience, we incur the duty of giving an account that invokes certain significant properties of works of art. Those properties presumably cause the experiences which are then directed back onto them. Until we specify those significant properties, the appeal to some art-audience relation is crucially incomplete.

I am not pushing the strong view that we might as well cut through the unnecessary detour via our experience of art and directly discuss the properties of the work of art that the audience experiences. My point is the weaker one that appealing to a relation to an audience's experience (understanding, emotion or pleasure) yields little progress in locating the essence of art until we specify the properties of the object that figure, or that are intended to figure, in the content of the experience. The point is not that the audience-based account has *evaporated* but that it needs to be *completed* with a specification of the properties of the work of art that the audience experiences.[6]

I will argue that once the audience theorist fills this gap, the theory becomes vulnerable to a powerful objection.

## 2.2 Rational Explanation: Audience vs. Artist Theories

What we need above all in the theory of art is *rational explanation*. I highlighted this in the first chapter of this book, and so I will not argue for this approach here. We want to know what art *is*, of course. But we cannot pursue that unless we can explain why art *matters* to us. We want a theory of art which explains why people are *interested* in art. The following are real questions: Why do artists create works of art? Why is there an audience for art? And why do artists present their works to an audience? These matters are not just *given*. The philosophy of art needs to address them. The relevant kind of explanation of the fact that human beings go in for artistic activities is not an explanation from a perspective outside human experience, but an explanation of what we see as worthwhile or desirable in making and experiencing art. This

---

[6] Malcolm Budd holds that the aesthetic value of a work of art is a disposition to provoke (and also warrant) an experience of the work which is "intrinsically valuable" (*Values of Art*, London: Alan Lane, 1995). But he says little about these experiences and about why they might be intrinsically valuable. We need to understand our experience of art as an experience *of* features that we value. For other problems with Budd's appeal to experience, see Jerry Levinson's critical notice "Art, Value, and Philosophy", *Mind*, 1996; and Peter Lamarque's book review in the *British Journal of Aesthetics*, 1997.

kind of explanation makes our concern with art intelligible, familiar and reasonable.[7]

Suppose that some theory of art picks on certain significant properties of works of art. Call these S properties. These S properties might be properties such as being beautiful, embodying truths about life, causing moral improvement, expressing emotions, having brass knobs or whatever. S properties could even be disjunctive, dispositional or functional. Let us leave open what S properties are. There will be a variety of different theories that take different properties to be the explanatorily interesting properties of works of art. But if a theory is to be explanatory, it must show how it is intelligible that the proffered properties are valued or thought desirable. Such properties might, of course, be variously realized in different works of art. But these realizations must be realizations of the sort of property which we can imagine valuing or finding desirable. The appeal to these properties must cast light on our concern with art. It must help explain why art matters to us. (Note that this does not assume that the S properties are themselves evaluative properties, only that they are properties that we can understand valuing and desiring. Furthermore, it does not imply the implausible view that all works of art are of value and so there cannot be bad art. The argument only implies that works of art have properties which we can understand being *thought valuable* or *thought desirable* by artists and audiences.)

An anti-audience theorist might be tempted to put forward the simple argument that audience theories rule out the possibility of a non-trivial answer to these questions because a relation to an audience is said to be part of the essence of art. The idea would be that we need to maintain the gap between art and audience if we are to appeal to one in order to explain the other; and if we collapse the gap, no explanation is possible. To say that art *is* something which bears an essential relation to an audience is to *preclude* an explanation of that very relation. Therefore

---

[7] This line of argument is not the same as Richard Wollheim's argument in "The Institutional Theory of Art" (essay 1, in *Art and Its Objects*, second edition, Cambridge: Cambridge University Press, 1980). Wollheim argues that if members of the artworld deem something to be art, they must have reasons for doing so. So, we might as well take their reason to tell us what art is, and circumvent the unnecessary detour through the artworld. But that objection says nothing about the rationality of *making* and *experiencing* art. All it draws attention to is the rationality of *calling* something art. The point I am making is quite different. Anyway, Wollheim's point is obviously ineffective against Dickie, since Dickie can say that the content of the thoughts of the executive members of the artworld is not that the thing is art, but, for example, that the thing is a candidate for appreciation. See Dickie, "Wollheim's Dilemma", *British Journal of Aesthetics*, 38, 1998.

if a theory of art is to do the explanatory work that we want, it must not be an audience theory. However, this simple argument is too quick. For an audience account could be compatible with *some* explanation of our interest in art, even though that theory did not provide the explanation. Given the 'intentional' nature of an audience's experience, all we can maintain is that until we say something about the properties of a work of art onto which an audience's experience is directed, we fail to have anything that provides a basis for an explanation of why an audience might be interested in art. But that is only to say that there is a *gap* in the theory, not that the gap cannot be filled. If we want to appeal to rational explanation in order to embarrass audience theories, we had better not try to argue that audience theories definitely rule out the possibility of rational explanation. The argument needs to be more subtle.

Before we go on, it will be a good idea to have in mind what the alternative to an audience theory looks like. For there will be those who wonder where else we can look if we agree that being a work of art is a relational property (because of the possibility of indiscriminables) but deny that it involves reference to an audience. The alternative is an *artist*-based theory of the kind advanced in Chapter 2, where we look to a relation between the artist and the work of art. Given an artist-based theory, which postulates certain valued or desired properties in works of art, it would be understandable that people want to realize those properties in objects and events. We would then have an explanation of the artistic activity of producing works of art. What is more, we would have a *rational* explanation of those activities: artists want to create works of art because those works of art embody properties which they value or desire. On an artist-based theory, the sort of rational understanding we seek is relatively easy to come by. On such an account, we would not need to deny that audiences exist and are important in some ways. It is natural that artists want their works to be appreciated by others. And it is true that the demands and inducements from patrons often partly determine which works are made and what they are like. Even so, on such a theory, an audience plays no *essential* role in what it is to be a work of art.

## 2.3 Convergence and Minimal Explanation

Let us be uncynical about the motives of artists and audiences. Let us assume that their interest in creating and experiencing a work is not completely extrinsic to it. For example, the artist's interest does not derive solely from the fact that the artist can use the work of art to make money, achieve fame or change society. And the audience's interest does not derive solely from the fact that contemplating certain works of art expresses their social status or makes them feel sophisticated. Let us uncynically assume that the artist and audience are concerned with something they find valuable in the work. (I deal with cynical motivations in section 4 of this chapter.)

The presence of the valued S properties explains the audience's concern to experience those properties. For the audience's belief that the object possesses the valuable S properties makes it *rational* for them to want to experience the object, or to want to continue experiencing it. This is *why* audiences are often prepared to pay to experience works of art. And this is why audiences often try to induce artists to create what they think will have valuable S properties. (The crucial point is that the audience's experience has content. This is often overlooked by audience theorists. Their experiences are *of* the S properties.)[8]

But—the argument goes—if the S properties are thought to be valuable or desirable, we can understand why the creation of the valued S properties is the goal, or at least *a* goal, of the artist. Given that the artist thinks that the properties are valuable or desirable, the intention to realize them is rational. (For simplicity, I shall henceforth ignore the 'desirable' disjunct.)

So the question of why artists want to make works of art and the question of why audiences want to experience them can both be answered by a theory which appeals to the fact that works of art have the valued S properties.

An audience theory involves a reference to an audience's experience of S properties or their disposition to experience them, or else it involves a reference to the intention that an audience should experience the S properties or have a disposition to experience them. An artist-based theory, on the other hand, appeals directly to the S properties and an artist's (intentional or real) relation to S properties. But in either case, the S properties that a successful theory of art selects must be ones people judge to be valuable. This is necessary if we are to explain why artists want to create works of art and why audiences want to experience them. The belief that an object would come to have S properties rationalizes an

---

[8] Here I draw on Paul Boghosian and David Velleman, "Colour as a Secondary Quality", *Mind*, 1989.

artist's intention to make the thing. And someone's belief that the object has S properties rationalizes their desire to experience or to continue experiencing it.

This means that there is *rational convergence*, by the artist and the audience, on the same valued S properties, but from different temporal directions.

Thus far, the artist's intentions and the audience's experiences seem to be on a par. The argument has been that we need a conception of art according to which it is intelligible that people value making and perceiving works of art; and that means that it must be intelligible that the property or properties that we single out as the object of the artist's intentions and the audience's experiences are thought by them to be valuable. It might be thought that this shows that the artist and the audience are *equally* constitutive of what it is to be art. But the argument now turns on what we *have* to say in order to obtain the sort of rational explanation that we need. What is the *minimum* that we can postulate in order to attain a rational explanation of artistic creation? The answer is swift. The intention to realize S properties would suffice to rationally explain an artist's activity, and no appeal to intentions concerning an audience is required. This follows from rational convergence. If an audience would be rational to take an interest in the S properties because they are thought by the audience to be valuable properties, then an artist who thought that S properties were valuable would be rational to try to realize them, irrespective of an audience. So we can give a rational explanation of the creation of art solely by reference to an artist's desire and intention to realize S properties.

## 2.4  Triangulation and Minimal Explanation

Let us now go further and consider the rationality of an artist's intentions on those occasions when they *do* concern an audience. All theories should admit that *sometimes* artists have audience-directed intentions. The rational explanatory questions are not just: "Why do artists create works of art?" and: "Why do audiences want to experience them?" but also: "Why do artists want audiences to experience their art?"

Once again, assuming that artists are not completely cynical, the answer must be that when artists have audience-directed intentions, it is because they intend the audience to find (or have a disposition to find) something of value in their work.

The support for this is the following. Why on earth would an artist want an audience to experience the object? Surely—cynical cases apart—it is because the artist thinks that the experience would be *worthwhile*. When an audience figures in an artist's intentions, it must be because the artist hopes that the audience will experience (or have a disposition to experience) the valued S properties. The artist's thought is not just that the audience *will* experience the S properties, but that the audience's experience of them will be worthwhile. At this point, we can run a minimal explanation argument again. If the artist is appraising the audience's experience of the S properties as worthwhile, that is only because the artist holds the S properties to be valuable. But if *that* is right, the belief that these valued S properties would be realized in an object could rationally explain why an artist intentionally realizes those properties. And that means that the production of art can often be rationally explained without invoking a relation to an audience. Of course, on many occasions, the artist's intentions are complex, involving attitudes to the audience as well as to the object. But this is only possible if there are, or can be, cases where the thought of the valued S properties rationally explains the creation of art, irrespective of thoughts about the audience.

Audiences may be aware of the fact that artists intend that they experience those properties. And artists may be aware that audiences are aware of their intentions concerning them. There can be complications. But any complications are layers built on what is essential—that some actual or envisaged object is thought to have valuable properties. That's why artists create works of art. That's why audiences want to experience them. And that's why artists want audiences to experience them. It follows that the intention to realize the valued properties could be a sufficient rational causal explanation of why the thing was created. It could both explain and justify an artist's action.

The situation is no different with a dispositional audience theory. On the *non*-dispositional audience theory that we have so far been considering, I have argued that the audience's experience (pleasures, emotions and so on) are *of* properties that we can understand being thought valuable. So if we say that an artist creates something for an audience to experience, this is incomplete: we must specify the properties that the artist intends the audience to experience. But if they are valuable properties, then the minimal explanation argument goes ahead: the thought of realizing these properties could rationalize the creation of art. Even if we say that the artist's intention is to create something that an audience has a *disposition* to experience, it merely delays the inevitable. This is also incomplete. We can only understand the disposition being thought valuable if *manifestations* of the disposition are thought valuable. But manifestations of the disposition are particular experiences *of* the work of art. So we must specify the properties of the work of art that are thought valuable. On the dispositional audience theory, the artist would only intend that the audience has a disposition to experience certain S properties because he thinks that it would be worthwhile for the audience if the disposition were manifested and they actually experienced the S properties. But then the minimal explanation argument goes ahead. If the manifestation of the disposition would be valuable because the audience would have a worthwhile experience of the S properties, we can, in at least some cases, explain the creation of art directly by appealing to the artist's concern to realize those S properties.

## 2.5 From Minimal Explanation to Essence

The essence of a thing cannot be irrelevant to the explanation of its existence. For example, if water comes into existence that must have to do with hydrogen and oxygen molecules; and if, when water comes into existence, it sometimes has nothing to do with carbon molecules, then carbon is not part of the essence of water. Similarly, if the creation of art can sometimes be rationally explained without any reference to an audience's experience, then we cannot maintain that a relation to an audience's experience is part of the essence of art. If a relation to an audience's experience were part of that essence, the explanation of the existence of works of art could not by-pass that essence. But, as we have seen, a relation to an audience may play no part in the rational explanation of artistic creation. So a relation to an audience is not part of the essence of art. The minimum that we need for a rational explanation of the creation of art is the existence of the intention to realize valuable properties in the object or event. Therefore that is all we should include in the essence of art. Moreover any role that an audience actually plays can only be explained on the assumption that art has an essence that is independent of the audience.

It is sometimes said or presumed that a theory of the essence of art is one thing and a theory of why we value it is another. So we should have a value-neutral audience theory which is *supplemented* by an account of why art is thought to be valuable. But this is not an option. The convergence argument shows that the mental states of the artist and the audience must be directed to the same valued properties of works of art. And the triangulation argument shows that if an artist intends an audience to experience those valued properties, it is because it is thought that the experience of those properties would be worthwhile. But then if the artist thinks that the properties are valuable, that would rationalize the creation of things that are thought to have them. Thus, the appeal to those valued properties is needed for a rational explanation of the creation of works of art, and the intention to realize those valued properties is part of what we should include in the essence of art. The minimal explanation argument shows the implausibility of the attempt to divorce the theory of the nature of art from the theory of why we value it.

## 3 DISPOSITIONAL AUDIENCE THEORIES

### 3.1 Actual and Dispositional Audiences

The minimal explanation argument leads us to think that, on *some* occasions, it is *sufficient* to explain and rationalize an artist's behaviour to suppose that the artist desired and intended to endow something with the valued S properties. Once we have isolated S properties that are desired, we can move from the rationality of the audience's desire to experience them, and from the rationality of the artist's desire that the audience experience them, to the possibility of a rational explanation of artistic activity that appeals solely to the artist's desires and intentions concerning the S properties of the work of art. So that is all we should include in the essence of art.

But what does this tell us about the S properties themselves? Despite what we have been through, we have nothing yet that makes trouble for a certain sort of *dispositional* audience view. On some theories, the salient S properties of works of art, which rationalize our interest in them, are identical to, or depend on, a disposition to produce a certain sort of experience in a certain sort of perceiver.[9] Suppose, for example, that it is *aesthetic* properties that are the valued S properties, and suppose that the right account of aesthetic properties is that they are

---

[9] I preserve neutrality between theories that *identify* a property with a disposition and theories which merely say that the property *depends* on a disposition. See Colin McGinn, "Another Look at Color", *Journal of Philosophy*, 1996. However, I shall drop the disjunction and say that the property is the disposition.

dispositions to produce experiences of a certain sort in a certain sort of perceiver.[10] Perhaps beauty is a disposition to provoke pleasure in those who experience it, who are 'standard' or 'ideal' observers. If some such dispositional account is true, it seems that a work of art might *indirectly* involve an audience. The idea would be, roughly, that an object is a work of art because and only because an artist intentionally endows it with a disposition to produce experiences in a certain audience. This is the shape of Beardsley's view, and it presupposes a kind of instrumentalist theory of aesthetic value because the properties of the work are only valuable because they stand in a causal relation to the experiences of an audience.

So, although the minimal explanation argument led to the conclusion that the rational explanation of artistic creation need only appeal to the artist's intentions concerning S properties of works of art, those S properties might or might not be dispositional relations to an audience. If the valued S properties are *not* dispositional relations to an audience, we can run the minimal explanation argument that a rational explanation for the creation of some works of art can be had without involving beliefs and desires about actual or dispositional relations to an audience. But if the valued S properties *are* dispositional relations to an audience, that argument will not be sufficient; and it seems that we will be forced to admit that such a relation is part of the essence of art—by the back door.

I would have liked my argument against audience theories to remain metaphysically neutral about aesthetic properties. But the argument I will present in what follows may make trouble for one common form of dispositionalism about aesthetic properties. This is not my immediate aim. But if it is a side-effect of the argument, I shall not shed any tears.

## 3.2  Kinds of Dispositionalism

Let us separate different versions of the dispositional audience theory.

We have already disposed of one sort of dispositional audience theory in section 2.4 of this chapter. That theory did not involve dispositional S properties, and it was no threat to the thesis of this chapter. The idea was just that the artist intends the audience to have a disposition to experience the S properties. But on the sort of audience theory that we are now considering, the S properties themselves are dispositions.

[10]  See, for example, Alan Goldman, *Aesthetic Value*, Boulder, CO: Westview, 1995.

Let us assume, for simplicity, that the S properties are aesthetic properties. There are various distinctions one can make among dispositional theories of aesthetic properties.

There are problems over the content of the audience's experience, on a dispositionalist theory. Suppose someone finds a statue beautiful. Is the content of the viewer's pleasure the beauty itself, or is it the tangible nonaesthetic properties of the statue? Suppose we say that beauty is a disposition to provoke experiences and those experiences are of beauty. This is problematic for an audience theorist because if beauty figures in the content of the audience's experience then the minimal explanation argument will become active. If the audience's experience is *of* beauty, that beauty could motivate an artist to make an object. So it is probably best for an audience theorist to say that the pleasure is in the nonaesthetic properties of the work, not in its beauty.

We could worry about exactly what kind of disposition is in question. For example, we can distinguish 'rigid' theories, which appeal to a disposition to affect creatures of the sort we actually are now, from 'non-rigid' theories, which allow that if we were to change then the disposition would change.[11]

But of more interest to us is the distinction between theories which appeal to the experience of those like us and theories which appeal to the experiences of more rarefied 'ideal observers'. Sometimes ideal observers are simply those with full information, but sometimes they are those who feel or judge *as they should*. Such theories build in a *normative* element. One sort of theory says that a thing is beautiful if it has a disposition to *cause* pleasure, whereas the other says that a thing is beautiful if it is such that it *warrants* pleasure. We can call these 'pure' and 'normative' dispositional theories.

## 3.3 Wollheim and Representational Works

There is a complication over representational works of art. Richard Wollheim writes:

. . . the artist paints in order to produce a certain experience in the mind of the spectator . . .

Wollheim then introduces a distinction either as support for his statement or as an elucidation of it.

[11] Martin Davies and Lloyd Humberstone, "Two Notions of Necessity", *Philosophical Studies*, 1980.

. . . if an artist aims to give pleasure, he paints so as to produce a certain experience. But my claim is that, equally, when he aims to produce content or meaning, which is his major aim, he also paints so as to produce a certain experience. He does so because this is how pictorial meaning is conveyed, and this is so because of what pictorial meaning is.[12]

This is Wollheim's dual claim. He goes on then to advance the following argument in its support:

In the simpler of the two cases in which the artist paints so as to produce a certain experience—that is to say, when he is concerned solely with the production of pleasure—his reliance on the experience that he himself has in front of the picture is straightforward. He is interested in the experience solely in order to discover whether it is or isn't pleasurable. . . .

whereas in the case of pictorial meaning

. . . his interest in experience is . . . to ensure that the experience that the picture is calculated to produce in others is attuned to the mental condition, or the intention, out of which he is painting it.[13]

Wollheim is right to distinguish between questions of pleasure and questions of content or meaning. We should agree with what Wollheim says about representational properties, but we should contest what he says about the pleasurable aspects of works of art. Furthermore, what he says about representational works of art does not generalize to all works of art.

Consider representational works of visual art—those which have content or meaning. It seems that artists who make representational works must have in mind someone who experiences them. In my view, Wollheim is right that pictorial representation involves seeing-in or seeing-as.[14] An artist who makes a representational work of art must intend that the work has a disposition to produce certain seeing-in or seeing-as experiences. So whether a work of art has a certain sort of representational property is audience-dependent in that it involves a relation to the artist's audience-directed intentions. Moreover, a work of art's being the precise work it is is also audience-dependent, if it is a representational work, since a work presumably has at least

---

[12] Richard Wollheim, *Painting as an Art*, London: Thames and Hudson, 1987, p. 44.
[13] *Painting as an Art*, p. 45.
[14] Richard Wollheim, *Painting as an Art*, p. 45; and "Seeing-In, Seeing-As, and Pictorial Representation", *Art and its Objects*, second edition, Cambridge: Cambridge University Press, 1980.

many of its representational properties essentially. So it looks as if an audience theory must be true for works that have representational properties.

One reply to this argument would be to say that, although being a *representation* is audience-dependent, this does not imply that the *art status* of a representational work is audience-dependent. Many representations are not works of art and many works of art are not representations. So what makes a thing a representation and what makes it art are distinct. Some things are both representations and works of art. But this does not mean that, for representational works, the property of being art essentially involves whatever relations to an audience are essential for those works to be the particular works that they are. Consider a play: it is true that a play is meant to be presented to an audience. That is what a play is. The status of the work as *a* play is dependent on the writer's audience-directed intentions. And that the play is the *particular* play it is depends on the writer's *specific* audience-directed intentions. But it does not follow that the play's status as a *work of art* is dependent on those audience-directed intentions. There are simple plays for children about road safety that lack art status. And there are simple plays in the business world which deal with customer relations. And in some forms of therapy, patients act out situations in order to help them with their problems. So being a play does not make something a work of art.

On the other hand, we might decide to make it stipulative that representational paintings and plays are works of art. In that case, it turns out that although *some* works of art essentially involve a relation to an audience, others don't. This would mean that we would have lost the quite general claim that *all* works essentially involve a relation to an audience.

So let us put aside questions arising from the representational properties of works of art.[15] What is questionable is Wollheim's view of those aspects of art which only concern pleasure.[16] So while Wollheim is right about representational properties, what he says can not generalize to all works of art, and thus it does not supply any pressure towards a quite general audience theory.

---

[15] There are other cases where works of art involve a relation to an audience even though they are not representational works. Examples are abstract street murals and music for advertising. And gardeners typically make gardens for the enjoyment of other people or for their own future enjoyment. But, again, not all works of art are like this.

[16] On the distinction between representational and aesthetic properties, see chapter 2 of the *Metaphysics of Beauty*.

## 4 ARTISTIC AUTONOMY

### 4.1 Artistic Altruism?

Presumably, behind audience theories there lies something like the idea of art as communication; but there is no natural sense in which one communicates with oneself, just as one cannot give oneself a present. So let us operate for a while with an 'exclusive' conception of an audience, which does not include the artist. Of course, an artist might be a member of the artworld or a human being with an interest in art. The artist can be an audience for *other* artists' works of art. But when artists make a work of art, let us assume for a while—as a matter of stipulation—that they do not count as part of the audience for that particular work. This assumption will be discharged in section 5 of this chapter. The strategy is to divide and conquer.

It is obvious why members of an *audience* might be interested in objects that have a disposition to give *them* experiences. But why on earth would *artists* be concerned to realize a disposition to affect an audience if they are not members of that audience?

*One* possibility is that they are *altruistically* motivated—they are moved by love for their audience. Well, that's very nice of them. But this is surely a special and unusual sort of case. In reality, it is often not the case that artists care about any actual or dispositional effects of their work on other people.[17]

Moreover, although altruism is normally viewed as being morally praiseworthy, a concern for others can be viewed in a negative light when we think about the motivations for making art. Stravinsky urged young composers to forget the audience and compose for themselves. He was surely not urging the impossible.[18] And Suzie Gablick complains that one major source of the decline of visual art in the latter half of the twentieth century has been the pursuit of career success by artists

---

[17] Bernard Williams' Gauguin is precisely a man who is concerned with his art at the expense of altruistic concerns. See his "Moral Luck", reprinted in *Moral Luck*, Cambridge: Cambridge University Press, 1981.

[18] Igor Stravinsky and Robert Craft, *Memories and Commentary*, London: Faber and Faber, 1960, pp. 91–95. See also Jorge Luis Borges' short story "The Secret Miracle", *Labyrinths*, Harmondsworth: Penguin, 1970. Contrast Richard Strauss's first 'golden rule for young conductors': "Remember that you are making music not to amuse yourself but to delight your audience", in (ed.) Richard Strauss, *Recollections and Reflections*, London: Boosey and Hawkes, 1953, p. 38.

who are concerned to please the public or the artworld at the expense of making art for its own sake. By contrast, she praises the more ascetic tendency of the early modernists to eschew public acclaim and critical success.[19] It is not plausible that pleasing an audience motivates the production of all art, given that many artists say that they make their art for its own sake or for themselves.

The point here is not merely that artists sometimes have no altruistic concern with whether their work *actually* pleases the audience, they sometimes also have no altruistic concern with whether their work has a *disposition to* please an audience—where that audience is an audience of ordinary folk as opposed to some abstract, idealized audience that is by definition capable of recognizing the valuable properties that artists believe they have realized in their work.

One interesting case is that of the inmates of the Nazi concentration camps who played music for their murderous captors. Of course, they performed primarily in order to save their lives. But they also took some pride in playing music for its own sake. This pride did not stem from any intrinsic concern with the effect of their work on their captors—whether that effect was actual or dispositional, or whether that effect was pleasure or some other valuable effect. Most likely they either regretted any such positive effect or had no intrinsic concern with it.

Motivations are sometimes neatly divided into selfish and altruistic motivations, but in fact there is a third possible kind of motivation—which is neither altruistic nor selfish in any ordinary sense. Those whose hobby is collecting butterflies have a motivation that is neither selfish nor altruistic. It is neither directed towards themselves nor other people. To say that painters sometimes paint for themselves or that composers compose for themselves is not to say that their actions are selfishly motivated. It is a way of emphasizing *artistic autonomy*—a lack of concern for others in making art.

## 4.2 Patronage and Sociology

Altruism is not the only reason that artists might be concerned with how their work strikes others. It will be objected that the sort of artist-centred theory that I favour is naively romantic about the nitty-gritty social, political and economic facts which surround art-production. Most importantly, there are the facts of patronage and the art market.

[19] Suzie Gablick, *Has Modernism Failed?* London: Thames and Hudson, 1984.

Audiences might be prepared to pay for certain kinds of work but not others. This often influences artists.

I do not deny this. What is crucial, however, is that, although these social factors determine *many* features of the work of art, they do not determine *all* of them. Such factors *underdetermine* the final product. They are often *necessary* but they are never (or very rarely) *sufficient* to explain a work of art. *Some* artistic behaviour is dictated by an audience in the sense that it is motivated by a concern for an audience. But it is not remotely plausible that *all* artistic behaviour is explainable in this way.

We need not ask whether an artist would have made *something* even if there had been no audience for it. That is too much. The claim is that there are some *properties* of works of art such that their realization by the artist is not dependent on an audience. The audience may determine a broad range of alternatives, but within that range there are significant choices open to the artist. The final selection within that range was his choice.

Here are two illustrations. First, the architectural historian Colin Rowe writes of Le Corbusier's *La Tourette*:

The programme for the building was explicit. There was to be a church to which the public could, on occasion, be admitted. There were to be a hundred cells for professors and students, an oratory, a dining room, a library, classrooms and spaces for conference and recreation. There was a certain problem of institutional decorum. But, though the architect was therefore subjected to certain very definite limitations, and though he was involved with a religious order whose regime was established rather more than seven centuries ago, it cannot truthfully be claimed that the operational requirements with which he was confronted were so very rigid and inflexible as to predicate an inevitable solution.

It is possible to imagine the Wrightian version of this programme: a major hexagonaloid volume, proliferating by an inward impulse a variety of minor hexagonaloids, terraces and covered ways. A Miesian solution can be conceived. Embryos of the Aalto-esque, the Khanian and a whole forest of other variants swarm in the imagination. But the number of choices available to any one man, like those available to any one epoch, are never so great as those which, in fact, exist. Like the epoch, the man has his *style*—the sum total of his emotional dispositions, the mental bias and the characteristic acts which, taken together comprise his existence; and in its essential distributions (though with one great exception), Le Corbusier's building is coordinated very much along the lines that previous evidence of his style would lead one to predict.[20]

[20] Colin Rowe, "La Tourette", *The Mathematics of the Ideal Villa, and Other Essays*, Cambridge, MA: MIT Press, 1976, p. 193.

Le Corbusier's brief determined much, but it also left much open. He had considerable freedom. And in that space he exercised his artistry. An imaginary patron who determined *every* feature in advance would no longer be a patron in any sense, since the employed person would be deprived of any artistic freedom. Instead the patron would *be* the artist, and the employed person merely like a studio assistant who does no more than take orders. An artist must have some freedom, given the brief.

Second, Serge Guilbaut has argued that abstract expressionism thrived when it did, not because of its formal excellence, as argued by Clement Greenberg, but because it reflected peculiarly American ideals which were useful during the initial phase of the cold war.[21] Guilbaut charts the rise of abstract expressionism in the post-war years; and he explains how the politicians who were pursuing the Cold War found it useful and appropriate for their ends. He also explains how it helped with the difficult position of theorists on the political left who favoured avant garde art. But Guilbaut's sociological analysis leaves out the sort of factors that Clement Greenberg appeals to, which are visual matters, internal to the works themselves.[22] And the natural thought is: why couldn't Guilbaut and Greenberg both be partly right? That is: without the ideological usefulness, formal superiority would not have ensured the dominance of abstract expressionism; but also without the formal excellence of the works, it would not have been so ideologically useful. If American art at the time had not been very good in itself, it could not have played the political role it did. So there are two factors, and only *together* do they explain the dominance of abstract expressionism, whereas Guilbaut presents the ideological aspect as being a *sufficient* cause.[23] We should see the formal and the ideological factors as *individually necessary* and *jointly sufficient* causes.

These two cases illustrate the fact that when all the influencing factors constraining art production have been taken into account, there is a

[21] Serge Guilbaut, *How New York Stole the Idea of Modern Art*, Chicago: University of Chicago Press, 1983.

[22] See Clement Greenberg, *Collected Essays and Criticism*, (ed.) John O'Brian, in 4 volumes, Chicago: University of Chicago Press, 1986. See also Greenberg's spirited contributions to *Modernism and Modernity*, (eds.) Benjamin Buchloch, Serge Guilbaut and David Solkin, Vancouver, BC: Nova Scotia Press, 1981, pp. 161–168, 188–193, 265–277.

[23] In the introduction to his book, Guilbaut seems to accept this distinction, since he says that he will argue that the dominance of abstract expressionism cannot be explained *solely* in terms of its formal excellence (op. cit., p. 2). But that 'solely' word gets quickly dropped; and by the conclusion of the book he is telling us why dominance was achieved solely by reference to ideological usefulness.

residual space in which the artist has *freedom*. This freedom implies a lack of concern with actual or dispositional effects of the work on others—except in the sense that the artist is concerned that the audience will recognize or have a disposition to recognize the values that the artist believes have been realized in the work. The passage from Rowe nicely highlights the fact that some of Le Corbusier's decisions were autonomous. By contrast Guilbaut, and many others who write about art from a sociological perspective, wrongly shut down on this creative space. Maybe Greenberg opens it up too far, but he was right, as against Guilbaut and others, to allow some measure of autonomy in art production.[24]

I argued in section 4.1 of this chapter that there are some cases where artistic creation can be explained without any reference to any person other than the artist. Although some art production is bound up with an audience, some is not. But we have now seen that even where there *are* external influencing factors which impinge on the artist's decision-making, there are always some *properties* of the work which cannot be explained without reference to the artist's (intrinsic) desire that the work should be a certain way.

## 4.3 Autonomy and Dispositionalism

Dispositional theories can be pure or normative. In a pure audience theory, there is an intention to create a disposition to affect an actual audience—an audience of flesh and blood people that the artist knows about, directly or indirectly. But on a normative theory, the artist has

---

[24] The audience exerts its influence on art production in different ways in different economic systems. Some artists in the last few decades have thought of themselves as struggling to escape the commodity-driven artworld by engaging in alternative forms of art, such as performances or environmental art. But in reality this is just an exchange of one form of control for another, which is less healthy in many ways, because less honest. Whether art is produced as a commodity in capitalist fashion, or for a patron, such as the church, the Medicis, or contemporary government funded arts organizations, makes no fundamental difference to the threat it poses to artistic autonomy. Here I disagree with some of what Suzie Gablick says in her otherwise insightful book *Has Modernism Failed?* She blames the decline in recent visual art on the ascendancy of one particular market-driven form of production. But I do not think that it can be said that the official quasi-monopolistic state art institutions, which do not answer to the market, are more open-minded and concerned with excellence than the capitalist art market. Many art writers and artists have a sanguine view of the situation when artists abandon selling their art as commodities, and turn to what they take to be more 'progressive' forms of financial support by state patronage.

some *ideal* audience in mind, and it is possible that all actual audiences fall short.

We have seen that if we strip away the artist's concern with what an actual audience experiences, there is much artistic freedom remaining. There is an *autonomous remainder*. And even if we strip away the artist's concern with what an actual audience would be *disposed* to experience, there is still such a remainder. So we cannot countenance a purely dispositional theory.

Perhaps we cannot strip away an *ideal dispositional* audience factor to see if there is anything left. Perhaps artists do have in mind an abstractly conceived ideal audience—but that audience is necessarily one that appreciates the values of the work. In so far as artists want an audience to appreciate their work (and not just *purchase* it), they want the *right* audience to appreciate it.[25] But that is a *normative audience*—it is an audience that is imagined to be like an all-knowing God judging our actions. A normative audience necessarily recognizes the S properties of works of art, which artists believe to be valuable and which they believe they have placed there. So we can put this normative form of the audience theory to one side, since what makes an audience ideal is their capacity to recognize the S properties. If artists think of an ideal audience, it is an audience that has perfect *discrimination*, and therefore finds in their works or art the valuable properties that they believe they have realized.

Perhaps there is a necessary relation between artists and ideal audiences.[26] But there is no necessary relation between artists and non-ideal audiences. Artists *may* seek reassurance from other people of the worth they believe their work possesses. And they *may* be charitably motivated to benefit and please others. But they may not. This means that we should not see art as always or usually being produced with the intention that it will have an actual effect on others or with the intention that it will have a disposition to have an effect on others. And this, in turn, means that we should not see that intention as part of the essence of art. The principle of minimal explanation bids us eschew reference to anyone but the artist when we give an account of the essence of art. While a normative, idealized form of

---

[25] Asked "For whom do you compose?", Stravinsky answered "For myself and the *hypothetical* other" (my emphasis, op. cit., p. 91).

[26] But that would not imply an *essential* connection. See my "Moore, Morality, Supervenience, Essence, Epistemology", *American Philosophical Quarterly*, 2005.

dispositional theory of aesthetic properties may be correct (I leave that open here), we must eschew a pure dispositional audience theory of art, given the assumption that an artist is not a member of the audience.

## 5 EGOISTIC ART: THE ARTIST AS AUDIENCE, INTEGRITY AND CREATIVE THINKING

### 5.1 Egoistic Rationality

Either S properties are valued intrinsically or instrumentally. That is, either S properties are valued in themselves or they are valued because they are dispositions to provoke experiences that are valued. If the former holds true, then the minimal explanation argument immediately cuts out the audience. If the latter holds true, then the experiences in question must either be those of the artist or of others. We saw in the last section that artists often have no concern with others, whether altruistic or cynical. And even where such a concern does exist, it does not determine all aspects of the work. So the only plausible remaining hope for a dispositional audience theory of art is to say that artists always intend and hope that the created thing will produce (or have a disposition to produce) an effect on *themselves*. (Presumably they would only value a *disposition* to give themselves experiences if they valued the *manifestation* of the disposition in their actual experiences of the work.) This would be an odd kind of audience theory, but perhaps we can nevertheless classify it as such.

So let us now operate with an 'inclusive' definition of the audience, according to which artists can be the audience for their own work.

### 5.2 Artistic Integrity: The Accordion Effect

Assuming a lack of altruism and a lack of cynical concern with an audience, on an inclusive audience theory, artists must be motivated by the thought that they will produce an experience in themselves. The initial problem with this is that it doesn't seem to be *true* that artists always have an interest in experiencing their work on future occasions. If artists never intend to look again at something they have made, then it would be irrational for them to care about whether the art has a disposition to produce future experiences in them. The dialectic over artists' future selves is similar to the one that is played out in the case of other people. Artists might not just create 'for themselves', but also 'for the present'. It is not plausible that in making a work, artists are always interested in investing the thing with a disposition that they exploit in the future. This is clearest in the case of music. When we play a musical instrument by ourselves, do we always keep a recording device running so that we can listen to ourselves later on? No. Sometimes, we just want to *play*. On those occasions when we *do* review our creation, we *might* admire what we have done and feel pride in it. This would be a pleasure which we take to be *warranted by* its valuable properties. But we did not produce it *in order* to feel pride in it. That gets the evaluative direction the wrong way round.[27] When we admire our own work, in retrospect, we are related to the work just as any another person, except for the added thought, "I did it". We might, however, be appalled on listening to what we played. We might even know while playing that we would be appalled if we listened, but we might nevertheless still enjoy playing.

However, it might be suggested that we play music in order to experience it *as we play it*. But this doesn't seem right at all. For, art-making would amount to a kind of auto-stimulation. But one does not make art merely to be the means by which experiences are produced in oneself. On Kant's insightful analysis of fine art, art-making stems from both our critical and our productive faculties—genius and taste.[28] The auto-stimulation notion of artistic activity ignores the *productive* aspect of artistic creation—the fact that artistic ideas flowed from a particular person. The realization of those ideas by artists has a value which is distinct from the value of merely producing an experience in themselves or in others. The point of making art for artists is not just the value of the art they produce but also the value of their producing it.[29]

Sometimes I decide to play my accordion. Do I do so because I want to have certain experiences? That is, do I do so because I have no recording of an accordionist better than myself? Or is it because some superior accordionist, such as my accordion teacher Igor, is not to hand, so that I can listen as a passive spectator? Surely not. But

[27] Compare P. H. Nowell-Smith's discussion of psychological hedonism, in *Ethics*, London: Penguin, 1954, chapter 10.
[28] See Kant, *Critique of Judgement*, Oxford: Oxford University Press, 1928, sections 48–54.
[29] In Chapter 2, I stress the importance of individual artistic insight and creation.

on the inclusive audience theory, it would be irrational for me to play my accordion when I can listen to a recording of a far better accordionist or when I can listen to Igor. If artistic activity were merely a means of producing experiences in oneself, then it would be quickly rendered irrational in most cases. I want to *play* the accordion, not just be the means in the causal nexus by which certain sounds are produced. It is crucial to the *point* of my action that the sounds are produced by my agency. I want to be active, not passive.[30] This point is the analogue of Bernard Williams' famous insistence on integrity in ethics.[31] Like consequentialism in ethics, the audience theory of art, when widened to become an 'inclusive' audience theory, falls foul of considerations of integrity. This point is especially strong where my artistic behaviour stems from my own artistic ideas—when I am improvising or creatively interpreting another's composition. But it also holds when all I want is to give a rendition of some extant work of another's creation, with no creative interpretive input of my own. It is true that there is room for reflection on one's artistic projects from a more detached, impartial, spectator point of view. But artistic activity, while one is engaged in it, cannot be so detached. It is this engagement which explains why musicians or painters sometimes take *pride* in their productions. They value the experience of their work not only because of its valuable S properties (assuming everything has gone well) but also because they have the thought that the S properties were of their doing. Alternatively, they might feel shame if things have turned out badly.[32]

---

[30] Similarly, why bother to write philosophy when one can read Plato, Descartes, Hume and Kant?

[31] See Bernard Williams, in (eds.) J. J. C. Smart and Bernard Williams, *Utilitarianism: For and Against*, Cambridge: Cambridge University Press, 1973. Jean-Paul Sartre applies something like the integrity point to the process of artistic creation in his "Why Write?", *Literature and Existentialism*, New York: Citadel, 1994. Sartre goes as far as to stress the *impossibility* of the writer's experiencing his own work as others do. But Sartre goes on to embrace an audience view about literature. Some of his reasons have to do with the fact that works of literature have a meaning, which is okay by me. But he also has reasons that generalize to non-representational arts, which I reject.

[32] Could an audience theory take artistic integrity on board? The idea would have to be that it is important that I produce the music on my accordion but what I produce is still something for me to take pleasure in. But how could this be? Why should I have such a bizarre conjunctive desire—to take such contemplative pleasure in music which just happens to be of my own making? There is sometimes a normative aspect to this: playing an instrument is pleasurable, not just because we are listening to the music that we are making, but because we can take ourselves to be making music *worth* listening to. It can be a source of pride.

## 5.3 The Role of the Artist's Experience: Monitoring and Exploration

It might seem mysterious, on my account, that artists *ever* experience their own work while making it. We need an account of the role of artists' experience of their work. I do not mean to underplay the artists' experience of what they do when they are producing a work. While I play my accordion, I both play and listen to what I am playing, just as visual artists look at what they are doing as they make marks on a surface. But what role is experience playing? The question is not *whether* artists perceive their work while they are making it, but *why* they do so. As we have seen, the idea that their aim is to produce experiences in themselves is implausible in the light of considerations of artistic integrity. But then I need to offer some other account.

Let us distinguish a 'blueprint' model of artistic thought from an 'exploration' model.[33]

On a blueprint model of artistic thought, an artist has an artistic idea, and mechanically realizes it. (For example, musicians or poets might wake up with a complete work before their mind, which they then write down.) Experience then merely serves to *monitor* whether the work has turned out as expected. If it has turned out well, the work can remain as it is. If not, modification is required. Or if it has turned out much worse than expected, the artist might start again from the beginning. This monitoring role is the primary and simplest role that experience plays in the creation of art. Someone hopes and intends to invest a work with certain valuable properties, and the experience serves to check whether these properties really have been realized as intended.

On the dispositional audience view, an artist makes a work in order to create something with a disposition to produce certain experiences. Producing those experiences would be the aim of the artist's action. But in fact the monitoring role of the artist's experience is quite different. One experiences the work of art in order to check that one's artistic actions have been successful—that they have resulted in the realization of the intended S properties. The success of a work does not consist

---

[33] See Monroe Beardsley, "The Creation of a Work of Art", *The Aesthetic Point of View*, Ithaca: Cornell University Press, 1982. See also Andrew Harrison, *Making and Thinking*, Indianapolis: Hackett, 1978.

in the production of those experiences, rather those experiences are our mode of recognizing its success.

Consider pottery and gardening, which are unlike most art-forms in that considerable time must elapse between an artist's actions and the intended effect. We watch what we are doing while we make pots or garden, so that we squeeze the clay in the right places, or prune the right plants in the right way, because we know what effect this will have. But there is no immediate monitoring of the results. We must wait some hours to see how our pot has turned out when it emerges from the kiln. The wait is more dramatic with gardening; if a gardener is waiting for trees to grow, it takes many years. In both cases, artistic feedback is considerably extended. But the situation with pottery and gardening is not fundamentally different from music and painting where feedback is usually immediate. In neither case is the *point* of the action to create experiences in the artist. Rather the point of the experiences is to *monitor* the action, which has an independent point. (We want to see how things have turned out.) It is just that, with pottery and gardening, it takes longer to see the fruits of one's labour than it takes with music and painting.

However, what an artist does is often modified by his experience of what he is doing. I have stressed that when I play my accordion, what I enjoy is the activity of *playing* it, and *making* certain sounds, not *listening* to the sounds I happen to produce. But there is *aesthetic feedback*. Sometimes I play and it sounds wrong or unpleasant. Or I am told or work out how to make it sound better. And as a result I modify my actions. I do it differently. Moreover, experience can also play an important role in affecting future artistic ideas and actions. Experience might lead me to modify my plan because I might be surprised by an effect that I have produced which opens up a new direction. There can be *experimentation* where I do something without knowing quite how it will turn out, in the sense that I do not know exactly which aesthetical properties will be realized.

We could describe this in language drawn from the philosophy of science; we could talk of artistic 'conjectures', 'confirmations' and 'refutations'. A *conjecture* is a variation of something in progress—it is an idea for an improvement, which may or may not succeed. A *confirmation* is the recognition of an improvement in the next stage; and the artist should probably retain the variation, and try another variation from that improved position. A *refutation* is the recognition of a decline in value from one stage to the next; and an artist should probably retreat to the previous stage, and try another variation from there. A refutation need not reduce the equation to zero (as the scientific Popperian thinks), merely to the previous stage.

We could also use the evolutionary language of "variation", "selection" and "de-selection" to describe the three phases of creative experimentation that I have separated. During the process of making something, a variety of experimental artistic ideas are thrown up. Some of those ideas are better than others. The better ones are selected and the worse ones abandoned. Acting on selected ideas makes a difference to the next phase of what we are doing.[34]

In this process, experience has a secondary monitoring role, and allows artists to redirect their artistic activity. After each development, we must monitor our progress, and see how things are going.

This is an account of how we *reason* from experience in artistic activity. But I do not mean to play down the non-rational aspect of creative insight, when we have artistic ideas.[35] Arriving at ideas for variation might not be random but a matter of *insight*. Plato might be right in the *Ion* that artistic insight is a non-rational matter—a matter of divine madness, of inspiration by the muse. But having *received* our artistic insights, from whatever non-rational source, we must do something with them. At this point we can engage in rational deliberation about our activities.

At any rate, it is clear that we can explain why artists experience their works while making them, without lapsing into an audience theory.

## 6 REVIEW AND CONCLUSION

Let us now review the dialectic of this chapter, since it has become quite complex.

Either S properties have intrinsic value or they have instrumental value. If artists take them to have intrinsic value, then they are rational to intend to realize them, and the audience's experiences of the S properties are a recognition of that distinct value. But if artists take S properties to have instrumental value, then they are rational to realize S properties

---

[34] In some respects, artistic experimentation conforms to the workings of evolutionary design described by Richard Dawkins in *The Blind Watchmaker*, Harmondsworth: Penguin, 1986.
[35] See further Chapter 2.

because they know that they are disposed to cause something else which they value. For example, if beauty is an intrinsic value, then it is intelligible that people want to promote this value. But if beauty is an instrumental value, then it is rational to promote beauty only if one has some concern with what beauty is an instrument for. On a hedonistic instrumentalist theory, the creation of beauty is only rational because one values the pleasure taken in the experience of beauty.

But whose pleasure? That of the artist? Or of others?

Not always others, since we can add the independently plausible premise that artists often do not care what others think. Art is sometimes made by people who have no concern with whether other people take pleasure in their art (or have other valuable experiences). Moreover, works of art have properties which are independent of various inducements and pressures from other people (patrons, buyers, consumers). Much art-making is not motivated either by altruism or by other influencing factors. So what rationalizes the artist's creation of art is not always a concern with others.

If one has no other-directed concerns in making art, then does one make art in order to experience it oneself? No. Not at the time of making it. The point of making it is not to have an experience. That ignores the existential value in making it oneself. And one often has no interest in experiencing the work again in the future.[36]

In brief, we must attribute to works of art properties that are intelligibly held to be valuable properties. But once we do so, artists' thoughts about these valuable properties can rationally explain why they made one work of art rather than another, or none at all. Either the valuable properties are dispositions with respect to an audience, or not. If not, the audience drops out immediately. But if the valuable properties *are* dispositions to affect an audience, we then lose the rationality of making a work of art in cases where artists have no concern for others. And even if we consider artists' experience of their own work while producing it, they are not making the work in order to produce the experience. Instead the experience serves either to monitor that the work has the intended valuable properties or else it serves to provide feedback as a source for future experimentation. So, neither

---

[36] I do not see why there should not be a work of art which was created in the knowledge that not even the person who made it would see its completion. Imagine a garden created by the last remaining survivor on earth, which will only mature one hundred years after the last survivor dies.

a concern with another's experiences nor a concern with one's own experiences can explain the creation of many artworks. It follows that purely dispositional audience theories fail the rationality requirement.[37]

I conclude that reference to an audience in a theory of the nature of art is unnecessary. And what is needed to explain why an audience sometimes figures in an artist's intentions presupposes that some artistic behaviour can be explained without any reference to audience-directed intentions. All audience theories focus on the effects of art not on its essence. Once we have a satisfactory artist-based theory, an explanation of the role of audiences falls out as a welcome by-product. Audience-based theories have matters the wrong way round. They have the tail wagging the dog. On artist-based theories, it is the dog that wags the tail.

---

[37] I was striving to remain metaphysically neutral about the S properties. But I may have stumbled inadvertently upon a powerful argument against purely dispositional theories of aesthetic value. A parallel argument threatens moral dispositionalism. Such theories cannot account for the rationality of actions that are motivated by that value. See my "Against Moral Dispositionalism", *Erkenntnis*, 2003.

## APPENDIX: ON DICKIE

### 1

In this Appendix I wish to highlight some contrasts between aesthetic theories of art and a particularly clearly articulated version of an audience view—the institutional approach of George Dickie. I do not want to get too involved in the details of the various versions of his theory.[38] Suffice it to say that in Dickie's view, it is essential to art that it should stand in relation to a certain audience—the artworld. This relation can be real or intended, corresponding to the earlier and later versions of the theory. On the earlier theory, it is a necessary condition of art that it is "(1) an artefact (2) a set of aspects of which has had conferred upon it the status of candidate for appreciation by some person or persons acting on behalf of a certain social institution (the artworld)"; and on the later theory, it is a necessary condition of art that it is "an artefact of a kind created to be presented to an artworld public".[39] Let us grant Dickie some satisfactory specification of this audience. So far as I can tell, Arthur Danto's theory is also of this broad sort, despite some differences from Dickie, since for Danto what it is to be art, rather than some 'mere real thing' consists in some art–artworld relation.[40] But let us focus on Dickie's theory, which is a cleaner target.

### 2

Dickie emphasizes the artefactuality of art in all his accounts. I think that this is right and that works of art are essentially artefacts. Beautiful natural things such as (wild) flowers may be appreciated, but they are not works of art. However, merely adding a requirement that works of art are artefacts, as Dickie does, is not a satisfactory way of dealing with the artefactuality of art. There are many artefacts that are not art but which are beautiful and can be appreciated, such as industrial machines, surgical instruments, factory chimneys, slag-heaps and quarries. Many industrial machines are made with only industrial effectiveness in mind.

---

[38] For more details, see my "Doughnuts and Dickie", *Ratio,* 1994.

[39] George Dickie, *Art and the Aesthetic*, Ithaca: Cornell University Press, 1974, p. 34; George Dickie, *The Art Circle*, New York: Haven, 1984, p. 80.

[40] Arthur Danto, *The Transfiguration of the Commonplace*, Cambridge, MA: Harvard University Press, 1981.

It was no part of the intention of those who created these things that they should one day be appreciated by anyone—never mind the artworld. (I assume that they have not been 'appropriated' by the artworld, something that happens only to a minuscule proportion of such objects.) But we may decide in retrospect that they have turned out to merit aesthetic appreciation. We put old machines in industrial museums, and not just for their historical interest. Old machines can be beautiful, and they can be appreciated, but this does not make them works of art. Similarly, sporting events may be visually interesting, even beautiful or graceful. But football is not ballet. A visually interesting or appreciable artefact or action is not necessarily a work of art. A theory of art must say something about the content of the intentions of those who make these things. The intentions of those who make industrial machines or who perform beautiful or graceful sporting movements have nothing to do with beauty or grace. Aesthetic theories of art can easily deal with this, since they appeal to intentions with aesthetic contents. Although some artefacts can be aesthetically appreciated, they are not aesthetic artefacts, which is why they are not works of art. Such cases pose a difficulty for Dickie's earlier theory, but perhaps not for his later theory.

## 3

What, though, of ordinary designed things that contrast with industrial machines, surgical instruments, factory chimneys, slag-heaps and quarries in that they *are* designed partly with aesthetic considerations in mind as well as with other more prosaic considerations? Many ordinary things are designed with aesthetic care—such as cars, toasters, adverts, fireworks and tattoos. If it is said that industrial and graphic design, and even the arts of fireworks and tattooing have their institutions and traditions, we can reply that there is much of aesthetic interest that is produced even outside these bounds. For example, we should also bear in mind everyday creative activities, such as doodling in the margin during a lecture, whistling a tune, arranging a room, deciding what clothes to wear or decorating a cake. It is likely that almost everything surrounding the reader falls into this category: lamps, furniture, pens, clocks and clothes are all made with some aesthetic concern. Aesthetic theories of art categorize these things as art; or perhaps they say that they are art to the degree that aesthetic considerations made a difference to their design. By contrast, artworld theories, like Dickie's and

Danto's, exclude these things from art status. In Danto's terms, for example, a non-appropriated Brillo Box is a 'mere real thing' and not an artwork.

So we have two theories, which agree on the art status of many things and also disagree about the art status of many other things. We have discussed at length the fact that aesthetic theories of art *exclude* some avant garde works that institutional theories *include*, but our present interest is in the fact that they also *include* many things that institutional theories *exclude*. We obviously cannot adjudicate between these theories on the grounds of what they and do not include, since that is just part of the theory. That would be ineffectively question-begging. However, we can argue on the grounds of explanatory richness.

## 4

Let us describe these aesthetically designed manufactured things in terms of the Aesthetic Creation Theory, which is the particular aesthetic theory of art that I favour. To recall: in that theory, very roughly, art is the intentional product of aesthetical creative thought. Someone must intentionally endow something with certain aesthetic properties by giving it certain nonaesthetic properties, as envisaged in an insight into a dependence relation between the aesthetic and nonaesthetic properties. This theory includes ordinary designed things, such as cars, and everyday creative activities, such as marginal doodles. Cars and marginal doodles are often aesthetically attractive, and were designed to be so. Consider the classic 1950s Citroën DS car. Of course, it was *also* designed with other practical considerations in mind. Safe and fast road transportation were obviously important aspects of the design. Nevertheless, aesthetic considerations also had a considerable impact on it. Designing the car involved some degree of creativity. The designer (Flaminio Bertoni) had aesthetic ideas and intentions that explain why the design is one way rather than another, even though other considerations also impinged on the final product. In this respect, cars are no different from works of architecture or religious paintings, which balance aesthetic and nonaesthetic considerations. The aim of car designers is, in part, to make something aesthetically interesting or attractive. This is an understandable ambition; it makes sense. It is not just taken as an unexplainable datum that people do these things (as it is for artworld theories)—given the Aesthetic Creation Theory, we can understand it.

According to the Aesthetic Creation Theory, there is no requirement that the artist's intentions are directed towards any audience whatsoever. A work of art *can* be presented to an audience; but that connection is quite accidental. It is not essential for something to be art. An audience is only relevant in that if they were to perceive the work of art, they might appreciate it and recommend it to others; and if they did, they would do so *because* of its aesthetic properties. This is a point in favour of the Aesthetic Creation Theory since it is not just a datum that people contemplate works of art (as it is for artworld theories); we are given some basis for an explanation of why they might do so.

Let us focus on the aesthetic property of *beauty*. (Other aesthetic properties, such as *grace* or *daintiness* are the sort of properties that one can appeal to in order to explain *why* something is beautiful. So an explanation of why we are interested in beauty will also provide an explanation of why we might be concerned with other aesthetic properties.) Perceiving and making beautiful things yields *pleasure*. To be sure, it yields pleasure of a special, rich sort, but pleasure nonetheless. In general, it is not too difficult to explain why people go in for pleasurable activities. Pursuing pleasure is wholly understandable and rational. So if making and experiencing beautiful things is pleasurable, then we would be on the road towards acquiring a rational explanation of these activities. It would not be a brute, explained, fact that people want to make or experience artworks, as it is on the institutional theory.

## 5

The Aesthetic Creation Theory embraces both ordinary designed things and things in galleries. It encompasses non-fine arts, such as industrial and graphic design and also fireworks and tattooing, as well as doodling in the margin during a lecture, whistling a tune, arranging a room, deciding what clothes to wear and decorating a cake. These involve creativity of the sort that is involved in 'high' artworld art. And we can understand the exercise of creativity. To explain these things, we need to look at the creativity that produces such things and their properties. Things which are art, according to the Aesthetic Creation Theory, are unified by being the product of a certain mental process. We are therefore on the road to an explanatory story about why people make certain things. We can see why someone might see the point of endowing a thing with aesthetic properties. Some art is indeed 'Great Art', and I do not want to denigrate it. (Perhaps the difference between artworld art and the rest is that non-artworld art does not *aspire* to be Great Art.) But we will not understand Great Art unless we have a theory that also encompasses industrial and graphic design, tattooing, fireworks, doodling, whistling, dressing and cake decoration. If we want to understand art, we do better not to dwell excessively on the artworld and its quirks. We should also consider more humble everyday examples of creative thought and its products, as well as artworld art. To appropriate Wittgenstein, we should avoid a 'one sided diet of examples' from the fine arts. (This approach might be called 'methodological philistinism'.)

# 6

The Aesthetic Creation Theory is richer than an institutional theory when it comes to explaining the making and consuming of art. Dickie's institutional theory tells us nothing at all about why people make art and why they experience it. We remain completely unilluminated about the motivation for making artworks, and we remain completely unilluminated about what those who encounter them get out of them. And this means that we have failed to begin to understand the phenomenon. We need an account that provides us with some understanding of these matters. Not only does the institutional theory say nothing about these questions, but there is nothing that it *could* say about them from within the confines of the theory. While Dickie may have found something in common between the things that he groups together—let us grant him that—it is not an explanatorily interesting grouping.

The interesting issue is not whether some theory is or is not subject to counterexamples. Perhaps different theories include and exclude different things. We need not object to the concept of art that Dickie is defining or perhaps constructing. We can grant that Dickie's definition of *his* concept is just fine. It is just that such a concept provides little philosophical illumination. There is indeed a concept of art, perhaps 'fine art'—which only concerns those things that are hung in galleries, and there is *a* concept of an 'artist' as a professional who produces things which are 'of a kind' intended to be hung in galleries, or who produces them as an art student. Some artworld theory, such as Dickie's, might be an accurate analysis of *that* concept. The problem is to see the philosophical *interest* of a concept of art that excludes ordinary designed things and everyday creative activities. We are not analysing a concept for its own sake, but seeking a concept that can figure in a theory that explains phenomena. The institutional theory is unilluminating because it explains little. Dickie may have succeeded in explicating a certain concept, but he has penetrated very little distance into the phenomena. If Dickie is right, he is superficially right. The phenomena to be explained are untouched.

What is taken as given in an institutional theory—art-making and art-consuming—is explained in the Aesthetic Creation Theory. Furthermore, by appealing to pleasure, the Aesthetic Creative Theory can explain why there is an artworld in the first place, which is, again, just a brute, unexplained fact for an institutional theorist and other artworld theorists. There is an artworld because people value art-making and art-experience. They value art-making and art-experience because of the pleasure that these involve. The artworld is, in part, a community of pleasure-lovers!

It is true that the Aesthetic Creation Theory fails to include some of the more avant garde excursions of twentieth century art. Such works—of Duchamp and his followers—are the inspiration for institutional theories. I discussed this in Chapter 3. But in the present context we can note that if what is in question is explaining our interest in avant garde art, then the institutional theory is no better off. For, on that theory, it is just a brute fact that people find such works of interest. No attempt is made, or could be made, within the confines of the theory, to explain that fact. The institutional theory is entirely *mute* on the question of *why* certain things get into the artworld and it is mute on the fundamental question of why the artworld exists at all.

Dickie might reply that his theory is not supposed to be an explanatory theory—he is doing something different. I would respond that he *should* be seeking an explanatory theory, for reasons given in Chapter 1. Given that art is a human product, understanding it necessarily involves interpretation and thus rational explanation. The same goes for all artefacts. So even if Dickie is not seeking such an explanatory theory, we can evaluate his theory on those grounds. (I suspect that my primary disagreement with Dickie, and with those who pursue the philosophy of art in roughly his way, is meta-philosophical—a matter of what the goals of philosophical speculation about art are and ought to be.)

This, then, is the basic reason why the institutional theory is unsatisfactory. It is unsatisfactory because it is explanatorily shallow. And because Dickie's presentation has the virtue of clarity, it makes that shallowness obvious. A theory of art should give us some basis for explaining why people make these works of art and why people want to experience them. We need rational explanation of art activities. It is in this respect that I am claiming that the Aesthetic Creative Theory is better than Dickie's as a theory of what art is.

# 7

# Against the Sociology of Art

## 1 AESTHETIC VS. SOCIOLOGICAL
## EXPLANATIONS OF ART ACTIVITIES

Those who approach the theory of art from a *sociological* point of view tend to be sceptical about any theory of art that appeals to aesthetic properties in a fundamental way. An aesthetic theory of art maintains that we need a general theory of art that makes essential appeal to beauty, elegance, daintiness and other aesthetic properties.[1] And the Aesthetic Creation Theory—the version of the aesthetic theory I have proposed in this book—adds a view about the source of aesthetic ideas. The aesthetic theory is a theory about how art comes to be produced. Sociological scepticism about any view of this kind takes two overlapping forms, only one of which I will pursue here. The form of scepticism I will address here denies that we need to appeal to aesthetic considerations in explaining the *production* of art. Let us call this *production scepticism*. This form of scepticism is not the same as scepticism about the appeal to aesthetic considerations in explaining our experiences and judgements about art. Let us call that *consumption scepticism*. Examples of consumption sceptics are Pierre Bourdieu and Terry Eagleton, who think that aesthetic value judgements about art really reflect social status rather than being a response to qualities of the works.[2] In my view, the reasons, such as they are, that Bourdieu and Eagleton put forward in favour of consumption scepticism are very weak, and based on multiple uncharitable misunderstandings of

---

[1] If we hold such a view, we can be shy of committing ourselves to a particular theory of aesthetic properties. We can bracket off that issue as a separate topic. The point is to see how far we can get in understanding art by giving an account that draws on aesthetic properties—whatever their nature. Such a theory can be constructed with the true nature of aesthetic properties as a variable.

[2] Pierre Bourdieu, *Distinction*, London: Routledge & Kegan Paul, 1984; Terry Eagleton, *The Ideology of the Aesthetic*, Blackwell: Oxford, 1984.

the category of the aesthetic. Moreover, there are obvious difficulties with the view. I have argued this elsewhere.[3] Consumption scepticism, however, is not the same as production scepticism, which needs to be considered separately. Production scepticism might be true even though consumption scepticism is false. Consumption scepticism does indeed remove one particular remote role for the aesthetic in the story about how and why works of art are produced. Audiences for works of art do often determine what artists produce, since they tend to demand more of what they like and less of what they don't like. But this role for the aesthetic is less *immediately* efficacious in art production than the role that the aesthetic plays in art-production according to an aesthetic theory of art. An aesthetic theory of art says that in order to explain art-production, we must grant the aesthetic a role in the mind of artists who produce works of art: minimally, artists must desire and intend to create things with specific aesthetic qualities. An aesthetic theory of art also grants the aesthetic a role in the mind of audiences who experience works of art and who generate demand for them, but their role in determining the production of art is dependent on the role of the aesthetic in the minds of artists. By contrast, production scepticism denies the aesthetic any role either in the minds of artists or in the minds of audiences.

To quote one example of production scepticism, Griselda Pollock writes in her book *Vision and Difference*:

I am arguing that feminist art history has to reject all this evaluative criticism and stop merely juggling the aesthetic criteria for appreciating art. Instead it should concentrate on historical forms of explanation of women's art *production*.[4]

Notice the opposition she assumes here between aesthetic criteria of appraisal, on the one hand, and art-production, on the other. The idea that artists might have aesthetic motives for production has been silently erased.

In her book, *The Social Production of Art*, Janet Wolff struggles to avoid taking an eliminativist or reductionist position about the aesthetic.[5] She officially affects neutrality about whether the 'aesthetic' is a category we should retain or dispense with in talking about art. She

---

[3] See chapter 12 of *Metaphysics of Beauty*, Ithaca: Cornell University Press, 2001.
[4] Griselda Pollock, *Vision and Difference*, London: Routledge, 1988, p. 27 (her emphasis).
[5] Janet Wolff, *The Social Production of Art*, London: Macmillan, 1981, see especially p. 7 and the conclusion.

says that she is not saying that the aesthetic is an illusion. (Perhaps her common-sense deployment of the notion of aesthetic value in thinking about her own experience gives her qualms about trashing the notion too thoroughly.) Despite this, Wolff does not allow appeal to the aesthetic in explanations of art production. The aesthetic, if it is tolerated, is epiphenomenal in this respect. It does not in any way *drive* the history of art. Wolff allows that those who *consume* art might be responding to aesthetic value. But the aesthetic plays no role in the minds of individual artists. When she describes the factors that she thinks influence artistic production, they appear to be entirely economic or ideological. The aesthetic as a motive in artist's minds has been omitted or tacitly silenced in what she says about the production of art.

Another writer in this vein is Howard Becker. In his book *Art Worlds*, he does not *explicitly* reject aesthetic explanations of art production and replace them with some other explanation; instead he is content to describe (in neutral terms) the social structures in which art is produced.[6] But this is to presume the de-aestheticizing strategy without openly saying so. Becker says nothing about *why* the participants in the social structures bother to engage in those social structures. In a sense, then, he offers no explanation at all of art-making, and is content merely to describe at a superficial level how people relate to each other when producing art. The idea that the participants might have a *motive* for participating has slipped from view. Becker's book is premised on the idea that art production is work like any other form of production,[7] which is fair enough to an extent. But the general principle that all kinds of productive work have the same kind of explanation is dubious. The absence of reference to individual mental content, or any fine-grained details of mental content, inevitably makes such descriptions superficial. Even if there are artworlds and collective activity that yield works of art, there is still the puzzle of why there are artworlds and why it is that we engage in such collective activity. That is something to be explained. But it cannot be explained so long as we retain the exclusively sociological explanatory framework.

In my view (and as should be familiar from the first chapter of this book), the central issue in the theory of art is an explanatory one. We need a theory which gives a good explanation of why people create and consume art. On an aesthetic theory of art, the explanation of

---

[6] Howard Becker, *Art Worlds*, Berkeley: University of California Press, 1982.

[7] Ibid., pp. ix–x.

the fact that people make art and contemplate it is that they want to create things that have aesthetic value and they think they find aesthetic value in those created things. Crucially, this explanation is not just a *causal* explanation but also a *rational causal* explanation. It reveals to us what people see in making and contemplating art. It makes art-making and art-contemplation *intelligible.* By contrast, according to production and consumption scepticism, the real explanation of the fact that people make art and contemplate it is *not* that they want to create things that have aesthetic value or that they think they find aesthetic value in things, although this is what they think. Instead art has some other social property that really moves them to make and perceive it. For example, perhaps art reinforces certain social power relations. These sociological explanations thus involve attributing self-deception or false consciousness. They are non-rational explanations. The question we have to consider is whether the aesthetic hypothesis is as good as sceptical hypotheses that deny the role of the aesthetic.

## 2 SOME/ALL, STRONG/WEAK

In my view, sociologists of art have given us very little to support scepticism about the role of the aesthetic in art production. The normal procedure is to appeal to various nonaesthetic influences on art production. But the step from there to the sceptical conclusion about the role of the aesthetic in art production is problematic, to say the least. Of course, it is true that there are important nonaesthetic influences on art production. It would be odd if there were not. For example, the prices of different pigments may determine the colours that a patron demands.[8] And the work may reinforce, prescribe or reflect ideas which are connected with social power relations. Newly wealthy burghers might want still-life paintings of the produce from which they make their living. But the question is to what extent such factors provide an explanation of the existence and character of works of art. The fundamental problem is that such considerations explain *some* aspects of works of art but not *all* of them. The nonaesthetic influences do not tell the whole story. They *underdetermine* what the work of art is

---

[8] Michael Baxandall, *Painting and Experience in Fifteenth Century Italy,* Oxford: Oxford University Press, 1972.

like. The fact that some features of a work of art are determined by social factors does not mean that they all are. Let us call this the 'some–all' fallacy'. Theorists who talk about art from a sociological point of view often commit this some–all fallacy.

Although the social conditions set certain parameters, within those parameters, the artist can exercise free choice about what to create. And some of those choices are made on aesthetic grounds. It is not remotely plausible that every choice that artists make are extrinsically determined by social conditions. To some degree their choices are autonomous, even if the options among which they choose are not up to them. Heinrich Wölfflin famously said that not everything is possible at every time, but it is equally plausible that not everything is *necessary* at every time. For example, perhaps the political conditions surrounding the cold war led to a premium on bold, flat, abstract works in post-war New York, as Serge Guilbaut has argued.[9] But even so, Pollock's drip paintings—celebrated by Clement Greenberg—were underdetermined by those social conditions. Pollock was the source of that aesthetic idea. It was up to him—to drip or not to drip.

That at least is the appearance. But it is not *mere* appearance. The appearance derives from the common-sense folk wisdom that we bring to bear in explaining art-production. Of course, common-sense folk theory of any sort can be wrong, and it can embody misguided ideology. But folk theory can also be a lot better than what is supposed to supplant it. Some have argued that our folk conception of the mind is misguided. And atheists think that folk theology is false. But where folk theory offers explanations that seem to be the basis for successful predictions, then there is a burden on the sceptic to show how the phenomenon can better be explained and predicted in other terms, and there is also a burden on the sceptic to show how the folk explanations are successful or apparently successful, even though they are not in fact true.

I take it that the burden of proof is against the production sceptic, since aesthetic explanations are part of our common-sense folk theory about our transactions with art, which seems to work well. I concede that a sceptical sociological explanation is *sometimes* better than the folk aesthetic explanation. For example, people are indeed

[9] See Serge Guilbaut, *How New York Stole the Idea of the Avant Garde,* Chicago: University of Chicago Press, 1983. See also David Wise, "Spook Art", *ArtNews,* September 2000, and Frances Stonar, *The Cultural Cold War,* New Press, 2000.

sometimes moved to make judgements of taste which are 'impure', as Kant would say (since their actual determining ground includes the representation of various social circumstances, not just our pleasure or displeasure in our representation of the object).[10] And we are indeed sometimes moved to make works of art for reasons that have nothing to do with aesthetic properties. Such partial truths account for the popularity of sociological theorizing. It is not that such theories have no degree of plausibility. Sometimes they are correct. What I dispute is the idea that *all* or *most* folk aesthetic explanation is erroneous. We have not been presented with any evidence to suggest this. Our folk aesthetic explanations work well enough for everyday purposes. And the replacement sociological theory cannot explain all the phenomena which the folk aesthetic explanations explain. So we should retain the folk explanations.

Note that there is absolutely no reason to think that an aesthetic theory of art is committed to some overly strong doctrine of the 'autonomy' of art. That is setting up a straw man: a work of art can have aesthetic values that depend on the meaning of the work, and aesthetic values need not be the only values of a work. Moreover, an aesthetic theory need not privilege high or fine art forms. Nor need it be committed to extreme formalism about aesthetic properties. Kant, for example, was committed to *none* of this.

Production scepticism about aesthetic value is indulged in more by sociologists who consider art rather than art-historians who consider the social context of art.[11] In fact there seems to be an inverse correlation: the more empirical evidence is cited, the less the resulting theories exclude reference to the aesthetic. For example, Richard Peterson's sociological theory (which invokes 'gate-keepers' and the like) deploys quite a bit of evidence. Although the theory that he builds on that evidence is neutral about the role of aesthetic matters, it allows a role for aesthetic considerations as an explanatory factor. And he occasionally mentions aesthetic considerations but not with the sense that he is

[10] Kant, *Critique of Judgement*, trans. Meredith, Oxford: Oxford University Press, 1928, pp. 65–66.

[11] One very interesting art historian who respects social facts but does not reject aesthetic value is Michael Baxandall. See for example his *Painting and Experience in Fifteenth Century Italy* and *Patterns of Intention*, New Haven: Yale University Press, 1985. Contrast Janet Wolff's book, *The Social Production of Art*, which contains little or no empirical evidence. She merely cites the authority of other sociological writers. See also her *Aesthetics and the Sociology of Art* (London: Allen & Unwin, 1983) for the same flaws.

mentioning something inimical to his theory, but rather as something that has a natural place within it. For example, at one point he writes

. . . aesthetic innovation was associated with periods of high levels of competition among record companies.[12]

If only more sociologists of art were like Peterson!

We should distinguish *strong* and *weak* programs in the sociology of art. The strong program sets out to show how art production is *completely* determined by the socio-economic conditions under which it is produced, leaving *no* role for the way that artists think of their own activity. The weak programme, by contrast, allows that *both* social factors and the artist's self-conception are necessary but not sufficient conditions, which together, and only together, explain the production of art. The weak programme is acceptable. But most sociologists of art pursue the strong programme.[13]

The general problem with the strong programme in the sociology of art is that works of art themselves drop out of the picture, as it were. But this requires too much false consciousness. Purely sociological analyses can never provide a complete explanation of our social transactions with art, although they may be partial explanations. In so far as the strong programme in the sociology of art has such complete explanatory ambitions, it rests on the premise of ignoring the aesthetic. (This was explicit in the quotation from Pollock.) But the appeal to the aesthetic has an explanatory value that purely sociological accounts cannot replace. This is why the strong program in the sociology of art is explanatorily incomplete, in a debilitating way. No serious discussion of the general nature of art, its value and its explanation, can take place until we put this anti-aesthetic ideology behind us. In so far as post-modernist, Marxist and feminist aesthetics assume the strong sociological program, they are defective. Aesthetic explanations are indispensable.[14]

---

[12] See Richard Peterson "Cultural Standing Through The Production Perspective", in (ed.) Diana Crane, *The Sociology of Culture*, London: Routledge, 1994, p. 175.

[13] One part of cultural production which might be submitted for sociological explanation is the twentieth-century theoretical rejection of the aesthetic by sociologists of art.

[14] Proponents of the so-called 'new' art history were keen to unearth ideological properties of works of art (and also of writings about them). (See (eds.) A. L. Rees and Frances Borzello, *The New Art History*, London: Camden, 1986.) But in fact, the 'old' art history was never the naive stereotype that it was made out to be. Earnst Gombrich, for example, is as sensitive as any to these matters.

### 3 PIGGYBACK EXPLANATIONS

Defenders of the aesthetic can go on to make a stronger point, which is that ideological explanations *depend* on aesthetic explanations. The sociology of art faces the following question: since one can have ideological expression without art and without anything aesthetic significance, why is it that the ideological and the aesthetic get mixed? The answer, surely, is that propaganda is harnessed to aesthetically excellent products because aesthetic value is independent of propaganda or ideology. The ideological aspect of art rides piggyback on its aesthetic aspect, which the sociologically minded refuse to recognize. Those anti-aesthetic ideologists who reject the aesthetic as an ideological delusion undermine themselves. They shoot themselves in the foot, since they deprive themselves of plausible ideological explanations.

So it is not merely that works of art have *both* aesthetic and ideological properties, but that the aesthetic properties have explanatory *primacy*. We need to appeal to an independent aesthetic value to explain why those with an ideology to peddle enlist aesthetic art in their service. For example, much Egyptian art served as propaganda for the pharaohs. But there is no doubt that it did this effectively partly because of its aesthetic impact.

Or—moving swiftly from ancient Egypt to post-war New York—Clement Greenberg clashed with more sociologically minded theorists over the role of aesthetic explanations in explaining the phenomena of post-war American abstract expressionist art. Contrary to his numerous detractors, I believe that Clement Greenberg's criticism was sometimes (though not always, to be sure) an accurate response to the value in the works he discusses, and a subtle articulation of that value.[15] That articulation of value is something Greenberg had a gift for. And Greenberg should be celebrated for his dogged insistence on that value in the face of the complacent consensus that opposed him. There is, of course, more to be said about what drives the history of art. It is true that there are often ideological forces at work. But unless there were

---

[15] See *Clement Greenberg: Collected Essays and Criticism,* ed. John O'Brian, in 4 volumes, Chicago: University of Chicago Press, 1986. See also *Modernism and Modernity,* (eds.) Benjamin Buchloch, Serge Guilbaut and David Solkin, Vancouver, BC: Nova Scotia Press, 1981, "To Cope with Decadence", and his contributions to his discussion on T.J. Clark's paper (pp. 188–193) and to the general panel discussion (pp. 265–277). See also his *Homemade Esthetics,* Oxford: Oxford University Press, 1999.

what Greenberg notices and elegantly articulates, not only would there be nothing for the history of art to be the history of, but there would be nothing for ideology to latch on to. The aesthetic is an essential part of what drives the evolution of art.

Although Greenberg was in some sense a formalist, interested in what lay on the canvas, he also had a Hegelian belief in historical trajectory and progress. (In this he was unlike Bell and Fry and more like Gombrich.) And Greenberg tied his formalism and his Hegelianism together in his view of the evolution of twentieth-century art. For Greenberg, American art of the post-war years was where the *Geist* was, being the culmination of what was happening in Europe in the first half of the century.[16] But we need not swallow this story. We can peel away the Hegel in Greenberg. Moreover, we can admit that Guilbaut was right to argue that there is *some* truth in the accusation that the ascendancy of post-war American art had a lot to do with its political usefulness to those on the right who were pursuing the cold war. Nevertheless, Greenberg's analysis of what struck his eye, in many cases rings true—true to the works he discusses. And unless Greenberg were largely right about the aesthetic properties of those works, the ideological phenomena that those like Guilbaut highlight would not have been possible.

Works of art are often goods that are made and exchanged in different ways depending on the economic system in which they are exist. In the contemporary world, many works of art are, among other things, commodities in a capitalist economic system.[17] But they are, at least to an extent, *aesthetic commodities*. People desire works of art partly because of their valuable aesthetic qualities, and this is one reason why they are prepared to pay for them. While the production of art is usually profit-driven, this is only because there is a demand for those works that is due, in part, to the aesthetic satisfaction they supply. In other words, no aesthetic appreciation: no art production. The economic explanation does not supplant the aesthetic explanation—it depends on it. Like ideological explanations, economic explanations sit piggyback on aesthetic explanations.

[16] See "Modernist Painting", in (ed.) John O'Brian, *Clement Greenberg: Collected Essays and Criticism*, volume 4.

[17] See Michael Baxandall's *Painting and Experience in Fifteenth Century Italy*, where he describes an economic system in which works of art were exchanged differently from the way works of art have been bought and sold as commodities for most of the twentieth century.

However, many contemporary works are not capitalist commodities but are funded by the state. This is true of the avant garde works that particularly interest art theorists. Many avant garde works are commissioned by, and exhibited in, public museums and galleries or at least publicly subsidized museums or galleries. This form of support has more in common with traditional forms of patronage by the nobility or the church. Few of these works would be produced if they relied on the capitalist art market. Nevertheless, those who control the publicly owned, or publicly subsidized, art institutions commission and purchase works for reasons. No doubt there are often ideological forces at work influencing their decisions. But aesthetic considerations are sometimes among the reasons for commissions and purchases. One can be cynical to an extent, but one must allow that at *some* point aesthetic considerations play a role in determining choices, and hence in determining what gets produced. For example, an arts administrator may decide that only feminist art will be purchased and exhibited in an exhibition. Nevertheless, unless the supply of such works is very scarce, there will be a plentiful choice, and one range of reasons for choice among competing works or artists who satisfy the ideological criteria will be aesthetic reasons. The case of abstract expressionism is especially interesting in this respect. Guilbaut notes that many of those who supported abstract expressionism positively disliked the works. They backed it for political reasons, despite their low aesthetic assessment of it.[18] This degree of cynicism is unusual. Nevertheless, someone still had to choose some abstract expressionist works over others. The cynics on the political right were happy to delegate that task to less cynical arts administrators, who were nevertheless in the pay of the cynics. Choice still needed to be exercised between competing works. This is where critics like Greenberg come in. There were many more abstract expressionist artists than could be promoted, so choices had to be made. Abstract expressionism was thought, by the cynics, to embody distinctively American political values in a way that might appeal to European intellectuals who were enamoured of the Soviet system and ideology in the wake of the Second World War. Jackson Pollock, with his emphasis on individual expression and autonomous action, as opposed to the worthy and dull values that socialist realist 'tractor art' embodied, was just what the political right in America needed. But

---

[18] The CIA funded exhibitions in Paris in 1952 and in Vienna in 1959. See Wise, "Spook Art", p. 163.

Pollock expressed these values better than many of his contemporaries mainly because of the aesthetic virtues of his work. Hence aesthetic explanations are needed there.

So not only have we not been presented with remotely compelling sociological reasons to reject the non-sceptical common-sense aesthetic view, any plausible ideological or economic explanation presupposes non-scepticism about the aesthetic. Without a Greenberg to tell us why the works themselves are of value and are thought to be of value in themselves, no other explanation gets a grip.

If there is to be a sociology of art, what we need is a sociology of the aesthetic, not the sociology of the illusion of the aesthetic.

## 4 BEAUTY AND PLEASURE

There remains a question about exactly how the aesthetic explanation of art production works. We need to say something here if we are to have a viable alternative to production scepticism. As I have said, we can to a considerable extent leave open the further analysis of beauty and other aesthetic features.[19] But whatever analysis we embrace, we need to answer motivational and evaluative questions about why aesthetic properties motivate us and why we value them.

At this point, along with a very long tradition in aesthetics, stretching back at least to the ancient Greeks, we can appeal to *pleasure*.[20] On an aesthetic realist account, aesthetic pleasure is our mode of apprehending real aesthetic properties of the world. But on a non-realist account, aesthetic pleasure is a reaction to nonaesthetic perceptions and beliefs, as Hume and Kant thought. In either account, the pleasure must be a very special pleasure. Hume and Kant said many illuminating things about the kind of pleasure it is. For example, I think that some of what Kant claimed about the 'disinterestedness' of aesthetic pleasure can be defended.[21] There is a lot more to say on the subject. But it is

---

[19] See my book *Metaphysics of Beauty*.

[20] Plato says ". . . beauty is what is pleasant through hearing and sight . . ." (*Hippias Major*, 298a.). Aquinus says "Those things we call beautiful are those that please when they are seen" (*Suma Theologiae*, I.5.4.ad.I). Moreover, the idea that some things 'delight the eyes' can be found in *Genesis* (II.9 and III.6) and in Homer (*Odyssey*, book IV, line 51).

[21] See my "UnKantian Notions of Disinterest", *British Journal of Aesthetics*, 1992; and "Kant on Pleasure in the Agreeable", *Journal of Aesthetics and Art Criticism*, 1995.

clear that it is intelligible that pleasure motivates us and it is intelligible that we value it. Hence it is intelligible that we desire and value the contemplation of things that yield pleasure. Nelson Goodman poked fun at aesthetic theories of art, by contrast with his own high-minded cognitive theory, by the rhetorical device of calling pleasure theories 'tingle immersion theories'.[22] But I say that there is a lot to be said for a good tingle! Pleasurable tingles motivate most of us, even if they leave Goodman cold. And it could be that certain tingles are of special value in virtue of their distinctive contents, relations and norms.

While the appeal to pleasure in contemplating beauty is important, and is part of the story of art-production, it is not enough to explain the production of art; this is because it says nothing about the person or persons who produce art. It is not plausible that all art-making is motivated by the desire to produce pleasure, either in others or in oneself. The pleasure we get from art-*making* is often internal to the process of art-making. It is not a matter of pleasure in contemplating the work while making it, or after having made it, or that one takes in the thought that others will take pleasure in it, or even in thinking that one has made something worthwhile.[23] There is an intrinsic pleasure one takes *in* making something. This pleasure in making art is probably not usefully categorized as aesthetic pleasure, which is usually thought of as a *contemplative* pleasure. The pleasure of art-making is pleasure in an *activity*. (We enjoy the activities of *painting* paintings or *playing* music.) The pleasure in making something beautiful is not the same as the pleasure in contemplating something beautiful. Nevertheless, the pleasure in the activity of making art surely stands in some intimate relation to contemplative aesthetic pleasure. It is not likely that we would find making art pleasurable unless we also found contemplating it pleasurable.[24]

A theory of art that appeals to contemplative pleasures, and pleasures in activity, is surely starting off in a sensible place. For such a theory is in a position to explain why we value art activities without attributing an error to us. On such a view, the reason we value our activities is *transparent* to us. That is, it is something we are aware of; it is not something hidden from us which is nevertheless a subterranean cause

---

[22] Nelson Goodman, *Languages of Art*, Oxford: Oxford University Press, 1969, p. 112.

[23] See further Chapter 6.

[24] Kant notes that although art-making involves the productive imagination, it also involves taste or judgement. See Kant, *Critique of Judgement*, section 50.

of our activities. A pleasure theory avoids the widespread attribution of false consciousness or some hidden psychological payoff, which only sociological or psychoanalytic analysis can reveal. Rather we value art activities because we find in them a value that they do indeed possess. By contrast, a theory that purports to explain art in terms of some unknown sociological or psychological factor ('art as social control', 'art as play', etc.) will not be able to provide a plausible explanation of why we value the arts. For our view of why we value art, and the real reason that we value it, will have come apart. On such an account, the explanation of our experiencing and making art is not transparent to us. The difficulty then is to explain the ubiquitousness and universality of our valuing the arts. How is it that human beings are so widely and deeply deceived in so many different cultures, classes, races, creeds and eras, although this is almost never apparent to them? The delusion we would have to believe is just too widespread and too deep-seated in our psychology to be believable. It is far more likely—indeed overwhelmingly likely—that much of what we find valuable in contemplating and making art is transparent to us. Pre-eminent among what we value is the pleasure that making and contemplating beauty yields. The arts involve a specific kind of pleasure, which is of peculiar value, a value greater than what Kant calls "pleasure in the agreeable". But it is pleasure nonetheless.

Let us draw a line here. There is obviously a lot to be said about the nature of the pleasure in making and contemplating beauty, and about the nature of beauty and other aesthetic properties, and about the nature of the aesthetic creative imagination. We value and desire making and perceiving beautiful things in virtue of the pleasure we have when we create and appreciate them. Why this is so is a deep matter, but we undoubtedly do. On that foundation we can build a theory of art which does justice to its importance for us. Whatever else art is, it is the art of beauty. Creating and contemplating beauty yields pleasure of a distinctive sort. This is why we value much art as highly as we do. And this is why we are right to do so.

# *Acknowledgements*

The places of publication of the papers from which the chapters of this book derive are as follows:

"Doughnuts and Dickie", *Ratio*, 1994.

"Groundrules in the Philosophy of Art", *Philosophy*, 1995.

"The Creative Theory of Art", *American Philosophical Quarterly*, 1995.

"Art and Audience", *Journal of Aesthetics and Art Criticism*, 1999.

"Art Identity", *Dialogue*, 1999.

"Aesthetic Functionalism", in (eds.) Emily Brady and Jerrold Levinson, *Aesthetic Concepts: Sibley and After*, Oxford University Press, 2001.

"Are There Counterexamples to Aesthetic Theories of Art?", *Journal of Aesthetics and Art Criticism*, 2002.

"Against the Sociology of Art", *Philosophy of the Social Sciences*, 2002.

"The Unimportance of the Avant Garde", *Revista di Estetica*, 2007. (Published in Italian.)

I am grateful to the editors and publishers for permission to reuse this material.

# Bibliography

Thomas Aquinas, *Suma Theologiae*, Indianapolis: Hackett, 2002.

Christine Battersby, *Gender and Genius*, Bloomington, IN: Indiana University Press, 1989.

Michael Baxandall, *Painting and Experience in Fifteenth Century Italy*, Oxford: Oxford University Press, 1972.

_____ *Patterns of Intention*, New Haven: Yale University Press, 1985.

George Bealer, "The Limits of Scientific Essentialism", *Philosophical Perspectives*, 1, 1987.

Monroe Beardsley, *Aesthetics*, Indianapolis: Hackett, 1958.

_____ "The Creation of a Work of Art", *The Aesthetic Point of View*, Ithaca: Cornell University Press, 1982.

_____ "An Aesthetic Definition of Art", in (ed.) Hugh Curtler, *What is Art?*, New York: Haven, 1983, and reprinted in (eds.) Peter Lamarque and Stein Olsen, *Aesthetics and the Philosophy of Art*, Oxford: Blackwell, 2004.

Howard Becker, *Art Worlds*, Berkeley: University of California Press, 1982.

Anthony Blunt, *Guernica*, Oxford: Oxford University Press, 1969.

Paul Boghosian and David Velleman, "Colour as a Secondary Quality", *Mind*, xcviii, 1989.

Jorge Luis Borges, "The Secret Miracle", *Labyrinths*, Harmondsworth: Penguin, 1970.

Pierre Bourdieu, *Distinction*, London: Routledge & Kegan Paul, 1984.

Malcolm Budd, *Values of Art*, London: Alan Lane, 1995.

William Carter, "Salmon on Artifact Origin and Lost Possibilities", *Philosophical Review*, 92, 1983.

Gregory Currie, "Supervenience, Essentialism and Aesthetic Properties", *Philosophical Studies*, 58, 1990.

Arthur Danto, "The Artworld", *Journal of Philosophy*, 61, 1964.

_____ *The Transfiguration of the Commonplace*, Cambridge, MA: Harvard University Press, 1981.

_____ *The Philosophical Disenfranchisement of Art*, New York: Columbia University Press, 1986.

_____ *Beyond the Brillo Box*, Berkeley: University of California Press, 1992.

_____ *The Abuse of Beauty*, Chicago: Open Court, 2003.

Donald Davidson, "Intending", *Essays on Actions and Events*, Oxford: Clarendon, 1980.

_____ "What Metaphors Mean", *Inquiries into Truth and Interpretation*, Oxford: Blackwell, 1984.

_____ *Essays on Actions and Events*, Oxford: Clarendon, 1980.

Donald Davidson, *Inquiries into Truth and Interpretation*, Oxford: Clarendon, 1982.

Martin Davies and Lloyd Humberstone, "Two Notions of Necessity", *Philosophical Studies*, 38, 1980.

Stephen Davies, *Definitions of Art*, Ithaca: Cornell University Press, 1991.

―――"First Art and Art's Definition", *Southern Journal of Philosophy*, XXXV, 1997.

―――"Non-Western Art and Art's Definition", in (ed.) Noel Carroll, *Theories of Art Today*, Maddison, WI: University of Wisconsin Press, 2000.

―――"Essential Distinctions for Art Theorists", (eds.) Stephen Davies and Anata ch. Sukla, *Art and Essence*, London: Praeger, 2003.

Richard Dawkins, *The Blind Watchmaker*, Harmondsworth: Penguin, 1986.

Mark Della Rocca, "Essentialists and Essentialism", *Journal of Philosophy*, 93, 1996.

Daniel Dennett, "The Interpretation of Texts, People and Other Artifacts", *Philosophy and Phenomenological Research*, L, 1990.

George Dickie, *Aesthetics: An Introduction,* Indianapolis: Bobbs-Merrill, 1971.

―――*Art and the Aesthetic*, Ithaca: Cornell University Press, 1974.

―――*The Art Circle*, New York: Haven, 1984.

―――"Wollheim's Dilemma", *British Journal of Aesthetics*, 38, 1998.

―――*Art and Value*, Oxford: Blackwell, 2001.

Denis Dutton, "But They Don't have Our Concept of Art", in (ed.) Noel Carroll, *Theories of Art Today*, Maddison, WI: University of Wisconsin Press, 2000.

Terry Eagleton, *The Ideology of the Aesthetic,* Blackwell: Oxford, 1984.

Kit Fine, "Essence and Modality", *Philosophical Perspectives*, vol. 8, 1994.

―――"Ontological Dependence", *Proceedings of the Aristotelian Society*, XCV, 1995.

Cynthia Freeland, *But is it Art?*, Oxford: Oxford University Press, 2001.

Suzie Gablick, *Has Modernism Failed?*, London: Thames and Hudson, 1984.

Alan Goldman, *Aesthetic Value,* Boulder, CO: Westview, 1995.

Ernst Gombrich, *The Story of Art*, London: Phaidon, 1950.

―――*Art and Illusion*, London: Phaidon, 1959.

Nelson Goodman, *Languages of Art*, Oxford: Oxford University Press, 1968.

Clement Greenberg, "Modernist Painting", in (ed.) John O'Brian, *Clement Greenberg: Collected Essays and Criticism,,* vol. 4, Chicago: University of Chicago Press, 1986.

―――*Collected Essays and Criticism*, ed. John O'Brian, in 4 volumes, Chicago: University of Chicago Press, 1986.

―――contributions, in (eds.) Benjamin Buchloch, Serge Guilbaut and David Solkin, *Modernism and Modernity,* Nova Scotia Press: Vancouver, BC, 1981.

―――*Homemade Esthetics*, Oxford: Oxford University Press, 1999.

Walter Gropius, *The New Architecture and the Bauhaus*, Cambridge, MA: MIT Press, 1965.

Serge Guilbaut, *How New York Stole the Idea of Modern Art*, Chicago: University of Chicago Press, 1983.

Gilbert Harman, *Reasoning, Meaning and Mind*, Oxford: Clarendon, 1999.

Andrew Harrison, *Making and Thinking*, Indianapolis: Hackett, 1978.

Philip Johnson-Laird, *Computers and the Mind*, London: Fontana, 1988.

Mark Johnston, "Constitution is not Identity", *Mind*, 101, 1992.

Immanuel Kant, *Critique of Judgement*, Oxford: Oxford University Press, 1928.

Jaegwon Kim, "Concepts of Supervenience", *Philosophy and Phenomenological Research*, 45, 1984; reprinted in his *Supervenience and Mind*, Cambridge: Cambridge University Press, 1993.

Peter Kivy, "Is Music an Art?", *Journal of Philosophy*, 90, 1993; reprinted in *The Fine Art of Repetition*, Cambridge: Cambridge University Press, 1993.

—— *Philosophies of the Arts: An Essay in Differences*, Cambridge: Cambridge University Press, 1997.

—— *The Possessor and the Possessed*, Yale University Press, 2001.

Daniel Kolak, "Art and Intentionality", *Journal of Aesthetic and Art Criticism*, 48, 1990.

Hilary Kornblith, *Knowledge and Its Place in Nature*, Oxford: Oxford University Press, 2002.

Saul Kripke, *Naming and Necessity*, Cambridge, MA: Harvard University Press, 1980.

Paul Kristeller, "The Modern System of the Arts", in (ed.) Paul Kristeller, *Renaissance Thought and the Arts*, New York: Harper and Row, 1965. A shortened version of this essay can be found in *Aesthetics*, (eds.) Susan Feagin and Patrick Maynard, Oxford: Oxford University Press, 1997.

Peter Lamarque, book review of Malcolm Budd's *Values of Art*, *British Journal of Aesthetics*, 37, 1997.

—— "Aesthetic Essentialism", in Emily Brady and Jerrold Levinson (eds.), *Aesthetic Concepts: Sibley and After*, Oxford: Oxford University Press, 2001.

Jerrold Levinson, "Zemach on Paintings", *British Journal of Aesthetics*, 27, 1987.

—— "Aesthetic Supervenience", *Music, Art and Metaphysics*, Ithaca: Cornell University Press, 1990.

—— "Refining Art Historically", *Music, Art and Metaphysics*, Ithaca: Cornell University Press, 1990.

—— "A Refiner's Fire: Reply to Sartwell and Kolak", *Journal of Aesthetic and Art Criticism*, 48, 1990.

—— "Art, Value, and Philosophy", *Mind*, 105, 1996; critical notice of Malcolm Budd's *Values of Art*.

Colin McGinn, "Another Look at Color", *Journal of Philosophy*, 93, 1996.

Mara Miller, *The Garden as an Art*, Albany: SUNY Press, 1993.

Ruth Millikan, *White Queen Psychology*, Cambridge, MA: MIT Press, 1993.

—— "Biofunctions: Two Paradigms", in (eds.) Andre Ariew, Robert Cummins and Mark Perlman, *Functions*, Oxford: Oxford University Press, 2002.

Moses, *The Torah: The Five Books of Moses*, Philadelphia, PA: Jewish Publication Society, 1962.

P. H. Nowell-Smith, *Ethics*, London: Penguin, 1954; a discussion of psychological hedonism.

John Perry, "The Same *F*", *Philosophical Review*, 79, 1970.

Richard Peterson "Cultural Standing Through The Production Perspective", in (ed.) Diana Crane, *The Sociology of Culture*, London: Routledge, 1994.

Griselda Pollock, *Vision and Difference*, London: Routledge, 1988.

Sally Price, *Primitive Art in Civilized Places*, Chicago: Chicago University Press, 2001.

Hilary Putnam, "The Meaning of Meaning", *Philosophical Papers,* vol. 2, Cambridge: Cambridge University Press, 1975.

Plato, *Hippias Major*, in (eds.) John M. Cooper and D. S Hutchinson, *Complete Works*, Indianapolis: Hackett, 1997.

_____ *Ion*, in (eds.) John M. Cooper and D. S Hutchinson, *Complete Works*, Indianapolis: Hackett, 1997.

A.L. Rees and Frances Borzello (eds.) *The New Art History*, London: Camden, 1986.

Colin Rowe, "La Tourette", *The Mathematics of the Ideal Villa, and Other Essays*, Cambridge, MA: MIT Press, 1976.

Mark Sagoff, "On Restoring and Reproducing Art", *Journal of Philosophy*, 75, 1978.

Yuriko Saito, *Everyday Aesthetics*, Oxford: Oxford University Press, 2007.

Jean-Paul Sartre, "Why Write?", *Literature and Existentialism*, New York: Citadel, 1994.

Eva Schaper, *Prelude to Aesthetics,* London: Allen and Unwin, 1968.

Roger Scruton, *The Aesthetic Understanding*, London: Carcanet, 1983.

John Searle, *Intentionality*, Cambridge: Cambridge University Press, 1983.

Brian Sewell, *An Alphabet of Villains*, London: Bloomsbury, 1995.

Sydney Shoemaker, "Personal Identity: A Materialist's Account", in (eds.) Sydney Shoemaker and Richard Swinburne, *Personal Identity*, Oxford: Blackwell, 1984.

_____ "Identity, Properties and Causality", *Identity, Cause and Mind*, Cambridge: Cambridge University Press, 1984.

Frank Sibley, "Aesthetic Concepts", *Philosophical Review*, 68, 1959.

_____ "Aesthetic/Nonaesthetic", *Philosophical Review*, 74, 1965.

Anthony Smith, *The Ethnic Origins of Nations*, Blackwell: Oxford, 1986.

Francis Sparshott, *Off the Ground,* Princeton: Princeton University Press, 1988.

Stephen Stich, *From Folk Psychology to Cognitive Science*, Cambridge, MA: MIT Press, 1983.

Frances Stonar, *The Cultural Cold War*, New York: New Press, 2000.

Richard Strauss, *Recollections and Reflections*, London: Boosey and Hawkes, 1953.

Igor Stravinsky and Robert Craft, *Memories and Commentary*, London: Faber and Faber, 1960.

P. F. Strawson, *Individuals*, London: Methuen, 1959.

—— *Freedom and Resentment and other Essays*, London: Methuen, 1963.

Kendall Walton, "Categories of Art", *Philosophical Review*, 79, 1970.

Bernard Williams, "Utilitarianism", in (eds.) J. J. C. Smart and Bernard Williams, *Utilitarianism: For and Against*, Cambridge: Cambridge University Press, 1973.

—— *Moral Luck*, Cambridge: Cambridge University Press, 1981.

Vaughan Williams, *National Music*, Oxford: Oxford University Press, 1987.

David Wise, "Spook Art", *ArtNews*, 99, September 2000.

Ludwig Wittgenstein, *Philosophical Investigations*, Oxford: Blackwell, 1953.

—— *Culture and Value*, Oxford: Blackwell, 1980.

Janet Wolff, *The Social Production of Art*, London: Macmillan, 1981.

—— *Aesthetics and the Sociology of Art*, London: Allen & Unwin, 1983.

Richard Wollheim, "Seeing-In, Seeing-As, and Pictorial Representation", *Art and its Objects*, second edition, Cambridge: Cambridge University Press, 1980.

—— "The Institutional Theory of Art", *Art and Its Objects*, second edition, Cambridge: Cambridge University Press, 1980.

—— *Art and Its Objects*, Cambridge: Cambridge University Press, second edition, 1980.

—— *Painting as an Art*, London: Thames and Hudson, 1987.

Nicholas Wolterstorff, *Works and Worlds of Art*, Oxford: Oxford University Press, 1980,

Stephen Yablo, "Identity, Essence and Indiscernibility", *Journal of Philosophy*, 84, 1987.

Nick Zangwill, "UnKantian Notions of Disinterest", *British Journal of Aesthetics*, 132, 1992.

—— "Doughnuts and Dickie", *Ratio*, 7, 1994.

—— "Kant on Pleasure in the Agreeable", *Journal of Aesthetics and Art Criticism*, 53, 1995.

—— "Moral Supervenience", *Midwest Studies in Philosophy*, 20, 1996.

—— "Direction of Fit and Normative Functionalism", *Philosophical Studies*, 91, 1998.

—— *The Metaphysics of Beauty*, Ithaca: Cornell University Press, 2001.

—— "Aesthetic Realism", in (ed.) Jerrold Levinson, *Oxford Companion to Aesthetics*, Oxford University Press, 2003.

—— "Perpetrator Motivation: Some Reflections on the Browning/Goldhagen Debate", in (eds.) Eve Garrard and Geoffrey Scarre, Moral *Philosophy and the Holocaust*, Aldershot: Ashgate Press, 2003.

Nick Zangwill, "Against Moral Dispositionalism", *Erkenntnis*, 59, 2003.

—— "Moore, Morality, Supervenience Essence, Epistemology", *American Philosophical Quarterly*, 142, 2005,

Nick Zangwill, "The Normativity of the Mental", *Philosophical Explorations*, 18, 2005.

―――― "Moral Epistemology and the Because Constraint", in (ed.) Jamie Dreier, *Contemporary Debates in Moral Theory*, Blackwell: Oxford, 2005.

―――― "The Indifference Argument", *Philosophical Studies*, 135, 2007.

Eddy Zemach, "No Identity Without Evaluation", *British Journal of Aesthetics*, 26, 1986.

# Subject Index

# Author Index